The Catholic Biblical Quarterly
Monograph Series
27

Blood
and Water

The Death and Resurrection
of Jesus in John 18–21

BY

John Paul Heil

The Catholic Biblical Quarterly
Monograph Series
27

Produced in the United States of America

Library of Congress Cataloging-in-Publication Data
Heil, John Paul.
Blood and water : the death and resurrection of Jesus in John
18–21 / by John Paul Heil
p.   cm. — (Catholic biblical quarterly. Monograph series : 27)
Includes bibliographical references and index.
ISBN 0-915170-26-4 (pbk.)
1. Bible. N.T. John XVIII–XXI–Criticism, Narrative.   I. Title.
II. Series.
BS2615.2.H45   1995
226.5'066–dc20
95-10479
CIP

Contents

Abbreviations

Abbreviations used throughout this work are those found in the "Instructions for Contributors," *CBQ* 46 (1984) 393-408, with the following addition:

EDNT   *Exegetical Dictionary of the New Testament*

Preface

In previous studies we have presented narrative critical analyses of the passion, death, and resurrection of Jesus in both the Gospel of Matthew (*The Death and Resurrection of Jesus: A Narrative-Critical Reading of Matthew 26-28* [Minneapolis: Fortress, 1991]; see also "The Narrative Structure of Matthew 27:55-28:20," *JBL* 110 [1991] 419-38) and the Gospel of Mark ("Mark 14,1-52: Narrative Structure and Reader-Response," *Bib* 71 [1990] 305-32; "The Progressive Narrative Pattern of Mark 14,53 16,8," *Bib* 73 [1992] 331-58). In this book we apply the same narrative-critical approach with emphasis upon the responses of the implied reader/audience to the final chapters of the Gospel of John. Like the Gospels of Matthew and Mark, John does not merely record the events, but engages the audience in an intensely contrasting interplay between the characters and actions in order to accomplish a rhetorical strategy of communication. While the Johannine presentation of Jesus' death and resurrection exhibits a narrative process externally similar to the Matthean and Markan presentations, it possesses its own unique and richly symbolic dynamism. We hope to give a new insight into how and what the Fourth Gospel more precisely and so profoundly communicates to its implied audience.

CHAPTER 1

Introduction

This book presents a new interpretation of the final four chapters of the Gospel of John, the events dealing with the death and resurrection of Jesus. This interpretation employs narrative criticism with an emphasis upon the responses of the implied reader or audience.

Before we begin, therefore, we need to define some concepts basic to our particular approach to John's narrative. In our investigation of the Gospel of John as a communication process we are concerned with the "implied author," the author discoverable in the text, as distinct from the real, historical author, who has an identity beyond this particular text. The implied author is a purely textual reality, the image of the author as projected by the text. The implied author controls the communication and represents the strategy, values, concerns and objectives of the text. For our purposes the implied author can be considered equivalent to the "narrator," the one who tells the story.

As the counterpart to the implied author, who stands at the giving end of the communication process, the "implied reader" stands at the receiving end of it. Rather than a real, historical reader or audience, the implied reader is a theoretical construct that represents the responses the implied author intends or assumes on the part of the textual reader or audience of the narrative. The implied reader is the reader or audience that every text presupposes in order to be actualized as an act of communication; it is "the reader" anticipated and actually generated by the text in the process of reading or listening to it. Our reader-response approach will concentrate on the responses of this implied reader or audience as determined by the various presuppositions, strategies and indicators within the text. We are concerned with what the narrative does, how it operates, and how it affects its textual audience in order to produce the meaning of the text and bring its act of communication to completion.[1]

Our narrative-critical approach proposes that the final scenes of the Fourth Gospel work together as a dynamic, interrelated progression, an "architecture in motion, assembled as it goes."[2] More specifically, we shall illustrate how these scenes are arranged in several sets of ongoing literary "sandwiches" or intercalations in which each successive scene is contrastingly framed or sandwiched by two other mutually related scenes. Each set thus operates as an alternation or "interchange" of contrasting scenes that involves the implied audience in an intense interplay of competing and/or complementary narrative themes.[3]

Our approach can be characterized as a close reading or listening to the text that strives to account for all of the literary elements and details that contribute to what the narrative is communicating. It includes how these final scenes of the Gospel variously recall, resonate with, and bring to a climactic conclusion elements and themes from the previous narrative (John 1-17), as well as how

---

[1] For an explanation of the narrative-critical approach that we are following, see M. A. Powell, *What Is Narrative Criticism?* (Minneapolis: Fortress, 1990). See also R. A. Culpepper, *Anatomy of the Fourth Gospel: A Study in Literary Design* (Philadelphia: Fortress, 1983); J. L. Staley, *The Print's First Kiss: A Rhetorical Investigation of the Implied Reader in the Fourth Gospel* (SBLDS 82; Atlanta: Scholars, 1988) 21-49; W. S. Vorster, "The Reader in the Text: Narrative Material," *Reader Perspectives on the New Testament* (Semeia 48; ed. E. V. McKnight; Atlanta: Scholars, 1989) 21-39; M. W. G. Stibbe, *John as Storyteller: Narrative Criticism and the Fourth Gospel* (SNTSMS 73; Cambridge: Cambridge University, 1992) 5-29; A. Reinhartz, "Great Expectations: A Reader-Oriented Approach to Johannine Christology and Eschatology," *Journal of Literature and Theology* 3 (1989) 61-76; idem, *The Word in the World: The Cosmological Tale in the Fourth Gospel* (SBLMS 45; Atlanta: Scholars, 1992) 1-15; M. C. de Boer, "Narrative Criticism, Historical Criticism, and the Gospel of John," *JSNT* 47 (1992) 35-48; F. J. Moloney, "Who is 'The Reader' in/of the Fourth Gospel?," *AusBR* 40 (1992) 20-33; idem, *Belief in the Word: Reading John 1-4* (Minneapolis: Fortress, 1993).

[2] R. Alter, *The Pleasures of Reading in an Ideological Age* (New York: Simon and Schuster, 1989) 153: "Literary structure is not only dynamic—one might say architecture in motion, assembled as it goes—but also is constituted of heterogeneous elements (sound, imagery, diction, motifs, syntax, and so forth). This means that many poems, many narrative and dramatic works, have complex structures produced by the interaction of different heterogeneous elements."

[3] D. R. Bauer, *The Structure of Matthew's Gospel: A Study in Literary Design* (JSNTSup 31; Sheffield: Almond, 1988) 18, draws a distinction between "intercalation" as "the insertion of one literary unit in the midst of another literary unit (a, b, a)" and "interchange" as "the exchanging or alternation of certain elements (a, b, a, b, a)." He points out that "interchange is often used to strengthen contrasts or comparisons." Our proposed narrative patterns for John 18-21 thus involve a combination of "intercalation" and "interchange."

they allude to their Jewish scriptural background. The result is a demonstration of how the implied audience is affected by and called to respond to the total progression of events involved in the Johannine presentation of Jesus' passion, death, and resurrection.[4]

Although our division into scenes and the narrative patterns that they form show similarities to previous studies, our investigation differs from them in significant ways. Whereas others have discussed the structure of parts of John 18-21, we are attempting a detailed, narrative-critical treatment of the entire complex as an interrelated totality and unity.[5] Our presentation focuses more than others on the rhetorical strategy and effect of the structure of all these scenes as a progression that guides the way they are read or heard by the implied reader or audience.[6]

We begin with an overview of the five major sections of narrative patterns

[4] For a similar narrative-critical analysis of the Matthean and Markan presentations of Jesus' passion, death, and resurrection, see J. P. Heil, *The Death and Resurrection of Jesus: A Narrative-Critical Reading of Matthew 26-28* (Minneapolis: Fortress, 1991); idem, "The Narrative Structure of Matthew 27:55-28:20," *JBL* 110 (1991) 419-38; idem, "Mark 14,1-52: Narrative Structure and Reader-Response," *Bib* 71 (1990) 305-32; idem, "The Progressive Narrative Pattern of Mark 14,53-16,8," *Bib* 73 (1992) 331-58.

[5] Presentations of the structures of parts of John 18-21 include A. Janssens de Varebeke, "La structure des scènes du récit de la passion en Joh. XVIII-XIX," *ETL* 38 (1962) 504-22; C. H. Giblin, "Confrontations in John 18,1-27," *Bib* 65 (1984) 210-32; idem, "John's Narration of the Hearing Before Pilate (John 18,28-19,16a)," *Bib* 67 (1986) 221-39; I. de la Potterie, *The Hour of Jesus: The Passion and the Resurrection of Jesus According to John* (New York: Alba House, 1989); F. Genuyt, "La comparution de Jésus devant Pilate. Analyse sémiotique de Jean 18,28-19,16," *RSR* 73 (1985) 133-46; F. F. Segovia, "The Final Farewell of Jesus: A Reading of John 20:30-21:25," *The Fourth Gospel from a Literary Perspective* (Semeia 53; ed. R. A. Culpepper and F. F. Segovia; Atlanta: Scholars, 1991) 167-90; Stibbe, *John as Storyteller*, 96-120. G. Mlakuzhyil, *The Christocentric Literary Structure of the Fourth Gospel* (AnBib 117; Rome: Biblical Institute, 1987), briefly examines John 18-21 as a chiastic rather than narrative structure. D. Senior's presentation, *The Passion of Jesus in the Gospel of John* (Collegeville, MN: Liturgical Press, 1991), devotes only pp. 135-43 to John 20-21. J. D. M. Derrett, *The Victim: The Johannine Passion Narrative Reexamined* (Shipston-on-Stour, Warwickshire, England: Drinkwater, 1993) 1, treats only the passion narrative, which he takes to extend from John 18:1 to 20:29.

[6] K. A. Plank (*Paul and the Irony of Affliction* [Atlanta: Scholars, 1987] 9) describes the response of the implied reader in terms of the "rhetorical effect" the text produces: "The *rhetorical effect* refers to the particular changes and affects which the author would incite in the readers as they progress through the text. Taken broadly, the rhetorical effect is the possible actualization of the text which the author intends to promote in the reader. In this sense, the rhetorical effect coincides with the commitments summoned in the serious reception of the discourse."

formed by John 18-21. Each of the first four sections is composed of six alternating scenes that function together as a dynamic progression of four narrative intercalations or sandwiches, while the fifth section contains three scenes that function as one sandwich. A separate coda concludes both the fourth (20:30-31) and the fifth (21:24-25) sections. We must keep in mind that each of the sections operates in a dynamic sequence. After the first sandwich (A-B-A), as each successive scene is heard by the implied audience it works as "architecture in motion,"[7] forming another sandwich with the previous two scenes (B-A-B), until the section is concluded. The entire complex, then, functions for its implied audience as a series of progressive patterns of narrative sandwiches, as illustrated by the following charts:

Narrative Progression of the Passion, Death, and Resurrection of Jesus in John 18-21

I. 18:1-27: Jesus reveals his leadership to the Jewish leaders while Peter misunderstands and denies him.

Six Scenes

A^1 18:1-9: With his disciples Jesus reveals his identity to his opponents.

B^1 18:10-11: Peter cuts off the ear of the high priest's servant.

A^2 18:12-14: Jesus alone is led to the father-in-law of the high priest to die for the people.

B^2 18:15-18: Peter denies Jesus in the courtyard of the high priest.

A^3 18:19-24: Jesus confronts the high priest with his revelatory mission and is rejected.

B^3 18:25-27: Peter denies Jesus a second and third time before a servant of the high priest.

Four Sandwiches

(1) 18:1-14: A^1(18:1-9)–B^1(18:10-11)–A^2(18:12-14)

(2) 18:10-18: B^1(18:10-11)–A^2(18:12-14)–B^2(18:15-18)

(3) 18:12-24: A^2(18:12-14)–B^2(18:15-18)–A^3(18:19-24)

(4) 18:15-27: B^2(18:15-18)–A^3(18:19-24)–B^3(18:25-27)

---

[7] Alter, *Pleasures of Reading*, 153.

II. 18:28-19:11: Jesus is rejected by the Jews but reveals himself to Pilate.

Six Scenes

A¹ 18:28-32: Outside the praetorium the Jews refuse Pilate's offer to judge Jesus themselves.

B¹ 18:33-38a: Inside Jesus reveals his kingship to Pilate.

A² 18:38b-40: Outside the Jews reject Pilate's offer to release Jesus as their king.

B² 19:1-3: Inside Pilate's soldiers mock Jesus' kingship.

A³ 19:4-7: Outside the Jews reject Pilate's offer of the innocent Jesus, God's Son.

B³ 19:8-11: Inside Jesus reveals his divine origin to Pilate.

Four Sandwiches

(1) 18:28 40: A¹ (18:28-32)–B¹ (18:33-38a)–A² (18:38b-40)

(2) 18:33-19:3: B¹ (18:33-38a)–A² (18:38b 40)–B² (19:1-3)

(3) 18:38b-19:7: A² (18:38b-40)–B² (19:1-3)–A³ (19:4-7)

(4) 19:1-11: B² (19:1-3)–A³ (19:4-7)–B³ (19:8-11)

III. 19:12 42: The revelatory death and burial of Jesus advances God's plan of salvation.

Six Scenes

A¹ 19:12-22: Pilate invites the Jews to see and accept Jesus as king.

B¹ 19:23-24: Roman soldiers take Jesus' clothing and fulfill scripture.

A² 19:25-27: Jesus invites the beloved disciple to see and accept his mother.

B² 19:28-30: Jesus takes vinegar, dies and completes scripture.

A³ 19:31-37: Jesus' blood and water invite looking upon him.

B³ 19:38-42: Joseph and Nicodemus take the body of Jesus for Jewish burial.

Four Sandwiches

(1) 19:12-27: A¹ (19:12-22)–B¹ (19:23-24)–A² (19:25-27)

(2) 19:23 30: B¹ (19:23-24)–A² (19:25-27)–B² (19:28-30)

(3) 19:25-37: A² (19:25-27)–B² (19:28-30)–A³ (19:31-37)

(4) 19:28 42: B² (19:28-30)–A³ (19:31-37)–B³ (19:38-42)

IV.   20:1-31: The disciples see and come to believe in the risen Jesus.

Six Scenes

A¹   20:1-2:   Mary Magdalene announces that Jesus was taken from the tomb.

B¹   20:3-10:   Peter and the beloved disciple witness the burial cloths in the tomb of Jesus.

A²   20:11-18:   Mary Magdalene announces her vision of the risen Lord.

B²   20:19-23:   The disciples see the risen Lord and receive the Spirit.

A³   20:24-25:   Thomas announces his disbelief without seeing.

B³   20:26-29:   The disciples and Thomas see and believe in the risen Lord.

C   20:30-31:   What has been written is a basis for the faith of the audience.

Four Sandwiches

(1) 20:1-18:   A¹ (20:1-2)–B¹ (20:3-10)–A² (20:11-18)

(2) 20:3-23:   B¹ (20:3-10)–A² (20:11-18)–B² (20:19-23)

(3) 20:11-25:   A² (20:11-18)–B² (20:19-23)–A³ (20:24-25)

(4) 20:19-29:   B² (20:19-23)–A³ (20:24-25)–B³ (20:26-29)

C (20:30-31)

V.   21:1-25: The risen Jesus empowers Peter to nourish the disciples and follow him.

Three Scenes

A¹   21:1-14:   The beloved disciple directs Peter to the risen Lord who feeds the disciples.

B¹   21:15-19a: Jesus commissions Peter to feed the sheep.

A²   21:19b-23: Peter and the beloved disciple follow the risen Lord.

C   21:24-25:   What has been written is a true witness for the faith of the audience.

One Sandwich

A¹ (21:1-14)–B¹ (21:15-19a)–A² (21:19b-23) C (21:24-25)

Preliminary Literary Analysis

In the remainder of this chapter we offer a preliminary explanation and justification for the above arrangement of narrative patterns. In the following chapters we will conduct a more detailed analysis of the scenes and sandwiches of each major section in the dynamic progression in which the implied audience experiences them.

First Section: John 18:1-27

The six scenes of John 18:1-27 alternate between A scenes that involve Jesus in confrontation with the highest Jewish authorities and B scenes that involve Simon Peter in confrontation with subordinate Jewish officials. Three introductory references to "Simon Peter" (18:10, 15, 25), who is then named simply "Peter" in the remainder of each respective scene (18:11, 16-18, 26-27), indicate the transition from each A scene to each B scene. This arrangement points to a major thematic contrast between Jesus (A scenes) and Peter (B scenes).

A literary inclusion formed by the words "when he (Jesus) said (εἰπὼν) these things" in 18:1, which refer especially to John 13 17, and the words "to fulfill the word which he (Jesus) said (εἶπεν)" in 18:9, which alludes to 17:12, further delineates the unity of 18:1-9 as the first A scene. It contrasts with 18:10-11 as the first B scene dealing with Simon Peter.[8]

Another inclusion formed by occurrences of the term "high priest" in 18:19 and 18:24 further depicts the unity of 18:19-24 as the final A scene, in addition to its being sandwiched between the second (18:15-18) and third (18:25-27) B scenes concerning Simon Peter.

Various references to the "high priest" serve as a focal point that unifies the six scenes of this first section and distinguish it from the subsequent sections in which the term "high priest" no longer occurs. After the notice in the first scene that Judas brought "guards from the chief priests (ἀρχιερέων) and the Pharisees" (18:3), Simon Peter in the second scene strikes "the servant of the high priest (ἀρχιερέως, 18:10)." In the third scene Jesus is led before the father-in-law of Caiaphas, "who was high priest that year" (18:13). The other disciple who followed Jesus in the fourth scene "was known to the high priest

---

[8] R. E. Brown, *The Gospel According to John* (AB 29-29A; Garden City: Doubleday, 1966-70) 805-18, presents 18:1-12 as the first unit of John's passion narrative, although he views 18:12-13 as "a transitional passage between the scene in the garden and the scene in the palace of the high priest" (p. 813). R. Schnackenburg, *Das Johannesevangelium: Kommentar zu Kap. 13-21* (HTKNT 4/3; Freiburg/Basel/Wien: Herder, 1976) 249-57; C. K. Barrett, *The Gospel According to St. John* (2d ed.; Philadelphia: Westminster, 1978) 515-22; Giblin, "Confrontations," 215-21; de la Potterie, *Hour*, 27-40; Senior, *John*, 46-55; and Stibbe, *John as Storyteller*, 96-97, treat 18:1-11 as the first scene.

and entered with Jesus into the courtyard of the high priest" (18:15; see also v 16). The fifth scene begins as "the high priest questioned Jesus" (18:19). After his reply one of the guards struck him and said, "Is this the way you answer the high priest?" (18:22). The fifth scene concludes as Annas sent Jesus "bound to Caiaphas the high priest" (18:24). Finally, in the sixth scene "one of the servants of the high priest" (18:26) asks the question that results in Peter's third denial of Jesus.

The references to the "garden" (κῆπος) in 18:1 as the place where Jesus often met with his disciples and in 18:26 as the place where Peter was seen with Jesus form a literary inclusion that further unifies the scenes of this section.[9]

The Johannine implied audience experiences this first section as a progressive series of four narrative intercalations or sandwiches. When the third scene is read or heard, the first sandwich (A^1-B^1-A^2) occurs, in which the first two A scenes focusing on Jesus (18:1-9 and 18:12-14) frame or sandwich the first B scene focusing on Peter (18:10-11). Then, as the sequence continues and the fourth scene is read or heard, a second sandwich (B^1-A^2-B^2) occurs, in which the first two B scenes dealing with Peter (18:10-11 and 18:15-18) frame or sandwich the second A scene dealing with Jesus (18:12-14). Likewise, the fifth scene in the sequence produces a third intercalation (A^2-B^2-A^3), in which the second and third A scenes centering on Jesus (18:12-14 and 18:19-24) sandwich the second B scene centering on Peter (18:15-18). The sixth scene concludes the sequence as it forms a fourth and final sandwich (B^2-A^3-B^3), in which the second and third B scenes concerning Peter (18:15-18 and 18:25-27) frame the third A scene concerning Jesus (18:19-24).

Second Section: John 18:28-19:11

The six scenes of John 18:28-19:11 alternate between A scenes that involve Pilate and the Jews outside the praetorium and B scenes that involve Pilate and Jesus inside the praetorium. This pattern thus indicates a major thematic contrast between the Jews in confrontation with Pilate (A scenes) and Jesus in confrontation with Pilate (B scenes).

References to "coming out" of and "going into" the praetorium define the scenes in this sequence. After the Jews led Jesus from Caiaphas to the praetorium in the first scene, they themselves "did not enter into" (οὐκ εἰσῆλθον εἰς)

---

[9] F. Manns, "Le symbolisme du jardin dans le récit de la passion selon St Jean," *SBFLA* 37 (1987) 61.

the praetorium in 18:28. So Pilate then "went out" (ἐξῆλθεν) to confront them "outside" (ἔξω) in 18:29. That Pilate "entered" (εἰσῆλθεν) again "into" (εἰς) the praetorium in 18:33 serves as the transition to the second scene, in which Pilate confronts Jesus inside the praetorium. The third scene begins in 18:38b when Pilate again "went out" (ἐξῆλθεν) to the Jews. That Pilate took Jesus and had him scourged in 19:1 introduces the fourth scene, which implicitly takes place inside the praetorium where Jesus is located. The introduction to the fifth scene in 19:4 confirms this, as Pilate again "went out" (ἐξῆλθεν) to the Jews "outside" (ἔξω) and told them that he is bringing Jesus "outside" (ἔξω) to them. Jesus then "went out" (ἐξῆλθεν) to them "outside" (ἔξω) (19:5).[10] The sixth scene begins when Pilate again "entered into" (εἰσῆλθεν εἰς) the praetorium after he heard what the Jews said and became more afraid in 19:8-9.

This second section functions as a dynamic sequence of four narrative sandwiches. Once the reader experiences the third scene, the first sandwich (A¹-B¹-A²) occurs, in which the first two A scenes involving Pilate in dialogue with the Jews outside the praetorium (18:28-32 and 18:38b-40) frame the first B scene involving Pilate in dialogue with Jesus inside the praetorium (18:33-38a). As the reader hears the fourth scene, a second sandwich (B¹-A²-B²) occurs, in which the first two B scenes pertaining to Pilate and Jesus inside the praetorium (18:33-38a and 19:1-3) sandwich the second A scene pertaining to Pilate and the Jews outside the praetorium (18:38b-40). As the fifth scene is heard, it forms a third intercalation (A²-B²-A³), in which the second and third A scenes concerning Pilate and the Jews outside the praetorium (18:38b-40 and 19:4-7) frame the second B scene concerning Pilate and Jesus inside the praetorium (19:1-3). The sixth and final scene in the sequence creates a fourth sandwich (B²-A³-B³), in which the second and third B scenes dealing with Pilate in relation to Jesus inside the praetorium (19:1-3 and 19:8-11) enclose the third A scene dealing with Pilate and the Jews outside the praetorium (19:4-7).

Third Section: John 19:12-42

The six scenes of John 19:12-42 alternate between A scenes that contain invitations to see and accept revelations in conjunction with the death of Jesus with B scenes that advance God's plan by the taking or accepting of something associated with the death of Jesus. This sequence involves the audience in both

---

[10] Although as Senior, *John*, 69, points out, an "explicit reference to going 'inside' is missing at the beginning of the scourging scene (19:1)," the context indicates that this scene takes place inside the praetorium.

a contrast and complementarity between what the death of Jesus reveals (A scenes) and accomplishes (B scenes) with regard to God's plan of salvation.

The first A scene begins in 19:12 as Pilate "at this" or "therefore" (ἐκ τούτου), that is, as a result of Jesus' statement to him inside the praetorium (19:11), sought to release him.[11] That the Jews' objection to this is now heard by Pilate inside the praetorium (19:13) breaks the pattern of the previous section in which the words of the Jews to Pilate were heard only outside the praetorium (18:28-32, 38b-40; 19:4-7).[12] This is a first indication of the beginning of a new section. But in 19:13 Pilate brings Jesus "outside" (ἔξω), so that this scene also serves as the final scene outside the praetorium. This first A scene, then, both concludes the alternation of scenes "inside" and "outside" the praetorium and begins a new sequence of alternating scenes, as it moves the action to new locations—the judicial bench at a place called Stone Pavement (19:13) and the Place of the Skull, where Jesus was crucified (19:17-18).

Occurrences of the term "king" (βασιλεύς) define the first A scene. References by the Jews to Jesus' claim to be a "king" serve as the literary inclusion that introduces and concludes the scene. When Pilate seeks to release Jesus in 19:12, the Jews object that "everyone who makes himself a king opposes Caesar." And after Pilate places on the cross an inscription designating Jesus as the King of the Jews (19:19), the chief priests of the Jews in 19:21 object, "Do not write, 'The King of the Jews,' but, 'This one said, I am the King of the Jews.'" The insistent and decisive reply of Pilate, "What I have written, I have written," then closes the scene in 19:22. The other occurrences of the term "king" in 19:14, 15 (*bis*), 19 unify this scene under the theme of kingship and distinguish it from both the preceding (19:8-11) and following (19:23-24) scenes, in which the term "king" does not occur.[13]

---

[11] Schnackenburg, *Johannesevangelium*, 3. 299-304; Giblin, "John's Narration," 222; de la Potterie, *Hour*, 80-82; C. Panackel, *ΙΔΟΥ Ο ΑΝΘΡΩΠΟΣ (Jn 19, 5b): An Exegetico-Theological Study of the Text in the Light of the Use of the Term ΑΝΘΡΩΠΟΣ Designating Jesus in the Fourth Gospel* (AnGreg 251; Rome: Gregorian, 1988) 253-55, 267-69; and Senior, *John*, 69, 90-94, treat 19:12 as the conclusion of the previous scene. But, as we explain below, 19:12 introduces the kingship theme that unifies 19:12-22 as an integral scene.

[12] Senior, *John*, 69, notes this inconsistency with the previous alternation of "inside" and "outside" settings: "in 19:12 the Jews who are 'outside' seem to be present for the 'inside' interrogation of Jesus by Pilate."

[13] We have found no other interpreter who recognizes 19:12-22 as an integral scene unified by the theme of kingship. The following regard 19:16 or 19:16a as the conclusion of a scene that marks the end of the trial before Pilate and 19:16b as the beginning of a new scene dealing with Jesus' death: Janssens de Varebeke, "La structure," 506-9; Brown, *John*, 785, 873-96; idem, *The Death of the Messiah: From Gethsemane to the Grave: A Commentary on the Passion Narra-*

Various references to "seeing" and "taking" delineate as well as unify the scenes in this section. After Pilate leads Jesus outside the praetorium in the first scene (19:13), he invites the Jews to "see" and accept Jesus as their king, "Behold ("Ἴδε) your king!" (19:14). Later in the same scene the Jews "received" or "took" (παρέλαβον) Jesus after Pilate handed him over to them to be crucified (19:16). When the soldiers crucified Jesus in the second scene, they "took" (ἔλαβον) his clothes (19:23), which fulfilled scripture (19:24). When the crucified Jesus "saw" (ἰδὼν) his mother and the beloved disciple in the third scene, he invited his mother to "see" and accept the disciple as her son, "Woman, behold (ἴδε), your son!" (19:26). He likewise invited the disciple to "see" and accept her as his mother, "Behold ("Ἴδε), your mother!" (19:27). The third scene concludes as the disciple "took" (ἔλαβεν) her to his own (19:27). In the fourth scene Jesus "took" (ἔλαβεν) the vinegar offered him (19:30), bringing scripture to completion (19:28, 30). When the soldiers "saw" (εἶδον) that Jesus was already dead in the fifth scene (19:33), they did not break his bones, but one of them pricked his side and "immediately blood and water came out" (19:34), to which the one who "saw" (ἑωρακὼς) testified (19:35). The fifth scene concludes with a quote from Zechariah 12:10, "They will look ("Ὄψονται) upon him whom they have pierced" (19:37). In the sixth scene Joseph of Arimathea and Nicodemus "took" (ἔλαβον) the body of Jesus and buried it in accord with Jewish custom (19:40).

A Greek μὲν . . . δὲ construction enhances the contrast between the second (19:23-24) and third (19:25-27) scenes: "On the one hand (μὲν) the soldiers did these things (19:24), but on the other hand (δὲ) standing by the cross of Jesus were his mother . . ." (19:25).[14]

---

tives in the Four Gospels (ABRL; 2 vols.; New York: Doubleday, 1994) 821-61; Barrett, *John,* 530-46; Schnackenburg, *Johannesevangelium,* 3. 304-9; B. D. Ehrman, "Jesus' Trial before Pilate: John 18:28-19:16," *BTB* 13 (1983) 124-31; E. Haenchen, *A Commentary on the Gospel of John* (2 vols.; Hermeneia; Philadelphia: Fortress, 1984-85) 2. 176-88; Genuyt, "La comparution," 133-46; Giblin, "John's Narration," 221-39; de la Potterie, *Hour,* 82-86; Panackel, *ΙΔΟΥ Ο ΑΝΘΡΩΠΟΣ,* 247-72; P. D. Duke, *Irony in the Fourth Gospel* (Atlanta: John Knox, 1985) 126-36; Mlakuzhyil, *Fourth Gospel,* 339-42; D. Rensberger, *Johannine Faith and Liberating Community* (Philadelphia: Westminster, 1988) 91-106; Senior, *John,* 94-98; D. A. Carson, *The Gospel According to John* (Grand Rapids: Eerdmans, 1991) 596-608; Stibbe, *John as Storyteller,* 105-13; J. W. Pryor, *John: Evangelist of the Covenant People. The Narrative & Themes of the Fourth Gospel* (Downers Grove, IL: InterVarsity, 1992) 76-79; T. L. Brodie, *The Gospel According to John: A Literary and Theological Commentary* (New York: Oxford University, 1993) 538-39; A. Charbonneau, "Jésus en croix (Jn 19,16b-42); Jésus élevé (3,14ss; 8,28ss; 12,31ss)," *ScEs* 45 (1993) 5-23, 161-80; M. Sabbe, "The Johannine Account of the Death of Jesus and Its Synoptic Parallels (Jn 19,16b-42)," *ETL* 70 (1994) 34-64.

[14] Janssens de Varebeke, "La structure," 512; BAGD, 502; Carson, *John,* 615 n. 1.

A literary inclusion formed by occurrences of the word "accomplished" (τετέλεσται) in 19:28 and 19:30 establishes the unity of the fourth scene.

Different requests of Pilate indicate the contrast between the fifth and sixth scenes. After the Jews asked Pilate (ἠρώτησαν τὸν Πιλᾶτον) that the legs of those crucified be broken and that they be taken away (ἀρθῶσιν), the soldiers then came (ἦλθον οὖν) and broke the legs of those crucified with Jesus in the fifth scene (19:31-32). But in the sixth scene Joseph of Arimathea, a secret disciple of Jesus for fear of the Jews, asked Pilate (ἠρώτησεν τὸν Πιλᾶτον) if he could take (ἄρῃ) the body of Jesus, and then came (ἦλθεν οὖν) and took (ἦρεν) his body after Pilate's permission (19:38).

This third section progresses for its reader in a sequence of four narrative sandwiches. With the hearing of the third scene, the first sandwich (A¹-B¹-A²) occurs, in which the first two A scenes containing invitations to see and accept revelations in conjunction with the death of Jesus (19:12-22 and 19:25-27) frame the first B scene containing an advancement of God's plan by the taking or accepting of something associated with the death of Jesus (19:23-24). As the audience hears the fourth scene, a second sandwich (B¹-A²-B²) occurs, in which the first two B scenes involving a "taking" in fulfillment of God's scriptural plan (19:23-24 and 19:28-30) sandwich the second A scene involving Jesus' invitation to his mother and the beloved disciple to see and accept one another as mother and son (19:25-27). With the hearing of the fifth scene, a third intercalation (A²-B²-A³) occurs, in which the second and third A scenes that invite a seeing and accepting of new revelations associated with the death of Jesus (19:25-27 and 19:31-37) embrace the second B scene in which the dying Jesus takes vinegar and accomplishes God's scriptural plan (19:28-30). The sixth and final scene in the sequence forms a fourth sandwich (B²-A³-B³), in which the second and third B scenes pertaining to a "taking" that advances God's plan of salvation (19:28-30 and 19:38-42) encompass the third A scene pertaining to "seeing" the blood and water that came out of the side of the dead Jesus (19:31-37).

Fourth Section: John 20:1-31

The six scenes in John 20:1-31 alternate between A scenes that focus on an individual's encounter with the resurrection of Jesus and B scenes that focus on a group's encounter with the resurrection of Jesus.[15] In this progression the audience experiences both a contrast and a complementarity between how

[15] On the unity and internal structure of John 20, see J. Smit Sibinga, "Towards Understanding the Composition of John 20," *The Four Gospels 1992: Festschrift Frans Neirynck* (BETL 100; ed. F. Van Segbroeck, et al.; 3 vols.; Leuven: Leuven University, 1992) 2139-52.

the resurrection of Jesus affects certain individuals on the one hand (A scenes) and the group of disciples on the other hand (B scenes). An aside inviting the reader to belief and life based on all that has been written in the book (20:30-31) concludes the section.

The focus on Mary Magdalene as the acting subject delineates the first scene. It narrates how she "comes" (ἔρχεται) "to the tomb" (εἰς τὸ μνημεῖον), sees the stone removed from the tomb, runs to Simon Peter and the beloved disciple, and informs them of the empty tomb of Jesus (20:1-2).

The second scene begins in 20:3 with a change in acting subjects as Peter and the other disciple "went out" (Ἐξῆλθεν) and likewise "came to the tomb" (ἤρχοντο εἰς τὸ μνημεῖον). After they entered the empty tomb, the scene closes in 20:10 as they "returned" (ἀπῆλθον) home. The inclusion formed by the notices that these two disciples "went out" and "returned" as well as the non-participation of Mary Magdalene in this scene establishes it as a scene in itself, distinct from the first scene.

A literary inclusion created by references to "Mary" in 20:11 and "Mary Magdalene" in 20:18 defines the unity of the third scene, which narrates Mary Magdalene's encounter with the risen Jesus. This scene is delimited from both the second (20:3-10) and fourth (20:19-23) scenes in which Mary Magdalene does not appear, and continues the story of Mary Magdalene introduced in the first scene (20:1-2).[16]

The temporal change to the "evening" of the first day of the week (see 20:1) as well as the spatial change from the "tomb" (20:1 [*bis*], 2, 3, 4, 6, 8, 11 [*bis*]) to the room behind locked doors where the disciples were for fear of the Jews indicate the beginning of the fourth scene in 20:19. In this scene the risen Jesus addresses the disciples as a group (20:19-23).

The notice in 20:24 that Thomas was not with the group of disciples when Jesus came introduces the fifth scene, in which the disciples tell Thomas that they have seen the risen Lord, but he refuses to believe unless he sees for himself (20:24-25). That the risen Jesus does not participate in this scene distinguishes it from the fourth (20:19-23) and sixth (20:26-29) scenes.

---

[16] We have found no other interpreter who divides 20:1-18 into these three scenes. The following treat either 20:1-10 or 20:1-18 as a unit, and thus neglect the intercalation of a scene concerning Peter and the beloved disciple (20:3-10) into a framework of scenes concerning Mary Magdalene (20:1-2 and 20:11-18): Brown, *John*, 979-1017; idem, "The Resurrection in John 20— A Series of Diverse Reactions," *Worship* 64 (1990) 194-206; Schnackenburg, *Johannesevangelium*, 3. 361-80; Barrett, *John*, 560-66; R. Mahoney, *Two Disciples at the Tomb: The Background and Message of John 20. 1-10* (Theologie und Wirklichkeit 6; Frankfurt/Bern: Lang, 1974) 228-77; de la Potterie, *Hour*, 159-75; Senior, *John*, 135-37; Brodie, *John*, 560-64. Carson, *John*, 635-46, divides 20:1-18 into two units: 20:1-9 and 20:10-18.

The temporal change to eight days later and the notice that Thomas was now with the disciples in the room behind locked doors initiates the sixth scene in 20:26. In this scene the risen Jesus addresses Thomas as an individual within the group of disciples (20:26-29).

The three scenes in 20:19-29, then, progress from a meeting between the risen Jesus and the disciples without Thomas (20:19-23) to an exchange between Thomas and the disciples without the risen Jesus (20:24-25) to a meeting between the risen Jesus and the disciples with Thomas (20:26-29). A separate statement of the purpose of the entire book concludes this section in 20:30-31.[17]

The six scenes in this section operate as a dynamic sequence of four narrative sandwiches. The first three scenes form the first sandwich (A^1-B^1-A^2), in which the first two A scenes focusing on Mary Magdalene at the tomb (20:1-2 and 20:11-18) frame the first B scene focusing on Peter and the beloved disciple (20:3-10). With the sequential occurrence of the fourth scene a second sandwich (B^1-A^2-B^2) becomes operative, in which the first two B scenes dealing with disciples (20:3-10 and 20:19-23) enclose the second A scene dealing with Mary Magdalene (20:11-18). As the audience hears the fifth scene, a third intercalation (A^2-B^2-A^3) occurs, in which the second and third A scenes concerning the individuals Mary Magdalene (20:11-18) and Thomas (20:24-25) embrace the second B scene concerning the group of disciples (20:19-23). The sixth scene in the sequence activates the fourth and final sandwich (B^2-A^3-B^3), in which the second and third B scenes narrating appearances of the risen Jesus to the disciples without (20:19-23) and with Thomas (20:26-29) encase the third A scene involving Thomas and the disciples without the risen Lord (20:24-25).

Fifth Section: John 21:1-25

A literary inclusion formed by the introductory notice that Jesus "manifested" (ἐφανέρωσεν) himself again to the disciples at the Sea of Tiberias and "mani-

---

[17] As far as we know, no other interpreter divides 20:19-31 in this way, which recognizes the intercalation of a scene involving Thomas and the disciples without the risen Jesus (20:24-25) into a framework of scenes involving the risen Jesus and the disciples without (20:19-23) and with Thomas (20:26-29). Brown, John, 1018-52, and Mlakuzhyil, Fourth Gospel, 336-37, treat 20:19-29 as a scene in itself; de la Potterie, Hour, 160-65, 175-90, divides 20:19-31 into 20:19-25, 20:26-29 and 20:30-31; Senior, John, 138-40, divides the same verses into 20:19-23 and 20:24-31; Schnackenburg, Johannesevangelium, 3. 380-405, Carson, John, 646-63, and Brodie, John, 567-73, divides them into 20:19-23, 20:24-29 and 20:30-31. Segovia, "Final Farewell," 167-90, treats 20:30-31 as the introduction to the last section of the Gospel.

fested" (ἐφανέρωσεν) himself in this way in 21:1 and the concluding notice that this was the third time that Jesus "was manifested" (ἐφανερώθη) to the disciples in 21:14 defines the first scene of this section. In this scene the beloved disciple directs Peter to the risen Lord, who feeds the disciples (21:1-14).

That the second scene consists of an encounter between the risen Jesus and Peter without the participation of the beloved disciple (21:15-19a) distinguishes it from both the first (21:1-14) and third (21:19b-23) scenes, in which the beloved disciple is a participant. This scene narrates how Jesus commissions Peter to the feed the sheep. It concludes in 21:19a with a reference to the kind of death with which Peter will glorify God. Jesus' command to Peter, "Follow ('Ακολούθει) me," introduces the third scene in 21:19b. A theme of "following" unifies this scene, as Peter sees the beloved disciple "following" (ἀκολουθοῦντα) in 21:20, and Jesus repeats his command to Peter, "You follow (ἀκολούθει) me" in 21:22. A repetition of Jesus' statement to Peter about the beloved disciple in 21:22, "If I wish him to remain until I come, what concern is it of yours," further unifies and concludes the third scene in 21:23.

An aside to the reader about what has been written in the book, which is similar to the aside that concludes the fourth section (20:30-31), likewise concludes the fifth section in 21:24-25.

The three scenes of this final section function as one narrative intercalation (A^1-B^1-A^2). The two A scenes involving both Peter and the beloved disciple in an encounter with the risen Jesus (21:1-14 and 21:19b-23) frame the B scene in which the risen Jesus commissions Peter to feed the sheep without mention of the beloved disciple (21:15-19a).[18]

---

[18] We have found no other interpreter who recognizes the intercalation of these three scenes in John 21:1 23. For other arrangements and treatments see Barrett, *John*, 576-88; Brown, *John*, 1065-1132; idem, "The Resurrection in John 21—Missionary and Pastoral Directives for the Church," *Worship* 64 (1990) 433-45; Mahoney, *Two Disciples*, 287-97; Schnackenburg, *Johannesevangelium*, 3. 406-48; Haenchen, *John*, 2. 220-34; Mlakuzhyil, *Fourth Gospel*, 343-47; Senior, *John*, 141-43; Carson, *John*, 665-86; Segovia, "Final Farewell," 167-90. On the close relation of John 21 to the rest of the Gospel, see P. S. Minear, "The Original Functions of John 21," *JBL* 102 (1983) 85-98; F. Neirynck, "John 21," *NTS* 36 (1990) 321-36; M. Franzmann and M. Klinger, "The Call Stories of John 1 and John 21," *St. Vladimir's Theological Quarterly* 36 (1992) 7-15; P. F. Ellis, "The Authenticity of John 21," *St. Vladimir's Theological Quarterly* 36 (1992) 17-25; J. Breck, "John 21: Appendix, Epilogue or Conclusion?," *St. Vladimir's Theological Quarterly* 36 (1992) 27-49; W. S. Vorster, "The Growth and Making of John 21," *The Four Gospels 1992: Festschrift Frans Neirynck* (BETL 100; ed. F. Van Segbroeck, et al.; 3 vols.; Leuven: Leuven University, 1992) 2207-21. On the narrative unity of John 21, see T. Wiarda, "John 21.1-23: Narrative Unity and its Implications," *JSNT* 46 (1992) 53-71.

CHAPTER 2

Jesus, the Jews, and Peter
(John 18:1-27)

With His Disciples Jesus Reveals
His Identity to His Opponents (A¹ 18:1-9)

1 Having said these things, Jesus went out with his disciples across the Kidron¹ valley to where there was a garden, into which he entered—he and his disciples. 2 Judas his betrayer also knew the place, because Jesus often met there with his disciples. 3 So Judas, taking a band of soldiers as well as officers from the chief priests and from the Pharisees, went there with lanterns and torches and weapons.

4 Then Jesus, knowing everything that was coming upon him, went out and said to them, "Whom do you seek?" 5 They answered him, "Jesus the Nazorean." He said to them, "I am he." Judas his betrayer was also standing with them. 6 When he said to them, "I am he," they withdrew backwards and fell to the ground.

7 Then he again asked them, "Whom do you seek?" They said, "Jesus the Nazorean." 8 Jesus answered, "I told you that I am he. If then you seek me, let these go." 9 This happened so that the word that he had said might be fulfilled, "I did not lose a single one of those whom you have given me."

---

¹ For the text-critical preference of the reading "of the Kidron" (τοῦ Κεδρὼν) rather than the variants, "of the cedars" (τῶν κέδρων) or "of the cedar" (τοῦ κέδρου), see B. M. Metzger, *A Textual Commentary on the Greek New Testament* (London/New York: United Bible Societies, 1971) 250-51. We shall employ our own translation of the Greek text throughout the book.

Judas takes armed men to Jesus and his disciples (18:1-3)

"Having said these things" (Ταῦτα εἰπὼν, 18:1) marks a transition from Jesus' preceding farewell prayer (John 17) and discourse (John 13-16). In this extended farewell discourse Jesus had repeatedly and emphatically "said things" (Ταῦτα εἰπὼν in 13:21; ταῦτα λελάληκα in 14:25; 15:11; 16:1, 4, 25, 33) to prepare his disciples not only for the hour of his departure from this world to the Father (13:1) but for his absence until he comes again to take them to himself (14:3).[2]

That "Jesus went out with his disciples" finally fulfills the command he uttered in the midst of the farewell discourse during his last supper with his disciples, "Rise, let us go from here" (14:31). Whereas Judas, the disciple who would betray Jesus, earlier went out (ἐξῆλθεν, 13:30-31) alone from this final table fellowship, Jesus went out (ἐξῆλθεν) still united with the rest of his disciples. That "he and his disciples" together entered a garden across the Kidron valley emphatically underlines their close union.[3]

This garden (κῆπος), mentioned here for the first time in the narrative, was the place where Jesus habitually met "with his disciples" (18:2) and thus serves as the symbol of their close union.[4] It functions as the spatial focus for the entire action of this first unit: Jesus and his disciples enter it (18:1); Judas knew "the place" as Jesus had often met "there" with his disciples (18:2); and Judas brings others "there" (18:3). That Jesus and his disciples entered (εἰσῆλθεν) the garden resonates with Jesus' previous metaphorical statement that "I am the gate; if anyone enters (εἰσέλθῃ) through me, he will be saved and will go in (εἰσελεύσεται) and come out and find pasture" (10:9). In accord with the extended shepherd metaphor (10:1-18, 26-30), the disciples (sheep) have heard the voice of Jesus (shepherd/gate) in the farewell discourse and have now followed him into the garden (sheepfold).[5]

---

[2] For a detailed analysis of the farewell discourse in 13:31-16:33, see F. F. Segovia, *The Farewell of the Word: The Johannine Call to Abide* (Minneapolis: Fortress, 1991).

[3] Our translation highlights the emphasis expressed here by the Greek construction and word order.

[4] For a possible biblical background to the symbol of the garden in John, see Manns, "Le symbolisme du jardin," 53-80; N. Wyatt, "'Supposing Him to Be the Gardener' (John 20,15): A Study of the Paradise Motif in John," *ZNW* 81 (1990) 21-38.

[5] For a discussion of the shepherd metaphor as part of the cosmological in addition to the historical and ecclesiological dimensions of the Johannine narrative, see Reinhartz, *The Word,* 48-104.

Jesus knew from the beginning that Judas, the son of Simon Iscariot, although one of the twelve disciples chosen by Jesus, was a "devil" (διάβολός, 6:70)[6] who would betray him (6:64-71).[7] At Jesus' last supper with his disciples the betrayal became imminent as "the devil (διαβόλου) had already put it into the heart of Judas, son of Simon Iscariot, to betray him" (13:2). After Jesus washed the feet of the disciples, Judas's separation from them began as Jesus declared that not all of them were clean, "for he knew who would betray him" (13:10-11). Jesus further singled out Judas as the one who would violate his close union of table fellowship with him in fulfillment of Ps 41:9, "The one who ate my bread lifted up his heel against me" (13:18). After Jesus gave Judas a dipped morsel during the meal, "Satan entered into him," and then the actual separation occurred as Jesus commanded him to do quickly what he was going to do and he went out immediately (13:27, 30). Now he has returned, using his knowledge as a disciple of where Jesus often met with his disciples (18:2), to perpetrate his betrayal of Jesus and of his discipleship.

When Mary anointed Jesus at Bethany, Judas protested that the oil could have been sold and the money given to the poor. The narrator, however, informed the reader that Judas had no concern for the poor but was rather a thief (κλέπτης), who used to steal from the money bag placed in his charge (12:1-6). In accord with the shepherd metaphor, then, Judas represents the

---

[6] O. Böcher, "διάβολος," *EDNT* 1. 297-98: "In the dualistic worldview that the NT shares with ancient Judaism, the heavenly βασιλεία stands in opposition to that of the demons. The devil is the highest sovereign of the demons; the demons are his 'angels' (Matt 25:41; Rev 12:7, 9). In accordance with ancient Jewish demonology the NT traces the διάβολος and his ἄγγελοι as creatures of God back to the fall of the angels in Gen 6:1-4 (Rev 12:9, 12). Before this fall the διάβολος had accused mankind before God (Rev 12:10; cf. Job 1:9-11; 2:4f.). . . . Anyone who succumbs to temptation is among the children of the διάβολος (John 8:44, of the Jews; Acts 13:10, of magus, Bar-Jesus—Elymas; 1 John 3:8, 10), and even becomes a διάβολος himself (John 6:70, of Judas; cf. Matt 16:23 par. Mark 8:33)."

J. V. Brownson, "Neutralizing the Intimate Enemy: The Portrayal of Judas in the Fourth Gospel," SBLASP 31 (1992) 52: "At the very point where the betrayer is introduced, even before he is named, he is identified as 'a devil' (John 6:70). . . . Later in 17:12, Judas is spoken of as the 'son of perdition' (ὁ υἱὸς τῆς ἀπωλείας). This phrase should probably be interpreted . . . as a genitive of origin, where ἀπώλεια stands for the Hebrew אבדן ('Abaddon'), a Hebrew term which can stand in general for Hell (Prov. 15:11, 27:20, 1QH 3:16, 19, 32), or more particularly for the devil or Hell personified (Job 28:22, Rev. 9:11). The reference to Judas as a son of Hell/the devil is in keeping with the use of 'child of Hell' and similar phrases as a common form of early Christian invective, and again cloaks Judas as a character with diabolical associations."

[7] On 6:64-71, see J. P. Heil, *Jesus Walking on the Sea: Meaning and Gospel Functions of Matt 14:22-33, Mark 6:45-52 and John 6:15b-21* (AnBib 87; Rome: Biblical Institute, 1981) 165-70.

thief (κλέπτης) and robber who has not entered through the gate (Jesus) into the sheepfold (garden) of the disciples (10:1). That he comes (ἔρχεται) with weapons (18:3) accords with his being the thief (κλέπτης) who comes (ἔρχεται) only "to steal and slaughter and kill" (10:10).

Judas also embodies Satan, "the ruler of this world" who, as Jesus has already informed the disciples, now comes (ἔρχεται) (14:30). Jesus has called Judas a "devil" (6:70), the devil has already put it into the heart of Judas to betray Jesus (13:2), and Satan has entered into Judas (13:27). But Jesus has predicted that "the ruler of this world will be cast outside" (12:31). And when the Paraclete (or Helper),[8] the holy Spirit (14:26; 15:26), comes, he will demonstrate to the world that "the ruler of this world has been condemned" (16:7-8, 11).

The chief priests and Pharisees had earlier sent officers (ὑπηρέτας) to arrest Jesus (7:32), but they returned without him, saying, "Never has anyone spoken like this!" (7:45-46). After Jesus raised Lazarus from the dead, the chief priests and Pharisees planned to put both Jesus and Lazarus to death (11:53; 12:10). They had given orders that if anyone knew where Jesus was, he should inform them, so that they might arrest him (11:57). Judas knew where Jesus was and now leads officers (ὑπηρέτας) from the chief priests and Pharisees to him, so that they can finally fulfill their plan of arresting and killing Jesus. In seeking to put Jesus to death the chief priests and Pharisees confirm Jesus' accusation that they are doing the work of the devil like Judas (8:37-44).

Judas takes a band or cohort (σπεῖραν) of Roman soldiers along with the officers from the chief priests and Pharisees. Whether this detachment of Roman soldiers numbers a full cohort of 600 or only a maniple of 200,[9] it functions as hyperbolic irony to exaggerate the violent strength of the diabolic forces of unbelief coming against Jesus with weapons.[10] That the chief priests and Pharisees are aligned with the very Romans they fear will come and take away their temple (literally "place") and nation if they do not prevent belief in Jesus (11:48) adds to the irony.

That Judas, the Roman soldiers, and the officers from the chief priests and Pharisees come with lanterns and torches corresponds with the notice that when Judas went out from the supper it was night (13:30). Since in John darkness and night symbolize the absence of the revelation that Jesus brings and the unbelief that leads to eternal death, the lanterns and torches they need because

---

[8] BAGD, 618.

[9] Brown, *John*, 807; idem, *Death*, 248-49; Barrett, *John*, 520; Carson, *John*, 577; L. Morris, *The Gospel According to John* (NICNT; Grand Rapids: Eerdmans, 1971) 741.

[10] Duke, *Irony*, 109.

of the night symbolically indicate their unbelief. The weapons taken along with the lanterns and torches underline the threat to Jesus and his disciples. But Jesus is the Word of God in whom is the Life[11] that is the light of human beings; it still shines in the darkness that did not overcome it (1:4-5). He is the true light who gives light to every person (1:9). Whoever believes in Jesus as the light of the world will not walk in darkness, but will have the light of Life (8:12; 12:46). Those coming in darkness to bring about Jesus' death are ironically coming to the light who could give them Life if they would believe in him.[12]

This first unit (18:1-3) prepares the audience for a dramatic life and death confrontation. Jesus is the good shepherd who lays down his life for his sheep (10:11) and the light of the world whose followers will not walk in darkness but have the light of Life (8:12). He went out with his disciples (sheep) to the garden (sheepfold), representative of the life of close union they have habitually shared. It points to the abundant, eternal life Jesus can give believers (10:10). But Judas, Roman soldiers, and Jewish officers, representative of the diabolical powers ruling the world, come as "thieves and robbers" (10:1-10). In the darkness of unbelief indicated by their lanterns and torches and weapons they have come to take away the life of the "shepherd" who offers the world the light of Life.

Jesus surrenders/reveals himself (18:4-6)

In correspondence to his "knowing (εἰδὼς) that his hour had come to pass from this world to the Father" (13:1), Jesus now "knows (εἰδὼς) everything that was coming upon him" (18:4). Judas has not taken him by surprise, for Jesus "knew (ᾔδει) who would betray him" (13:11). Indeed, Jesus is in command as he himself directed Judas to do quickly what he was going to do (13:27). And once Judas went out to betray him, Jesus declared, "Now is the Son of Man glorified, and God is glorified in him" (13:31).

Whereas Jesus went out (ἐξῆλθεν) from the supper united with his disciples (18:1), now he went out (ἐξῆλθεν) from the garden alone (18:4). In control of the situation he acts as the good shepherd who lays down his life for his sheep (10:11). He went out of the garden (sheepfold) to meet the "thieves and rob-

---

[11] Since in John "life" (ζωή) is equivalent to "eternal life" (ζωὴ αἰώνιος), we have capitalized it; see J. G. van der Watt, "The Use of αἰώνιος in the Concept ζωὴ αἰώνιος in John's Gospel," NovT 31 (1989) 217-28.

[12] For occurrences of the light/day and darkness/night symbolism, see 1:4-5, 7-9; 3:2, 19-21; 5:35; 6:17; 8:12; 9:4-5; 11:9-10; 12:35-36, 46; 13:30; 19:39; 20:1; 21:3.

bers" (10:8) who come "to steal and slaughter and kill" (10:10). He has not abandoned the sheep and fled like a hired hand when he sees a wolf coming (10:12-13).

The question Jesus puts to them, "Whom do you seek?" (Τίνα ζητεῖτε), recalls his question to the first two disciples who follow him, "What do you seek?" (Τί ζητεῖτε) (1:38). After they accepted his invitation to come and see where he stays, they remained with him that day (1:39) and eventually believed in him (2:11). In asking his opponents a question that leads to his surrender and arrest, Jesus is ironically asking a question that could lead them to believe in him.

Their answer, "Jesus the Nazorean" (18:5), continues the irony. When Philip found Nathanael and informed him that "Jesus son of Joseph from Nazareth," was the one about whom Moses and the prophets wrote, he sarcastically replied, "Can anything good come from Nazareth?" (1:45-46). After he accepted Philip's invitation to come and see, his encounter with Jesus led him to confess his belief (1:50) that "you are the Son of God, you are the King of Israel!" (1:49). In answering, "Jesus the Nazorean," the opponents are ironically identifying the one whom they are seeking to kill as the one who could bring them to the faith of Nathanael.

The reply of Jesus, "I am he," or more literally, "I am" (Ἐγώ εἰμι, 18:5), not only identifies him as the Nazorean but resonates with all of his previous "I am" predications,[13] especially with his absolute statements that "I am."[14] Believing in Jesus as "I am" means believing in him as *the* revealer of the Father, who offers believers Life. Jesus told his Jewish adversaries that they would "die" in their sins if they do not "believe" that "I am" (8:24). When they lift up Jesus as the Son of Man in crucifixion, then they will know that "I am," that Jesus does nothing on his own, but says or reveals only what the Father taught him (8:28). Jesus knows the Father and keeps his word, for as he tells the Jews, "Before Abraham came to be, I am" (8:58). He told his disciples about his betrayal (13:18) before it happened, so that when it happened they might believe that "I am" (13:19). In replying "I am" and surrendering himself to his opponents as the Nazorean to be put to death, Jesus is ironically giving them, his disciples, and the audience an opportunity to believe in him as "I am," the one who reveals the Father and gives Life.

---

[13] John 4:26; 6:20, 35, 41, 48, 51; 8:12, 18; 10:7, 9, 11, 14; 11:25; 15:1, 5.

[14] For a discussion of the Johannine "I am" statements, see Brown, *John,* 533-38; and on "I am" in John 18:4-8, see idem, *Death,* 259-62.

The parenthetical note that "Judas his betrayer was also standing with them" (18:5) indicates his continuing unbelief despite this opportunity to believe in Jesus as "I am." Indeed, Judas has completed his separation from Jesus and his disciples. He is no longer "with his disciples" (μετὰ τῶν μαθητῶν αὐτοῦ, 18:2) but has now associated himself "with them" (μετ' αὐτῶν), his fellow opponents, who along with Judas represent the powers of evil and unbelief.

The emphatic expression "they withdrew backwards" (ἀπῆλθον εἰς τὰ ὀπίσω) when Jesus pronounced his powerful "I am" (18:6) underlines the unbelief of Judas, the Roman soldiers, and the Jewish officers. Earlier, when many of his disciples "murmured" and were scandalized (6:60-61) by Jesus' Bread of Life discourse (6:22-59), he declared that "there are some of you who do not believe." For Jesus knew from the beginning those who would not believe and who would betray him (6:64). Coming to him in faith must be granted by the Father (6:65). Many of his disciples then confirmed the words of Jesus and demonstrated their unbelief as "they withdrew backwards" (ἀπῆλθον εἰς τὰ ὀπίσω) and no longer went around with him (6:66).

That his opponents "withdrew backwards and fell to the ground" (18:6) at the "I am" of Jesus illustrates his superior power and points to his ultimate victory over this large group of evil forces who have come with weapons to arrest him and lead him to death. This brings the irony of this unit (18:4-6) to a climax. By his "I am" Jesus both surrendered himself and revealed his profound identity as *the* revealer of God. Although this resulted not in belief but in emphatic unbelief, it assures the audience that Jesus rather than his evil, unbelieving adversaries is in ultimate control.[15]

Jesus saves all those given to him (18:7-9)

Illustrating his continued control, Jesus again takes the initiative by repeating his question, "Whom do you seek?," to which his foes repeat, "Jesus the Nazorean" (18:7). In reiterating his powerful "I am" Jesus not only reveals and surrenders himself to his enemies but wins the release of his disciples: "If then you seek me, let these go" (18:8). As the good shepherd Jesus is laying down his life for the sheep (10:11). Jesus has saved the disciples (sheep) who have entered the garden (sheepfold) through him (sheepgate) (18:1) and are now

---

[15] On the "quest" to arrest Jesus in John 18:1-11, see J. Painter, *The Quest for the Messiah: The History, Literature and Theology of the Johannine Community* (Edinburgh: Clark, 1991) 32.

allowed to go out freely (10:9). This points to the fulfillment of Jesus' pronouncement that an hour is coming and has come when each of the disciples will be "scattered" (like sheep) to his own home and leave Jesus alone with his Father (16:32). Indeed, it is through his intimate "aloneness" and unity with his Father that Jesus is freely laying down his life for the disciples. His enemies are not taking his life from him. In majestic control over them he is laying his life down in obedience to the command of his Father (10:17-18).

That Jesus secures the escape of his disciples by revealing and surrendering himself allows, as the narrator announces, the word which he had previously spoken to be fulfilled: "I did not lose (ἀπώλεσα) a single one of those whom you have given me" (18:9). This refers, first of all, to what Jesus said in his farewell prayer to the Father for his disciples as those whom the Father has "given" him (17:2, 6, 9). He asserted that "when I was with them I guarded them in your name that you gave me, and I protected them, and none of them was lost (ἀπώλετο) except the son of destruction (ἀπωλείας), in order that the scripture might be fulfilled" (17:12).

With his powerful "I am" pronouncements (18:5-6, 8), through which he revealed the name of the Father, Jesus, the good shepherd, has guarded and protected his disciples, the sheep, so that not one of them was lost. That he did not "lose" one of them means not only that he has not allowed the "thieves and robbers" (10:8) to "steal and kill and destroy" (10:10) them, but that they did not lose their faith and join the forces of evil and unbelief like Judas. They have remained believing sheep who have heard the voice of the good shepherd and followed him (10:26-27). That Jesus did not "lose" (ἀπώλεσα) one of them means that in laying down his life for them as the good shepherd (10:11) he is giving them eternal life and "they shall not be lost/perish (ἀπόλωνται) for eternity" (10:28).[16] In contrast to the "thieves and robbers" Jesus came so that the sheep "might have life and have it more abundantly" (10:10).

Whereas in his farewell prayer Jesus declared that none of his disciples "was lost/destroyed except the son of destruction" (17:12), which refers to Judas,[17] now it is emphasized through a double negative that there is no longer an exception: "I did not (οὐκ) lose no one (οὐδένα) of those whom you have given me" (18:9).[18] Since Judas has separated himself from the disciples and

---

[16] The word ἀπόλλυμι means both to be lost and to be destroyed or perish; see BAGD, 95; A. Kretzer, "ἀπόλλυμι," *EDNT* 1. 135-36.

[17] See 6:70; 13:2, 27; Brownson, "Judas in the Fourth Gospel," 52.

[18] On John 18:8b-9, see Brown, *Death*, 289-91.

associated with the Jewish officers and Roman soldiers (18:5), he is no longer among those whom the Father has "given" to Jesus. Indeed, Judas, the "thief" (12:6), has come as a "son of destruction (ἀπωλείας)" to "destroy" (ἀπολέσῃ) the sheep, whereas Jesus, the good shepherd, came that they may have abundant, eternal life (10:10, 28).

"Those whom you have given (δέδωκάς) me" include not only the disciples but all listeners who respond with faith to the appeal for their belief. In the Bread of Life discourse (6:22-59) Jesus declared that all (πᾶν) that the Father gives (δίδωσίν) him will come to him, that is, will believe in him (6:35-37). His saving of the disciples from perishing in a sea storm by walking on the sea (6:16-21) illustrated and substantiated his proclamation that "this is the will of the one who sent me, that I should not lose/let perish (ἀπολέσω) all (πᾶν) of what he has given (δέδωκέν) me, but raise it up on the last day" (6:39).[19] In his farewell prayer Jesus disclosed that the Father gave him authority over all (πάσης) people, so that he might give eternal life to all (πᾶν) whom the Father has given (δέδωκας) him (17:2). As the narrator had earlier announced, God gave his only Son to the world, so that all (πᾶς) who believe in him may not perish (ἀπόληται) but have eternal life (3:16). That Jesus did not "lose" or "let perish" a single one of those "given" to him (18:9), then, assures the audience that in laying down his own life Jesus is providing eternal life for all who believe in him.

That Jesus did not let perish (ἀπώλεσα) "a single one" of those given him serves as an ironic understatement of the universalizing and unifying aspects of his life-giving death:

1) The high priest Caiaphas told the chief priests and the Pharisees that it would be better for them if one man died for the people so that the "whole" nation may not perish (ἀπόληται) (11:50). The narrator added that the high priest was actually prophesying that Jesus was going to die not only for the nation, but also to gather into "one" the dispersed children of God (11:51-52),[20] that is, those who accept Jesus and believe in his name (1:12).

2) As the good shepherd who lays down his life for the sheep, Jesus declared that he has other sheep not of this fold, those who are not yet

[19] Heil, *Jesus Walking on the Sea*, 155-57.
[20] J. Beutler, "Two Ways of Gathering: The Plot to Kill Jesus in John 11.47-53," *NTS* 40 (1994) 399-406.

believing disciples. He must lead them also, and they will hear his voice, and there will be "one flock, one shepherd" (10:15-16). He will thus give them also, as believing followers (10:26-27), eternal life and "they shall not perish (ἀπόλωνται) for eternity" (10:28).

3) In his farewell prayer Jesus prayed not only for his disciples but also for those who will believe in him through the word of his disciples, so that "all" may be "one" and share in the intimate unity that Jesus enjoys with his Father (17:20-21).

4) When the chief priests and the Pharisees sent officers to arrest Jesus, he said that he would be with them only a little while longer, and then go to the one who sent him. They will look for him but not find him, since where he is they cannot come (7:32-34). The Jews wondered where he was going that they could not find him. With ironic misunderstanding they ask, "Surely he does not intend to go to the dispersion among the Greeks and teach the Greeks?" (7:35).[21] Instead of Jesus going to the Greeks, some Greeks come to see him, which signals the arrival of the hour for Jesus as the Son of Man to be glorified through his death (12:20-23).[22] When he is "lifted up" from the earth in crucifixion, he will draw "all" to himself (12:32).

5) In not allowing a single one of those given him to perish (18:9), Jesus is providing eternal life not only for his disciples but for "all," including the whole nation (11:50), the scattered children of God (11:52), the "other sheep" (10:16), future disciples (17:20), and Greeks of the dispersion (7:35; 12:20). His death draws "all" who believe into "one," allowing them to participate in the intimate unity of Life that Jesus shares with his Father (10:16; 11:52; 12:32; 17:21).

This opening scene (18:1-9), then, involves a dramatic, life and death confrontation in which the diabolical forces of unbelief, represented by the Roman soldiers and Jewish officers led by Judas, a former disciple, come in darkness with weapons against Jesus and the disciples still united with him. In

---

[21] Duke, *Irony,* 90-92. J. Wanke, "Ἕλλην," *EDNT* 1. 436: "According to John 12:20f. there were 'Greeks' 'among those who went up [to Jerusalem] to worship at the feast' and these Greeks sought to see Jesus. The passage concerns 'God-fearers' (cf. Acts 17:4), i.e., Gentiles who are closely associated with Judaism without converting.... John 7:35 ... has the Greek-speaking Gentile world in view. The genitive phrase 'Diaspora of the Hellenes' refers to geographic area. . . . Thus the reference is not to Diaspora Jews. The Evangelist has the confused Jews express the later reality without realizing it: The gospel will be preached to the Gentiles."

[22] J. Beutler, "Greeks Come to See Jesus (John 12,20f)," *Bib* 71 (1990) 333-47.

surrendering himself Jesus is also revealing himself, both appealing for belief and demonstrating his superior power. Although they fail to believe, Jesus' surrender of himself assures the audience that Jesus is providing not only for his disciples, but for all who believe, the eternal life of unity with him and his Father.

Peter Cuts Off the Ear of the High Priest's Servant
(B¹ 18:10-11)

10 Then Simon Peter, who had a sword, drew it, struck the servant of the high priest, and cut off his right ear. The name of the servant was Malchus. 11 Jesus then said to Peter, "Put the sword into its sheath. The cup that the Father has given me, am I not to drink it?"

Peter strikes the servant of the high priest (18:10)

Simon Peter first appeared in the narrative as the brother of Andrew, a disciple of John the Baptist, who became a follower of Jesus (1:35-40). He brought Simon to Jesus as the Messiah, who distinguished Simon with the name Cephas, Aramaic for "Peter" (1:41-42).[23] When many disciples abandoned Jesus (6:66) after the Bread of Life discourse (6:22-59), Simon Peter, as spokesman for the Twelve (6:67) who still believed in Jesus, pronounced the climactic confession, "Lord, to whom shall we go? You have the words of eternal life, and we have come to believe and know that you are the Holy One of God!" (6:68-69).[24] Although he initially objected, Peter offered to allow Jesus to wash not only his feet but also his hands and head in order to have a "share" with Jesus and thus remain united with him (13:6-9). When Jesus announced his betrayal by one of the disciples, it was Peter who nodded to the "beloved disciple" to find out whom he meant (13:21-24). After Jesus told the disciples of his departure, Peter wanted to follow him and promised to lay down his life for him, but Jesus predicted that Peter would deny him three times (13:36-38).

---

[23] R. Pesch, "Κηφᾶς," EDNT 2. 292: "The predominant Aramaic meaning, which is reflected in the Greek tr. Πέτρος, is 'stone' (also: 'bundle,' 'lump,' etc.).... The original symbolism of the name, in view of its 'success,' was probably 'precious stone' = significant person (Peter as 'first' in the circle of the Twelve). Along with being an epithet or surname (preserved in the double name 'Simon Peter'), Cephas very early became a proper name, as the old Church creed in 1 Cor 15:3ff. attests, and gradually supplanted the name Simon (most often in the Greek tr. Πέτρος)."

[24] Heil, Jesus Walking on the Sea, 167-70.

Now Peter continues to distinguish himself. In contrast to the other disciples, Peter remains to defend Jesus (18:10) and demonstrate his willingness to lay down his life for him (13:37) rather than employ the escape Jesus has won for his disciples (18:8). Like the opponents Peter has a weapon (18:3), a sword. But in contrast to them he actually wields it, as he drew it and struck the servant of the high priest. By cutting off the servant's right ear, Peter effects a mutilation that disqualifies this important official from assisting the high priest in his priestly office.[25] That the narrator discloses the name, Malchus, of this member of the otherwise anonymous group of officers from the chief priests and Pharisees (18:3) further associates him with the high priest whose name, Caiaphas, has also been disclosed (11:49), and thus heightens his importance as a chief representative of the high priest.[26]

Despite his attempt to defend Jesus, in striking the servant of the high priest, Peter is assaulting a significant but subordinate official. It was the high priest, not his servant, who voiced God's plan for Jesus and has a leading role in executing it. It was the high priest Caiaphas who spoke "not on his own" but for God as he "prophesied" that Jesus was going to die not only for the nation but to gather into one the dispersed children of God (11:51-52).

Jesus must drink the cup the Father has given him (18:11)

The command of Jesus for Peter to put the sword back in its sheath confirms that Peter is actually obstructing God's plan for Jesus. Peter's violent defense is preventing Jesus from "drinking the cup" of suffering and death the Father has given him (18:11). In the biblical tradition the image of the "cup" one must drink refers to one's destiny as determined by God, often with bitter connotations.[27] Here the bitterness of drinking the cup refers to Jesus' impending death that the high priest Caiaphas has persuaded the chief priests and Pharisees to pursue (11:47-53).

That the Father has given (δέδωκέν) the cup to Jesus parallels the final statement of the previous scene, "I did not lose a single one of those whom you have given (δέδωκάς) me" (18:9). Drinking the cup of death "given" him by the

[25] Lev 21:16-23; B. T. Viviano, "The High Priest's Servant's Ear: Mark 14:47," *RB* 96 (1989) 71-80.

[26] D. R. Beck, "The Narrative Function of Anonymity in Fourth Gospel Characterization," *Characterization in Biblical Literature (Semeia* 63; ed. E. S. Malbon and A. Berlin; Atlanta: Scholars, 1993) 143-58.

[27] Pss 11:6; 16:5; 75:9; Isa 51:17, 22; Ezek 23:31-35; Jer 25:15-17; Hab 2:16; Lam 4:21; BAGD, 695.

Father will enable Jesus not to lose or let perish but to provide eternal life for those believers "given" him by the Father.

Peter does not respond to the question of whether Jesus is to drink the cup the Father has given him (18:11); it remains a question for him and the audience to answer and affirm. This has the rhetorical effect of reinforcing for the audience that in surrendering himself to death Jesus is accomplishing the plan of God. Jesus' willingness to "drink the cup" the Father has given him resonates with his earlier statement that "Now my soul is troubled, yet what should I say?—'Father save me from this hour'? But it was for this reason that I have come to this hour. Father, glorify your name" (12:27-28).

To drink the cup of death that "the Father" has given Jesus also resonates with his being the good shepherd who freely gives up his life for the sheep (10:11-14) in accord with the will of God, the Father. Just as "the Father" knows Jesus and Jesus knows "the Father," so Jesus will lay down his life for the sheep (10:15). "The Father" loves Jesus because he lays down his life in order to take it up again. No one takes it from him but he lays it down on his own. He has the "power" or "authority" (ἐξουσίαν) to lay it down and to take it up again. This command he has received from "my Father" (10:17-18).

This scene (18:10-11), then, contrasts with the previous scene (18:1-9) in a triple way: 1) In contrast to the other disciples Peter attempts to defend Jesus with a violent assault. 2) In contrast to the armed opponents Peter uses his sword to strike the servant of the high priest. 3) In contrast to Jesus Peter is thwarting rather than accomplishing God's will that Jesus "drink the cup" of death.

Jesus Alone Is Led to the Father-In-Law of the High Priest To Die for the People (A² 18:12-14)

12 Then the band of soldiers, the tribune, and the Jewish officers arrested Jesus and bound him. 13 They led him before Annas first, for he was the father-in-law of Caiaphas, who was high priest that year. 14 It was Caiaphas who had advised the Jews that it was better for one man to die for the people.

They take Jesus to Annas, father-in-law of Caiaphas (18:12-13)

As the final scene in this first A-B-A intercalation,[28] Jesus' being arrested, bound, and brought before Annas (18:12-14) not only contrasts with the

---

[28] See the outline and preliminary analysis in chapter 1.

middle B scene involving Peter (18:10-11) but also develops the action and theme of the opening A scene (18:1-9).

In contrast to Peter, who victimized the servant of the high priest with a strike of his sword (18:10), Jesus permits himself to be victimized by the Roman soldiers and Jewish officers (18:12-13). Whereas Peter attacked a subordinate high priestly official named Malchus, Jesus is forced to confront a higher official, the high priest's father-in-law named Annas. That he was led before Annas "first" implies that he will face the high priest himself later.

In development of the first A scene (18:1-9) now it is reported that those who came seeking Jesus the Nazorean include the tribune (χιλίαρχος, 18:12), the Roman military commander of the band or cohort of soldiers.[29] This gentile military leader, his band of soldiers, and the Jewish officers finally arrest (see 7:32; 11:57), bind, and lead Jesus before the Jewish leader, Annas, the father-in-law of Caiaphas, the high priest that fateful year (11:49, 51; 18:12-13).[30] Although Jesus surrendered himself to the opposing leaders as the good shepherd who lays down his life on his own so that no one takes it from him (10:18), he now allows himself to be a victim.

Caiaphas advised that one man die for the people (18:14)

The reminder of Caiaphas's counsel to the Jews (11:49-52) presents a double contrast with Peter's aggression in the previous scene. First, the advice "that it was better for one man *to die* for the people" contradicts Peter's valiant but vain attempt to protect Jesus from death by striking the servant of the high priest (18:10). Second, "that it was better for *one man* to die for the people" contradicts Peter's demonstration of his eager willingness to follow and lay down his life for Jesus (13:36-37). Despite his violent assault on an important member of the arresting party, Peter has not been arrested along with Jesus. Only the "one man" Jesus, not Peter also, will die for the people.

The recommendation of Caiaphas also contrasts with the reply of Jesus to Peter in the previous scene. Whereas Caiaphas was ironically unaware that he was not speaking on his own but prophesying God's plan when he advised that

---

[29] H. Balz, "χιλίαρχος," *EDNT* 3. 466-67: "As a rule it (χιλίαρχος) refers to the *leader of a cohort* (a group of five hundred to a thousand soldiers). . . . The Evangelist thus envisions a relatively large Roman and Jewish contingent gathered against Jesus and probably understands the χιλίαρχος to have been the Roman military tribune or at least a commanding officer (John does not use other designations for military officers)."

[30] Brown, *John*, 439-40.

"it was better" (συμφέρει) for Jesus to die for the people (11:50-51; 18:14), Jesus has resolved to die fully aware that it is God's plan for him: "The cup that *the Father* has given me, am I not to drink it?" (18:11). By dying in accord with the plan of the Jewish high priest, Jesus will ultimately accomplish the plan of God. Indeed, as Jesus told his disciples in his farewell discourse, "It is better (συμφέρει) for you that I go away, for if I do not go away, the Paraclete will not come to you; but if I go, I will send him to you" (16:7).

By drinking the cup of death that God, "the Father," has given him, Jesus, the good shepherd who freely lays down his life for the sheep in accord with the Father's will (10:11-18), becomes also a sacrificial victim, the "Lamb of God" that John the Baptist identified for the first disciples (1:29, 36). That Jesus is "the Lamb of God who takes away the sin of the world" (1:29) associates him with the rich sacrificial connotations of both the Passover lamb slaughtered for the benefit of the people (Exod 12) and the suffering servant of the Lord slaughtered as a lamb for the sins of the people (Isa 52:13-53:12).[31] In accord with both the sacrificial and leadership character of a high priest, Caiaphas aptly called for the death of Jesus as a sacrifice of one person for the people (18:14) Caiaphas is leading. As the good shepherd who sacrifices himself as the Lamb of God, however, Jesus is also performing the sacrificial and leadership roles of a high priest—a new and unique high priest who far exceeds what the Jewish high priest of "that year" (18:13) can do for "the people."

As a development of the first A scene (18:1-9) Caiaphas's counsel that only "one man die for the people" confirms Jesus' statement that "I did not lose a single one of those whom you have given me" (18:9). Jesus has effectively protected those given him from death. He alone, not Peter nor "a single one" of the other disciples, has been arrested to die for the people.

Furthermore, Caiaphas's advice reminds the reader that by dying Jesus is providing eternal life not only for "those given him" and for the Jewish people but for all the dispersed children of God that he will gather into one (11:51-52). Although Caiaphas advised "the Jews" that it would be better for them if only one man died so that the whole Jewish nation would not be destroyed by the Romans (11:48), the reader recognizes the irony that the death of Jesus will have a much greater significance. It will provide eternal life for *all* who believe

---

[31] Brown, *John*, 58-63; Barrett, *John*, 176-77; Carson, *John*, 148-51; Morris, *John*, 143-50; R. Schnackenburg, *Das Johannesevangelium: Einleitung und Kommentar zu Kap. 1-4* (HTKNT 4/1; Freiburg/Basel/Wien: Herder, 1972) 284-89; R. Summers, *Behold the Lamb: An Exposition of the Theological Themes in the Gospel of John* (Nashville: Broadman, 1979); G. L. Carey, "The Lamb of God and Atonement Theories," *TynBul* 32 (1981) 97-122.

(3:16), whether Jew (11:51-52; 18:14), Greek (7:35; 12:20), or even the Romans collaborating with the Jews (18:3, 12) in putting Jesus to death. Indeed, as John the Baptist pointed out, Jesus is "the Lamb of God who takes away the sin of the *world*" (1:29), and as the Samaritans proclaimed, he is "truly the savior of the *world!*" (4:42). By his death Jesus will draw all to himself (12:32) and unify all who believe in him (10:16; 11:52; 17:20-21).[32]

Peter Denies Jesus in the Courtyard of the High Priest
(B² 18:15-18)

15 Simon Peter and another disciple followed Jesus. That disciple was known to the high priest and entered with Jesus into the courtyard of the high priest, 16 but Peter was standing before the gate outside. So the other disciple, who was known to the high priest, went out and spoke to the gatekeeper and brought Peter in. 17 Then the maid who was the gatekeeper said to Peter, "You are not also one of the disciples of this man, are you?" He said, "I am not." 18 Now the servants and the officers were standing around a charcoal fire they had made, because it was cold, and were warming themselves. Peter was also standing with them and warming himself.

Another disciple brings Peter into the courtyard (18:15-16)

Creating a B-A-B intercalation with the two previous scenes, Peter's denial of Jesus (18:15-18) contrasts with Jesus' being arrested, bound, and brought before Annas (18:12-14). It also develops the theme of Peter's separation from Jesus introduced by his striking the servant of the high priest (18:10-11).

In contrast to the Roman soldiers and Jewish officers, who made Jesus a victim as they arrested, bound, and led him before the Jewish leader Annas (18:12-13), Simon Peter and another disciple relate to Jesus as a leader when they "followed" (ἠκολούθει) him (18:15). Those who became the first disciples of Jesus did so by "following" him (1:37, 38, 40, 43). Whereas the enemies have come in darkness "with lanterns and torches" (18:3), Jesus earlier proclaimed, "I am the light of the world; whoever follows (ἀκολουθῶν) me will not walk in darkness but have the light of life" (8:12). By "following" Jesus, Peter and the other disciple demonstrate that they are the "sheep" who follow (ἀκολουθεῖ) the good "shepherd" rather than another leader (10:4-5, 27).

---

[32] On the universalizing and unifying aspects of the life-giving death of Jesus, see also the above section on 18:7-9.

After declaring that whoever loves his life loses it, and whoever hates his life in this world will preserve it for eternal life (12:25), Jesus added, "If anyone would serve me, let him follow (ἀκολουθείτω) me, and wherever I am there also my servant will be" (12:26). Although Jesus had warned Peter, "Where I am going, you cannot follow (ἀκολουθῆσαι) me now, though you will follow (ἀκολουθήσεις) me later" (13:36), Peter objected, "Lord, why can I not follow (ἀκολουθῆσαι) you now? I will lay down my life for you" (13:37). Peter has now indeed "followed" Jesus. Will he now die for him?

In contrast to those who "arrested" or literally "took with" (συνέλαβον) them Jesus as victim (18:12), the other disciple followed and "entered with" (συνεισῆλθεν) Jesus as leader (18:15). That this other disciple "was known (γνωστὸς) to the high priest" (18:15, 16) associates him with the high priest Caiaphas, who advised that Jesus be the one sacrificial victim to die for the people (11:49-50; 18:14). It also associates him with the "high priest" Jesus, who offers himself to be that sacrificial victim as the good shepherd who lays down his life for the sheep (10:11, 15, 17) whom "I know (γινώσκω) and who know (γινώσκουσί) me" (10:14). That the anonymous, "other" disciple was known to the high priest Jesus links him to the anonymous disciple whom Jesus loved (13:23), the ideal representative of the disciples for whom Jesus will demonstrate his great love by laying down his life for them (15:12-13). As one of the sheep for whom the good shepherd lays down his life, the other disciple entered the courtyard (αὐλὴν, 18:15) of the high priest, which also represents the sheep "fold" (αὐλὴν, 10:1, 16) of the good shepherd and "high priest" Jesus.

Whereas the other disciple followed and entered with Jesus into the courtyard/sheepfold, Peter followed but did not enter with Jesus. He remained standing before the gate outside (18:16). In contrast to Jesus who was led before (πρὸς) Annas (18:13), Peter stands before (πρὸς) the gate outside of the courtyard/sheepfold. This develops the separation of Peter from Jesus begun in the first B scene (18:10-11), in which he did not understand the divine necessity for Jesus to die.

Although outside, Peter stands before the gate (θύρᾳ), a symbol of Jesus, who declared, "I am the gate (θύρα) of the sheep (10:7) . . . I am the gate (θύρα); if anyone enters through me, he will be saved and will go in and come out and find pasture" (10:9).[33] For a second, emphatic time the other disciple is described as one who "was known to the high priest" (18:15, 16), implying

---

[33] A. Bottino, "La metafora della porta (Gv 10,7.9)," *RivB* 39 (1991) 207-15.

that he is familiar with the necessity for the "high priest" Jesus to lay down his life for the "sheep." He went out and brought Peter, one of the "sheep," through the gate into the courtyard/sheepfold of the high priest and good shepherd (18:16).

That the other disciple spoke to the gatekeeper (θυρωρῷ) in order to bring Peter in (18:16) places Peter in the position of being not only a "sheep" but also a "shepherd." As Jesus stated, "Whoever enters through the gate is shepherd of the sheep. For him the gatekeeper (θυρωρὸς) opens..." (10:2-3). As a "sheep," Peter numbers among the disciples for whom Jesus, the good shepherd, lays down his life. But as a true shepherd and disciple, Peter must in turn lay down his life for the sheep (10:11). Just as Jesus washed the feet of his disciples, a symbolic gesture pointing to his death for them, so they must wash one another's feet (13:14-16).[34] He commanded his disciples to love one another as he loved them. And no one has greater love than to lay down his life for his friends (15:12-13). Peter indeed seemed more than willing to fulfill the role of both the good shepherd and disciple who lays down his life, when he promised Jesus, "I will lay down my life for you" (13:37).

Peter denies being a disciple of Jesus (18:17-18)

In contrast to Jesus whom they led (ἤγαγον) before Annas, a named, authoritative male leader, who was the father-in-law of the high priest Caiaphas (18:13), Peter, whom the other disciple led in (εἰσήγαγεν, 18:16), faces a lesser figure, an anonymous female maid who was the gatekeeper (18:17). Ironically, the very "gatekeeper" who allowed Peter to enter the courtyard/sheepfold through the "gate," placing him in the position not only of a sheep/disciple but also of a shepherd/disciple, induces him to deny his discipleship with a question expecting a negative answer, "You are not also one of the disciples of this man, are you?" (18:17). She asks whether Peter is "also," that is, in addition to the "other disciple," a disciple of this "man" (ἀνθρώπου), the one "man" (ἄνθρωπον) who as good shepherd and "high priest" will sacrifice himself by dying for the people (18:14) and laying down his life for the sheep/disciples.

Peter's denial of his discipleship further develops his separation from Jesus

---

[34] J. C. Thomas, *Footwashing in John 13 and the Johannine Community* (JSNTSup 61; Sheffield: JSOT, 1991) 16-17. On John 13, see also F. F. Segovia, "John 13:1-20, The Footwashing in the Johannine Tradition," *ZNW* 73 (1982) 31-51; F. J. Moloney, "The Structure and Message of John 13:1-38," *AusBR* 34 (1986) 1-16; J. A. du Rand, "Narratological Perspectives on John 13:1-38," *Hervormde Teologiese Studies* 46 (1990) 367-89.

begun in the first B scene (18:10-11). By boldly striking the servant of the high priest to prevent the death of Jesus (18:10), Peter demonstrated that he did not understand the divine necessity for Jesus to die (18:11). Now he continues to misunderstand the significance of Jesus' death by meekly denying that he is one of the disciples (18:17) for whom Jesus is dying to provide eternal life for all. The Peter who promised to lay down his life for Jesus (13:37) now dissociates himself from the disciples for whom Jesus is laying down his life. Peter's cowardly "I am not" (Οὐκ εἰμί) to the maid in this second B scene also stands in sharp contrast to Jesus' courageous "I am he" (Ἐγώ εἰμι) to his armed opponents in the first A scene (18:5, 6, 8).

In a further ironic contrast to the previous A scene (18:12-14), the Peter who vowed to die for Jesus (13:37) now associates with the officers (ὑπηρέται, 18:12, 18) who arrested, bound, and led Jesus to Annas to put him to death (18:12-13)! Instead of standing as a disciple with the other disciple, who entered "with" Jesus (18:15) and who led Peter as a disciple/sheep into the courtyard/sheepfold of the "high priest" who lays down his life for the sheep, Peter stands "with them" (18:18).

In a further ironic development of the previous B scene (18:10-11), the Peter who cut off the ear of the servant (δοῦλον) of the high priest to defend Jesus from death now stands with the servants (δοῦλοι) associated with those bringing about Jesus' death (18:18)! Like Judas his betrayer, who "was also standing (εἱστήκει) with them (μετ' αὐτῶν)," the enemies seeking to kill Jesus (18:5), Peter "was also standing with them" (μετ' αὐτῶν ἑστώς). Peter was "warming himself" with those who made a charcoal fire "because it was cold" (18:18), which symbolically characterizes the darkness and coldness of their unbelief, similar to the darkness that characterized the unbelief of those who came against Jesus with torches and lanterns (18:3). This accentuates his association with evil unbelievers who are not "sheep." When Jesus was in the temple during the coldness of winter, his Jewish adversaries demanded that he tell them plainly whether he is the Messiah. He insisted that he had already told them and they did not believe. They indeed did not believe, he asserted, because they are not among his "sheep" (10:22-26).

Jesus Confronts the High Priest with His Revelatory Mission and Is Rejected (A³ 18:19-24)

19 Then the high priest questioned Jesus about his disciples and about his teaching. 20 Jesus answered him, "I have openly spoken to the world; I always

taught in a synagogue and in the temple, where all the Jews gather, and in secret I spoke nothing. 21 Why do you ask me? Ask those who heard what I spoke to them. Behold, these know what I said." 22 When he said these things, one of the officers standing there gave Jesus a slap, saying, "Is that how you answer the high priest?" 23 Jesus answered him, "If I spoke wrongly, testify about the wrong. But if rightly, why do you strike me?" 24 Then Annas sent him bound to Caiaphas the high priest.

Jesus tells the high priest that he has taught openly (18:19-21)

Forming an A-B-A sandwich with the two preceding scenes, Jesus' interrogation by the high priest (18:19-24) contrasts with the B scene of Peter's first denial of Jesus (18:15-18). It also develops the A scene of Jesus' being arrested, bound, and brought before Annas (18:12-14) in order to be put to death.

In development of the previous A scenes, now that Jesus has surrendered to his opponents (A¹ 18:1-9) and they have led him to the high priestly leadership (A² 18:12-14), the high priest interrogates him (18:19). His question about the disciples and about the teaching of Jesus expands the previous focus on Jesus alone.[35] The opponents arrested none of the disciples but only Jesus (18:8), and despite Peter's attack of the high priest's servant (18:10), they brought to Annas only the "one man" Jesus to die for the people (18:13-14).

That the high priest inquires about Jesus' disciples when he is in fact concerned with putting Jesus alone to death begins an ironic contrast with the previous B scene (18:15-18). Although the high priest already knows about Jesus' disciples, since the "other disciple" has entered the courtyard of the high priest with Jesus and it is twice mentioned that he is known to the high priest (18:15-16), the high priest nevertheless questions Jesus about his disciples. But with the high priest's query about Jesus' disciples the reader also experiences a tragic irony because of Peter's abandonment of his discipleship. To the maid who was the gatekeeper he denied that he was "one of this man's disciples" and associated with those putting Jesus to death (18:17-18).

In asking Jesus about his teaching (διδαχῆς, 18:19) while seeking to put him to death, the high priest is unwittingly placing himself in a position of accepting or rejecting Jesus as the revealer of the Father, the one who teaches the will of God. When Jesus earlier taught in the temple he told the Jews amazed by his scriptural learning: "My teaching (διδαχὴ) is not mine but of the one who sent me" (7:14-16). If the high priest does not recognize Jesus' teaching as God's rev-

[35] Brown, *Death*, 411-14.

elation and fails to believe, he discloses his unwillingness to do the will of God. For, as Jesus continued, "Anyone who wishes to do his will shall know whether the teaching (διδαχῆς) is from God or whether I speak on my own" (7:17; see also 5:19, 30; 8:28; 12:49; 14:24).

The beginning of Jesus' reply to the high priest forms a chiasm in which statements (a) of the absolute universality and openness of his revelatory "speaking" to the world frame statements (b) of the more particular universality and openness of his teaching to "all" the Jews "always" in the synagogue or temple (18:20):

(a) I have openly spoken (λελάληκα) to the world;
(b) I always (πάντοτε) taught in a synagogue and in the temple,
(b) where all (πάντες) the Jews gather,
(a) and in secret I spoke (ἐλάλησα) nothing.

In always "teaching" all the Jews in a synagogue and in the temple Jesus thereby publicly offered to the whole world the revelatory word of God, as signified by the use of the Greek verb λαλεῖν for his revelatory "speaking."[36]

The retort of Jesus to the high priest broadens the issue. More than merely a teacher with disciples, Jesus has and still is openly (παρρησίᾳ) "speaking" (λελάληκα, perfect tense), that is, definitively revealing God's word to the world and not in secret (ἐν κρυπτῷ) (18:20). His rejoinder serves as a climactic summary of his mission as the divine revealer. Despite the attempt by the Jews to kill him (7:1), Jesus has done what his brothers had urged: "No one acts in secret (ἐν κρυπτῷ) if he seeks to be openly (παρρησίᾳ) known. If you do these things, manifest yourself to the world" (7:4).

As a development of the previous A scene (18:12-14), with an emphatic "I" (Ἐγώ, 18:20) Jesus indicates the transcendency of his alternative high priestly leadership to that of the Jewish high priest: "I," not you, the Jewish high priest, have openly spoken God's word to the world and "I" always taught the whole Jewish people. Whereas the Jewish high priest Caiaphas had advised "the Jews" (18:14), that is, only the chief priests and Pharisees gathered in a private session of the Sanhedrin, of the expediency for Jesus to die for the people (11:47-50),

---

[36] According to de la Potterie, *The Hour,* 44: ". . . in religious language the word λαλεῖν has acquired a higher significance: in biblical Greek it is one of the terms signifying divine revelation: the revelatory word of God through the mediation of angels, prophets, men of God, visions, etc.: it is par excellence the word of him who is himself the Word of God." See also idem, *La vérité dans Saint Jean* (AnBib 73-74; Rome: Biblical Institute, 1977) 40-42. On the response by Jesus to the high priest in John 18:20-23, see Brown, *Death,* 414-16.

Jesus has always taught "all the Jews" not in secret but in the public gatherings in the temple (2:14-15; 5:14; 7:14, 28; 8:2, 20, 59; 10:23) and synagogue (6:59).

In contrast to the previous B scene (18:15-18) Jesus courageously affirms his identity as the divine revealer to the authoritative high priest intent on putting him to death, while Peter timidly denies his identity to the maid who was merely the gatekeeper to the high priest's courtyard. Whereas Jesus firmly asserts that "I" publicly spoke to the world and "I" always taught all the Jewish people (18:20) despite the danger of death, Peter, when asked if he is one of Jesus' disciples, weakly disclaims, "I am not" (18:17).

The further reply of Jesus continues to insinuate the supremacy of his leadership over that of the Jewish high priest. Only some of the chief priests and Pharisees know what the high priest said privately about the benefit for the people of putting Jesus to death (18:14; 11:47-50). But anyone who has heard the open and public teaching of Jesus to all the people should be able to testify to the high priest what Jesus has "spoken," that is, revealed about God: "Why do you ask me? Ask those who heard what I spoke (ἐλάλησα) to them. Behold, these know what I said" (18:21). The final and emphatic "I" (ἐγώ) in the statement that (literally) "these know what said *I*" underlines that the people know what "I," Jesus, said but not what the Jewish high priest said. Emphatic "I" assertions thus open (18:20) and close (18:21) Jesus' aggressive rejoinder to the Jewish high priest.

This further retort of Jesus about those who have "heard" (ἀκηκοότας) and "know" (οἴδασιν) what he spoke/revealed about God also continues the ironic contrast with the previous B scene (18:15-18). After Jesus taught his revelatory Bread of Life discourse (6:22-58) in the synagogue at Capernaum (6:59), many of his disciples who "heard" (ἀκούσαντες) it rejected it, "This word is difficult; who can hear (ἀκούειν) him?" (6:60). But Simon Peter, spokesman for the twelve disciples who remained with Jesus (6:66-67), was able to "hear" and accept it. He told Jesus, "You have the words of eternal life; and we have believed and have come to know (ἐγνώκαμεν) that you are the Holy One of God!" (6:68-69).[37] But now that Peter has denied his discipleship and associated with those bringing about the death of Jesus (18:17-18), can he testify to the high priest what he "heard" and "knows" that Jesus revealed? It would seem that the "other disciple" known to both the high priest Caiaphas and the "high priest" Jesus (18:15-16) is in a better position to testify to what he has "heard" and "knows" Jesus said.

---

[37] Heil, *Jesus Walking on the Sea*, 167-70.

Jesus' deflection of the Jewish high priest's inquiry from himself to those who have and still are really "hearing" (ἀκηκοότας, perfect tense) his divine revelation and "know" (οἴδασιν) what he said (18:21) presents the reader with a poignant self-reflection. As one of those who has and even now "hears" and "knows" what Jesus has said throughout the narrative, is the reader able to testify that Jesus has indeed revealed the words of eternal life? Is the reader in the position of Peter or that of the "other disciple"? Is the reader like those who, despite "hearing" (ἀκούσαντες) the revelatory words of Jesus, say, "Who can hear (ἀκούειν) him?" (6:60) or, "Why hear (ἀκούετε) him?" (10:20)? Or is the reader among those who "hear" (ἀκούει) the voice of the good shepherd and follow him (10:3, 16, 27)? Is the reader able to testify with the Samaritans, "We ourselves have heard (ἀκηκόαμεν) and know (οἴδαμεν) that this is truly the savior of the world!" (4:42)?

One of the officers strikes the innocent Jesus (18:22-24)

That one of the officers (ὑπηρετῶν) standing there gave Jesus a slap (18:22) continues the ironic contrast with both of the previous B scenes. Whereas Peter had defended Jesus in the first B scene (18:10-11) by striking the servant of the high priest (18:10), he does not now come to his defense. Instead, by now standing with the "servants and officers (ὑπηρέται)" (18:18) in the second B scene (18:15-18), Peter associates with the group that includes the one now unjustly inflicting violence on Jesus.

In development of the previous A scenes, now that Judas has taken soldiers and officers (ὑπηρέτας, 18:3) in search of Jesus (A¹ 18:1-9) and now that the soldiers, the tribune, and the Jewish officers (ὑπηρέται, 18:12) have arrested, bound, and led Jesus before Annas (A² 18:12-14), one of the officers (ὑπηρετῶν) continues the victimization of Jesus by giving him a slap (18:22). His question, "Is that how you answer the high priest?" (18:22), rings ironic for the audience, since Jesus has indicated his superiority to the high priest as the divine revealer (18:20) and has himself demonstrated the leadership qualities of a true "high priest."

The reply of Jesus (18:23) to the officer who struck him challenges him to testify whether Jesus rightly or wrongly "spoke" (ἐλάλησα) God's revelatory word not only presently when he "spoke" (λελάληκα) to the Jewish high priest, but previously when he "spoke" (ἐλάλησα) to the world and the whole Jewish people (18:20). If Jesus truly and in transcendency to the Jewish high priest "spoke" divine revelation, then it is not he who has offended the high priest, but the officer who has inappropriately and unjustly offended Jesus as the superior "high priest": "But if (I spoke) rightly, why do you strike me?" (18:23).

The challenge to the officer to testify (μαρτύρησον) whether Jesus rightly "spoke" (ἐλάλησα) divine revelation (18:23) continues the challenge for the testimony of his present and future followers (the audience): "Why do you ask me? Ask those who heard what I spoke (ἐλάλησα) to them" (18:21). The persecution that Jesus undergoes and the "testifying" that he calls for and that he himself gives here serves as a model for his disciples. In his farewell discourse preparing his followers and the audience for the future he warned, "Remember the word that I said to you, 'No servant is greater than his master.' If they persecuted me, they will also persecute you. If they kept my word, they will also keep yours" (15:20). He went on to predict, "When the Paraclete comes whom I will send you from the Father, the Spirit of truth who comes from the Father, he will testify (μαρτυρήσει) about me. You also are to testify (μαρτυρεῖτε), because you have been with me from the beginning" (15:26-27).

The testifying by Jesus himself to his revelatory mission and his appeal for the testifying of those who heard what he revealed result not in the belief of the Jewish leadership but in his continued persecution and victimization as "Annas sent him bound to Caiaphas the high priest" (18:24). Not only has the innocent Jesus had to endure this humiliating interrogation by Annas, but now he is sent to Caiaphas as well. This fulfills an expectation of the previous A scene, in which Jesus was led "before Annas first" with the presumption that he would later be sent also to Caiaphas (18:13).

The statement that Annas sent Jesus to Caiaphas at this point, however, surprises the reader, who presumed that the "high priest" who conducted this inquisition of Jesus (18:19) was in fact Caiaphas, earlier identified as "high priest that year," rather than Annas, his father-in-law (18:13).[38] That both

---

[38] According to de la Potterie, *The Hour*, 43: "Annas had himself been high priest from the year 6 to the year 15, but he had been deposed by the Romans. He continued, however, to exercise considerable influence in the sphere of the Jewish politico-religious activity. He was considered a person of great authority, as a wise counsellor; he was respected and frequently consulted." According to Senior, *John*, 59: ". . . Annas may have continued to play an influential role in the religious affairs of Judaism at this period. He may also have been popularly addressed as the 'high priest' even though he did not formally hold that office." See also Brown, *John*, 820-21; idem, *Death*, 404-11.

Annas and Caiaphas are called a high priest creates confusion for the reader about who is truly the high priest leading the Jewish people.[39] This confusion reinforces the theme of the A scenes—the uniqueness of Jesus as the "one man" to die for the people (18:14), the one victim who offers his own life as the one and only true "high priest."

Peter Denies Jesus a Second and Third Time before a Servant of the High Priest (B³ 18:25-27)

25 Now Simon Peter was standing and warming himself. They then said to him, "You are not also one of his disciples, are you?" He denied it and said, "I am not." 26 One of the servants of the high priest, a relative of the one whose ear Peter had cut off, said, "Did I not see you in the garden with him?" 27 Then Peter again denied it, and immediately the cock crowed.

A second time Peter denies being a disciple of Jesus (18:25)

The scene of Peter's second and third denials of Jesus (18:25-27) concludes a B-A-B intercalation with the two previous scenes. It contrasts with Jesus' confrontation with the high priest (18:19-24) and develops Peter's first denial of his discipleship (18:15-18).

This third B scene takes up where the second left off. As the servants and the officers were standing around a charcoal fire they had made, the second B scene concluded with the notice that "Peter was also standing with them and warming himself" (18:18). The third B scene commences with Peter in that same position of separation from Jesus and association with his enemies: "Now Simon Peter was standing and warming himself" (18:25).

The behavior of the fully named "Simon Peter" contrasts with that of the anonymous officer in the previous A scene. Whereas one of the officers standing there (παρεστηκὼς) gave Jesus a slap on behalf of the Jewish high priest (18:22), Simon Peter was standing (ἑστὼς) and warming himself (18:25) rather than defending the true "high priest" Jesus, as he had done previously in the first B scene (18:10).

Peter's second denial of Jesus intensifies and reinforces his first denial in the previous B scene. Only the maid first questioned Peter about his discipleship, expecting a negative answer, "You are not also one of this man's disciples, are you?" (18:17). Now a whole group, "they," ask essentially the same question

---

[39] J. L. Staley, "Subversive Narrative/Victimized Reader: A Reader Response Assessment of a Text-Critical Problem, John 18.12-24," *JSNT* 51 (1993) 79-98.

again expecting a negative response, "You are not also one of his disciples, are you?" (18:25). In his first denial Peter merely "said" that "I am not" (18:17); now he both "denied it" and "said" again, "I am not" (18:25).

Peter's second denial that he is a "disciple" of Jesus continues the tragic ironic contrast with the high priest's query about the "disciples" of Jesus in the previous A scene (18:19). Although Jesus asserted that those who heard his revelatory "speaking" know what he said and can testify to the high priest about Jesus' teaching of divine revelation (18:20-21), Peter not only fails to testify on behalf of Jesus but even renounces his own discipleship. He serves as a negative model for the reader, who will likewise be called to "testify" as a believing follower of Jesus (15:27).

To his opponents seeking to arrest him in the first A scene Jesus bravely identified himself with bold "I am he" ('Εγώ εἰμι) assertions (18:5-7). And to the authoritative Jewish high priest in the previous A scene Jesus courageously identified himself as the divine revealer with forceful "I" pronouncements, "I ('Εγω) have openly spoken..."; "I (ἐγώ) always taught..."; and "...these know what said I (ἐγώ)" (18:20-21). In pathetic contrast Peter refuses to identify himself as a disciple for an emphatic second time to subordinate officials with whom he stands. He cowardly tells them, "I am not" (Οὐκ εἰμί) (18:17, 25).

A third time Peter denies his association with Jesus (18:26-27)

In a progression of the theme of the B scenes, after first a mere maid who was the gatekeeper of the high priest's courtyard (18:17) and then the general group standing there have questioned Peter (18:25), a more authoritative individual, "one of the servants of the high priest," confronts Peter (18:26). That this servant was a relative of the servant whose ear Peter had cut off (18:10) makes this third inquiry more difficult for Peter. Indeed, the first two questions, introduced with the Greek particle Μὴ (18:17, 25), expected a negative answer. But the third question, introduced by Οὐκ, expects an affirmative reply: "Did I not see you in the garden with him?" (18:26).[40] The first two questions concerned Peter's relationship to Jesus as a disciple in general. The third, however, progresses to his more specific and close association with Jesus. It recalls that the Peter who had defended Jesus had been "in the garden with him" (18:1, 26).

As Peter "again denied it" (18:27), he incredibly repudiated not only his

[40] BDF, 220, #427.

discipleship but also his close association with and earlier defense of Jesus. That "immediately the cock crowed" after Peter denied (ἠρνήσατο) a third time (18:27) inserts his failure within Jesus' ultimate control of his passion and death. It confirms Jesus' prediction that the Peter who vowed to lay down his life for him would deny (ἀρνήσῃ) him three times before the cock crowed (13:38).

In contrast to the previous A scene, whereas Jesus boldly affirmed his revelatory mission to the world and the Jewish people before their highest authority, the high priest (18:20), Peter timidly disowns his close association with Jesus before a subordinate servant of the high priest (18:26-27). Jesus challenged the high priest to ask not him but those who "heard" his revelatory "speaking." They "know" what he said and can surely answer the high priest's question about the disciples and teaching of Jesus (18:19-21). Jesus then defiantly rebuked the officer who struck him, challenging him to "testify" to the rightness or wrongness of his revelatory "speaking," and was sent bound to yet another high priest (18:22-24). But the disciple Peter, rather than testifying to Jesus' divine revelation, sadly denies to a high priestly servant whose relative's ear he had cut off that he was even in the garden with Jesus. Now that the cock has crowed (18:27), do Peter and the reader, who have "heard" the rightness of what Jesus "spoke" about Peter's triple denial (13:38), "know" what he said? Can they now testify to Jesus' divine revelation?

Summary

Through the complex narrative structure of John 18:1-27 the audience experiences a progression of contrasting scenes that produce a sequential network of intercalations. The A scenes develop the theme of Jesus as the divine revealer who challenges those who hear him to testify that he offers his own life as the good shepherd and singular "high priest" to provide eternal life for all who believe: In surrendering to his foes Jesus reveals himself as the good shepherd who lays down his own life so that his sheep might have eternal life (A¹ 18:1-9). As the one and only man who must die for the people, Jesus, the good shepherd, allows himself to be the sacrificial victim, the Lamb of God, who offers himself as a new and unique "high priest" (A² 18:12-14). In his confrontation with the Jewish high priest Jesus invites all who hear what he has divinely revealed to the whole world to testify on his behalf (A³ 18:19-24).

In continual contrast to the A scenes, the B scenes generate the theme of Peter's failure to understand what it means to be a disciple who follows Jesus and testifies to his divine revelation: Misunderstanding the divine necessity for Jesus to lay down his own life, Peter mistakenly attempts to prevent his arrest (B^1 18:10-11). Although he follows Jesus into the courtyard of the high priest, the Peter who vowed to lay down his life for Jesus denies being his disciple (B^2 18:15-18). In denying Jesus a second and third time, Peter fails to testify on his behalf, but the crowing of the cock confirms the revelatory words of Jesus (B^3 18:25-27). And so before Peter (and the reader) can be a disciple/shepherd who lays down his life for his friends (13:14-16, 37; 15:12-13) and testifies to Jesus' divine revelation, he must realize the need to be a disciple/sheep for whom only Jesus can provide eternal life by laying down his own life in accord with God's will.

This dynamic progression of contrasting scenes produces the following effects in the implied reader/audience:

1) The dramatic confrontation between Jesus and his evil foes in the first A scene (18:1-9) assures the reader that in surrendering himself Jesus is laying down his own life as the good shepherd, revealing his superior power to acquire eternal life for all who believe in him.

2) In contrast to Jesus' surrender of himself, the question put to Peter after he wrongly defended Jesus in the first B scene (18:10-11), whether Jesus is to drink the cup the Father has given him, provokes the audience to realize the divine necessity of Jesus' death.

3) In contrast to Peter's attempt to defend Jesus, but advancing the theme of Jesus' revelation, that his opponents lead Jesus to the Jewish high priestly leadership in the second A scene (18:12-14) as the one and only man to die for the people ironically reveals him as a new and unique "high priest" who sacrifices himself to lead all his followers to eternal life.

4) In contrast to Jesus' acceptance of his arrest, but advancing the theme of Peter's misunderstanding, Peter's denial of his discipleship in the second B scene (18:15-18) warns the reader of the difficulty of being a disciple called to follow Jesus in laying down his own life to win eternal life for others.

5) In contrast to Peter's denial of his discipleship, but advancing the theme of Jesus' revelation, Jesus, in the third A scene (18:19-24), challenges the

audience, who has heard what Jesus spoke, to bring others to faith by testifying to his divine revelation of eternal life.

6) In contrast to Jesus' being bound and sent to the high priest, but advancing the theme of Peter's misunderstanding, the crowing of the cock that Jesus predicted after Peter's second and third denials of him in the final B scene (18:25-27) empowers the reader to realize and testify to the ultimate control and reliability of Jesus' revelatory words offering eternal life to all who believe.

CHAPTER 3

Jesus, the Jews, and Pilate
(John 18:28-19:11)

Outside the Praetorium the Jews Refuse Pilate's Offer To Judge Jesus Themselves (A[1] 18:28-32)

28 Then they led Jesus from Caiaphas to the praetorium. It was early in the morning. And they themselves did not enter into the praetorium, in order not to be defiled so that they could eat the Passover. 29 So Pilate came outside to them and said, "What charge do you bring against this man?" 30 They answered and said to him, "If this one were not doing wrong, we would not have handed him over to you." 31 Pilate then said to them, "Take him yourselves and according to your law judge him." The Jews said to him, "We are not allowed to put anyone to death," 32 in order that the word of Jesus might be fulfilled that he said indicating the kind of death he was to die.

The Jews deliver Jesus as an evildoer to Pilate (18:28-30)

After the band of soldiers, the Roman tribune, and the Jewish officers had arrested Jesus and bound him, they led (ἤγαγον) him before Annas (18:12-13). After the high priest Annas interrogated Jesus (18:19-23), he sent him bound to the high priest Caiaphas (18:24). Then "they" led (ἄγουσιν) Jesus from his encounter with Caiaphas (unnarrated) to the praetorium, the residential headquarters of the Roman governor in Jerusalem (18:28).[1]

---

[1] Brown, *John*, 845; idem, *Death*, 705-10; G. Schneider, "πραιτώριον," *EDNT* 3. 144: "Πραιτώριον is a Latin loanword (*praetorium*) and in the NT designates the residence of a Roman provincial governor.... The *praetorium* was originally the tent in which the praetor lived, then, it designated the praetorian guard or its barracks or the residence of a political official."

Although they led Jesus to the praetorium, they themselves refused to enter into it. It was already early in the morning (the cock has crowed, 18:27), and Jesus' Jewish captors did not want to defile themselves for the sacred ritual of the Passover in the evening by entering an unclean gentile residence.[2] They thus continue the ironic theme about the Passover that runs throughout the narrative: In putting Jesus to death during the Passover the Jews are unwittingly establishing Jesus as the true Passover Lamb of God (1:29, 36).[3]

A subtle but dramatic narrative strategy has been building that associates the death of Jesus with the nearness of the Jewish feast of Passover. The Passover of the Jews was near (ἐγγὺς, 2:13) when Jesus drove out those doing business in the temple (2:14-17), a sign pointing to his death and resurrection (2:18-22). The Passover, the feast of the Jews, was near (ἐγγὺς, 6:4) when Jesus miraculously provided overabundant bread for five thousand (6:1-15), a sign pointing to the giving of his flesh (through death) as the bread that offers eternal life to the world (6:51). The Passover of the Jews was near (ἐγγὺς, 11:55) when many went up from the country to Jerusalem "before the Passover," seeking Jesus in the temple after the chief priests and Pharisees had given orders for his arrest (11:56-57), since they had decided to kill him (11:53). Six days "before the Passover" (12:1) Jesus went to Bethany and was anointed with precious oil (12:1-6) to be used for his burial (12:7). "Before the feast of Passover" (13:1) Jesus knew that his hour had come to pass from this world to the Father through his death. While observing the nearness of their Passover by not entering the praetorium, the Jews have ironically prepared for the arrival of the true Passover by leading Jesus to the praetorium to be put to death (18:28).

The Jews seek the death of Jesus because they fear that if all believe in him the Romans will come and take away both their temple ("place") and their nation (11:48). Yet they collaborate with the very Romans they fear! Those who arrested Jesus included a cohort of Roman soldiers as well as the Roman tribune (18:3, 12). And now the Jews lead Jesus to the Roman praetorium (18:28). Their concern not to enter into it themselves in order properly to celebrate the Passover aptly accords with their concern to preserve their freedom from Roman destruction. The Jewish Passover commemorated the exodus events that liberated the ancient Israelites from Egypt and established them as a nation. The irony is that the Jews continue to reject the Jesus who offered them a freedom that transcends the freedom they are concerned to preserve

---

[2] For a discussion of what this defilement may more precisely have involved, see Brown, *John*, 845-46.

[3] Brown, *John*, 866; Duke, *Irony*, 127-28; Senior, *John*, 77.

by bringing him to the Roman praetorium, which they refuse to enter in order to celebrate their freedom in the Passover.

Jesus had previously challenged the Jews who had only superficially believed him to become truly his disciples in order to experience the real freedom that comes from knowing the truth that Jesus as the Son of God reveals (8:31-38).[4] He told them that if they remain in his revelatory word, they will truly become his disciples, and know the truth and the truth will free (ἐλευθερώσει) them (8:31-32). They objected that as Jews they are descendants of Abraham and have never been enslaved to anyone, so how can Jesus say, "You will become free (ἐλεύθεροι)?" (8:33). Jesus assured them that everyone who "does the sin," that is, fails to believe in him, is a slave (8:34).[5] Whereas the slave does not remain in the household forever, the son does remain forever (8:35). If *the* Son, Jesus, frees (ἐλευθερώσῃ) them, they will be really free (ἐλεύθεροι) (8:36). But unfortunately, although the Jews are descendants of Abraham, they seek to kill Jesus, because his revelatory word has no place within them (8:37). They have the opportunity to believe, however, as Jesus urged them to do what they heard from the Father, just as he revealed what he saw from the Father (8:38).

Although they readily defile themselves morally by delivering the innocent Jesus to the praetorium, the Jews ironically do not enter it themselves lest they be cultically defiled (18:28). They want to remain purified along with those who came up to Jerusalem from the country before the Passover to purify (ἁγνίσωσιν) themselves for the ritual (11:55; see Exod 19:10, 14). But the Jesus they reject offers those who believe in him as the revealer of truth a new "sanctification" that transcends the purification associated with their celebration of the Passover. To his holy (ἅγιε) Father (17:11) Jesus prayed for his disciples: "Sanctify (ἁγίασον) them in the truth; your word is truth. As you have sent me into the world, so I have sent them into the world. And for them I sanctify (ἁγιάζω) myself, so that they also may be sanctified (ἡγιασμένοι) in truth" (17:17-19).[6] Rather than a sanctification that separates them from the ordinary world, Jesus sends his disciples into the world to extend the revelatory mission on which the Father sent him and to which he obediently sanctified or dedicated himself. They are likewise to be sanctified or dedicated to the truth, to

---

[4] For a detailed discussion of this passage dealing with the freedom that comes from the truth Jesus reveals, see de la Potterie, *La vérité,* 789-866.

[5] Ibid., 829-33.

[6] For a detailed discussion on these verses dealing with being sanctified in the truth, see de la Potterie, *La vérité,* 706-83.

offer the world the revelatory truth Jesus has offered them from the Father that the world may believe that the Father sent Jesus (17:21).

While leading Jesus to his death, the Jews are concerned to eat (φάγωσιν) the Passover meal that included the eating of unleavened bread as well as the Passover lamb (18:28). But Jesus, the Lamb of God (1:29, 36), had invited them to eat his own flesh in order to have eternal life: "I am the living bread that came down from heaven. Whoever eats (φάγη) of this bread will live forever; and the bread that I will give is my flesh for the Life of the world" (6:51). But among themselves the Jews questioned, "How can this man give us his flesh to eat (φαγεῖν)?" (6:52). Their question is now being ironically answered. The death of Jesus that they themselves are perpetrating will enable him to give his flesh to be eaten as the bread of eternal life. Unlike their ancestors of the exodus events commemorated in the Passover, who ate (ἔφαγον) the manna in the desert yet died (6:31, 49, 58), those who eat (φάγητε, 6:53) the bread/flesh that Jesus gives will never die but have eternal life (6:50-58).[7]

In an emphatic contrast to the Jews who refused to enter (εἰσῆλθον) into (εἰς) the praetorium (18:28), Pilate, the Roman governor, exited (ἐξῆλθεν) outside (ἔξω) to them (18:29).[8] His challenging question, "What charge do you bring against this man?" (18:29), corresponds to Jesus' earlier unanswered challenge to the officer who slapped him for his retort to the high priest, "If I spoke wrongly, testify about the wrong. But if rightly, why do you strike me?" (18:23). The implication is that they still have nothing with which to charge the innocent Jesus.

Pilate's reference to Jesus as only "this man" (ἀνθρώπου τούτου, 18:29) continues the denigration implicit in the gatekeeper's question to Peter, "You are not also one of the disciples of this man (ἀνθρώπου τούτου), are you?" (18:17). But it stands in ironic contrast to Caiaphas's reference to Jesus as the one and only "man" (ἄνθρωπον) whose death can save the Jewish people (18:14; 11:50). It recalls the "charge" the Jews have against Jesus, the real reason why they have brought him to Pilate: "This man (οὗτος ὁ ἄνθρωπος) is doing many signs. If we let him go on like this, all will believe in him, and the Romans will come and destroy both our place and our nation" (11:47-48).

To Pilate's implication of Jesus' innocence ("what charge") and insignificance ("this man") the Jews counter, "If this one (οὗτος) were not doing

---

[7] The Passover celebration may have anticipated the giving of the eschatological manna along with the arrival of the Messiah; see Brown, *John*, 265-66.

[8] For historical background on Pontius Pilate, see Brown, *Death*, 693-705.

wrong, we would not have handed him over to you" (18:30). The Jews' statement cleverly suggests that simply because they have handed Jesus over to
Pilate, he must surely be a prominent criminal, yet avoids a direct answer to
Pilate's request for a specific charge against him. Although they insinuate that
Jesus was doing wrong (κακὸν), their inability to answer Jesus' challenge, "If I
spoke wrongly (κακῶς), testify about the wrong (κακοῦ)" (18:23), ironically
underlines for the reader the innocence of Jesus.

The Jews' unproven insinuation that Jesus was doing (ποιῶν) wrong serves
as an ironic understatement of his revelatory activity (18:30). Not only has he
not "done" anything wrong, but he has been "doing" the signs, works, and will
of God that invite people to believe in him:

1) Nicodemus, a leader of the Jews, began his encounter with Jesus by
   saying, "Rabbi, we know that you are a teacher who has come from God,
   for no one can do (ποιεῖν) these signs that you are doing (ποιεῖς), unless
   God is with him" (3:2). Jesus concluded the encounter with an appeal for
   faith: "Whoever does (ποιῶν) the truth comes to the light, so that it
   might be manifested that his works have been worked in God" (3:21).[9]

2) While the Jews are concerned to eat (φάγωσιν) the Passover (18:28), to
   his disciples who exhorted him, "Rabbi, eat (φάγε)," Jesus said, "I have
   food to eat (φαγεῖν) which you do not know." So his disciples said to one
   another, "Surely no one has brought him something to eat (φαγεῖν)?"
   Then Jesus said to them, "My food is to do (ποιήσω) the will of the one
   who sent me and to complete his work" (4:31-34).[10]

3) To the Jews seeking to kill him Jesus said, "The Son can do (ποιεῖν) nothing on his own, but only what he sees the Father doing (ποιοῦντα); for
   whatever that one does (ποιῇ), the Son does (ποιεῖ) likewise (5:18-19)
   . . . the works that the Father has given me to complete, these works that
   I am doing (ποιῶ), testify on my behalf that the Father has sent me"
   (5:36). In the temple Jesus told the Jews, "The works that I do (ποιῶ) in
   the name of my Father testify about me (10:25) . . . I have shown you
   many good works from the Father (10:32) . . . If I am not doing (ποιῶ)
   the works of my Father, do not believe me; but if I am doing (ποιῶ) them,
   even though you do not believe me, believe the works, so that you may

---

[9] For other statements of the revelatory signs that Jesus "does," see 2:11, 23; 4:45-46, 54; 6:2,
14, 30; 7:31; 9:16; 11:47; 12:18, 37.

[10] For other statements of Jesus' revelatory "doing" of the will the Father, see 5:30; 6:38; 8:28-
29; 9:31, 33; 14:31.

know and understand that the Father is in me and I am in the Father" (10:37-38).[11]

The Jews' statement that they have "handed over" Jesus to Pilate because he was "doing wrong" (18:30) rings doubly ironic. First, the verb "hand over" (παρεδώκαμεν) also means "to betray." Indeed, this has been its primary meaning previously in the narrative in reference to Judas (6:64, 71; 12:4; 13:2, 11, 21; 18:2, 5).[12] The irony is that in "handing over" Jesus as one whom they falsely claim has done wrong the Jews are "betraying" the one who has in fact done the revelatory signs, works, and will of God that offer them the faith that leads to eternal life. Second, the Jews are able to "hand over" Jesus only because the devil had already put it into the heart of Judas to betray (παραδοῖ) him (13:2). Jesus then surrendered himself (18:1-9). Ironically, the Jews are handing over/betraying Jesus not because he was doing (ποιῶν) wrong but because they are doing (ποιεῖτε) the works of their father (8:41), the devil, whose murderous desires they wish to do (ποιεῖν) (8:44).

The Jews refuse to judge Jesus themselves (18:31-32)

In attempting to give Jesus back to the Jews (18:31) Pilate is unwittingly offering them the opportunity to believe in him as the God-sent revealer of *the* truth that would enable them to become children of God. Pilate's appeal to the Jews, "Take (Λάβετε) him yourselves," is oriented toward "taking," "accepting," or "receiving" Jesus in faith. As the narrator declared in the prologue, "To those who received (ἔλαβον) him he gave the power to become children of God, to those who believe in his name" (1:12). Jesus told his disciples that whoever receives (λαμβάνων) him receives (λαμβάνει) the God who sent him (13:20). Jesus' disciples wanted to take (λαβεῖν) him into the boat after he revealed to them his divine power to walk on the sea (6:16-21), which led to their profession of faith (6:68-69).[13] They received (ἔλαβον) his revelatory words and truly understood that he came from the Father and that the Father sent him (17:8). But to the Jews Jesus said that although "I came in the name of my Father, you did not accept (λαμβάνετε) me" (5:43). The Jews did not receive (λαμβάνετε) with faith either the revelatory testimony (3:11, 32-33) or

[11] For other statements about the revelatory "works" that Jesus "does," see 7:3-4, 21; 14:10, 12; 15:24; 17:4.

[12] Duke, *Irony*, 79.

[13] Heil, *Jesus Walking on the Sea*, 148-49.

the revelatory words (12:48) of Jesus. Indeed, although Jesus "came to his own, his own did not receive (παρέλαβον) him" (1:11).[14]

By telling the Jews to judge (κρίνατε) Jesus according to their own law, Pilate is ironically directing them to the evidence that should lead them to believe in him. Jesus exhorted the Jews seeking to kill him not to judge (κρίνετε) him by appearance, but to judge (κρίνετε) the right judgment (7:24). Nicodemus cautioned them that their law does not judge (κρίνει) a person without first hearing what he "does" (7:51). If they judge Jesus they would hear that he "does" the signs, work, and will of God, revelatory activity that calls for faith. Although Jesus and the Father who sent him provide them with the valid testimony required by their law, they know neither Jesus nor the Father and fail to believe (8:15-19). If Jesus had not "done" the revelatory works among them that no one else ever "did," they would have no sin. Instead, they have now seen yet hated both him and his Father (15:24). Their guilt of unbelief underlines the innocence of Jesus as they ironically fulfill what was written in their own law, "They hated me without cause" (15:25; Pss 35:19; 69:5). Not only does Jesus fulfill the messianic expectations written in the law and the prophets (1:45), but his revelatory truth transcends that of the law: "The law was given through Moses, but the gift of truth happened through Jesus Christ" (1:17).[15]

The Jews' rejoinder to Pilate, "We are not allowed to put anyone to death" (18:31), has a triple narrative function. First, it underlines that the Jews rather than Jesus are guilty of not doing their own law. That the Jewish law does not permit them to put to death the Jesus whose divine revelation not only fulfills but transcends the law serves as an ironic understatement.[16] Nevertheless, they seek to kill the Jesus who pointed out to them, "Did not Moses give you the law? Yet none of you does the law. Why do you seek to kill me?" (7:19; see also 5:18; 7:1, 25; 8:37, 40; 11:53). Second, it subtly reinforces that the Jews are under Roman subjugation. The Roman governor has forced the Jews, concerned to commemorate their national freedom in the Passover (18:28), to admit that they are not permitted to put anyone to death. Ironically, they need the help of the Romans to kill the one whose death they think will prevent the destruction of their freedom by the Romans (11:48). Third, by raising the seri-

---

[14] de la Potterie, *La vérité*, 345-46.

[15] Ibid., 138-41.

[16] Duke, *Irony*, 128.

ousness of the issue to that of the death penalty, the Jews' reply compels an unwilling Pilate to deal with Jesus.[17]

The narrator's notice that this scene fulfills the word that Jesus spoke about the kind of death he would die (18:32) assures the audience that these events are happening in accord with God's plan as spoken by Jesus. While the Jews and Pilate are manipulating one another to take responsibility for putting Jesus to death, it is Jesus who has taken ultimate responsibility for his own death. No one takes his life from him. As the good shepherd, Jesus lays down his life himself in accord with the authority he has received from the command of his Father (10:18).

The "indicating" (σημαίνων) by Jesus of "the kind of death he would die" (18:32) recalls his predictions that his death by crucifixion would be a "lifting up" or "exaltation" serving as his ultimate revelatory "sign" (σημεῖον).[18] Just as Moses "lifted up" the serpent in the desert (Num 21:9), so Jesus as the Son of Man "must" (δεῖ), in accord with God's plan, be "lifted up," so that all who believe may have eternal life in him (3:14-15). Once the Jews "lift up" the Son of Man, then they will know that "I am he," that Jesus is *the* divine revealer who does nothing on his own but reveals what the Father taught him (8:28). When Jesus is "lifted up" from the earth, he will draw all people to himself (12:32), "indicating (σημαίνων) the kind of death he would die" (12:33), a death that would unify all and offer eternal life to those who believe.

This opening scene (18:28-32) begins an intensely dramatic and ironic series of manipulative moves and countermoves between the Jews and Pilate with regard to Jesus. The Jews have delivered Jesus to Pilate, who taunted them to produce a charge against him. After they assured Pilate that Jesus is an evildoer, he ordered them to judge him themselves. Their counter that they are unable to put Jesus to death forces an unwilling Pilate to deal with him. That the Jews are unable and Pilate apparently unwilling to put Jesus to death underlines how he is laying down his own life as a "lifting up" in crucifixion that will serve as his final revelatory sign. That both Jews and gentile Romans are involved in putting Jesus to death already begins to fulfill Jesus' prediction that by his "lifting up" he would draw all people to himself (12:32).

[17] R. J. Cassidy, *John's Gospel in New Perspective: Christology and the Realities of Roman Power* (Maryknoll, NY: Orbis, 1992) 45; Rensberger, *Johannine Faith*, 92-93.

[18] For references to the revelatory "signs" of Jesus, see 2:11, 18, 23; 3:2; 4:54; 6:2, 14, 26, 30; 7:31; 9:16; 11:47; 12:18, 37.

Inside Jesus Reveals His Kingship to Pilate
(B¹ 18:33-38a)

33 Then Pilate again entered into the praetorium and summoned Jesus and said to him, "You are the King of the Jews?" 34 Jesus answered, "Are you saying this on your own or have others told you about me?" 35 Pilate answered, "I am not a Jew, am I? Your own nation and the chief priests have handed you over to me. What have you done?" 36 Jesus answered, "My kingdom is not of this world. If my kingdom were of this world, my officers would fight that I not be handed over to the Jews. But as it is, my kingdom is not from here." 37 Pilate then said to him, "So you are a king?" Jesus answered, "It is you who say I am a king. As for me, it is for this that I was born and for this that I came into the world, to testify to the truth. All who are of the truth hear my voice." 38 Pilate said to him, "What is truth?"

Pilate asks Jesus if he is the King of the Jews (18:33-34)

Forced by the Jews to deal with Jesus as a significant criminal deserving of death (18:30-31), Pilate entered (εἰσῆλθεν) again into (εἰς) the praetorium (18:33) the Jews had refused to enter (εἰσῆλθον) into (εἰς) (18:28). He summons Jesus and, continuing his denigration of "this man" (18:29), confronts him with a derisive, incredulous question: "*You* (of all people!) are the King of the Jews?" (18:33). But ironically for the reader Pilate's scornful question can also be heard on a deeper level as a true declaration: "*You* (surely) are the King of the Jews!"[19] Hence Pilate both mocks and unwittingly affirms the kingship of Jesus that others in the narrative have recognized. Nathanael confessed to Jesus, "You are the King of Israel!" (1:49). Those who were miraculously and overabundantly fed by Jesus tried to make him "king" (6:15). The crowd who met Jesus coming into Jerusalem for the feast of Passover proclaimed, "Hosanna! Blessed is he who comes in the name of the Lord—the King of Israel!" (12:13; see also 12:15).

Jesus counters Pilate's disdain with a sarcastic question of his own, "Are you saying this on your own or have others told you about me?" (18:34). The suggestion that others have told Pilate about Jesus makes him painfully aware that, although he was unwilling to deal with Jesus, "others," the Jews he holds in con-

---

[19] That these words are introduced by "he said" rather than "he asked" (cf. 18:19) and begin with an emphatic "you" (Σὺ) facilitate this double meaning. See also Duke, *Irony*, 189 n. 29.

tempt, have successfully manipulated him to ask about Jesus' kingship. Jesus furthermore implies ironically that Pilate has done what Jesus challenged the high priest to do—to listen to "others" who can testify to what Jesus has divinely revealed (18:19-21). But the words, "Are you saying this on your own?," compel both Pilate and the audience to decide for themselves, listening to the testimony of others, whether Jesus is King of the Jews.

Jesus' kingship is not from this world (18:35-36)

A piqued Pilate retaliates with a ridiculing retort, "I am not a Jew, am I?" (18:35). That Pilate is obviously not a Jew implies he has no personal interest in acknowledging whether Jesus is King of the Jews. But precisely because he is not one of the Jews who have decided to seek the death of Jesus (18:31), Pilate is eminently qualified to decide for himself whether Jesus is King of the Jews. Indeed, that Jesus' own Jewish nation and its chief priests have already handed over/betrayed (παρέδωκάν) him to Pilate leaves it to Pilate to decide. The Jews accused Jesus of doing (ποιῶν) wrong (18:30), although they refused to judge what he did (18:31). But Pilate, by asking, "What have you done (ἐποίησας)?" (18:35), unwittingly opens himself to hearing about the divine revelatory activity that Jesus has "done."

In reply to Pilate's humiliating reminder that the very nation and leaders of whom Jesus would be king have rejected him, Jesus reveals the nature of his kingship in a chiastically constructed pronouncement (18:36):

- (a) My kingdom is not of this world.
- (b) If my kingdom were of this world,
- (b) my officers would fight that I not be handed over to the Jews.
- (a) But as it is, my kingdom is not from here.

The statements that his kingdom is "not of this world" and "not from here" frame Jesus' explanation to Pilate of why his own people and leaders have abandoned him (18:35). Since his kingdom is not like other kingdoms of this world, his "officers" (ὑπηρέται) have not fought to prevent his betrayal to his Jewish enemies.[20] That Jesus' kingdom does not have its origin from this world or "from here" (ἐντεῦθεν) implies that it comes "from above," from God—that it is the kingdom of God. As Jesus told his Jewish opponents, "You are from

---

[20] For the activity of "officers" of this world, see 18:3, 12, 18, 22. Peter, who fought to prevent the arrest of Jesus (18:10), thus misunderstood the nature of Jesus' kingship.

below, I am from above (ἄνω); you are of this world, I am not of this world" (8:23). And Jesus instructed Nicodemus that anyone who would see and enter the kingdom of God must become a believer (3:11-15) by being born "again/from above" (ἄνωθεν) by water and the Spirit (3:3, 5, 7).[21]

Jesus' revelation to Pilate that his kingship is not of this world climaxes the way he has modified previous acknowledgments that he is a king. Although Nathanael proclaimed him to be the King of Israel, Jesus promised that he and others, thus including the audience, would see still greater things not of this world—heaven opened and the angels of God ascending and descending upon Jesus as the Son of Man (1:49-51).[22] Jesus refused to allow the crowd he had miraculously fed to make him a king of this world (6:15). When the crowd entering with Jesus into Jerusalem for the Passover feast exclaimed him to be the King of Israel, Jesus mounted an ass rather than a war horse, in fulfillment of scripture (Zech 9:9), to indicate how his humble and peaceful kingship differs from that of the kings of this world (12:12-15).[23]

Jesus came to testify to the truth (18:37-38a)

Pilate seizes upon Jesus' apparent admission that, although his kingdom is not of this world, he is nevertheless a king, "So you are a king?" (18:37). Without denying his kingship, Jesus places the responsibility for recognizing it upon Pilate with an emphatic "you" (Σὺ)—"It is *you* who say I am a king" (18:37). With an emphatic "I" (ἐγὼ) in contrast to "you" (Pilate), Jesus announces his revelatory mission that any realization of his kingship must embrace: "As for me, it is for this that I was born and for this that I came into the world, to testify to the truth" (18:37).[24]

That Jesus was "born" and "came" into the world to testify (μαρτυρήσω) to the truth (ἀληθείᾳ) sums up his revelatory mission as presented in the pro-

[21] For a discussion of the double meaning of ἄνωθεν (again/from above) in 3:3, 7, see G. R. O'Day, *The Word Disclosed: John's Story and Narrative Preaching* (St. Louis: CBP, 1987) 20-27; Duke, *Irony*, 144-45.

[22] Note the expansion from a singular "you" will see (ὄψῃ) greater things (1:50) to a plural "you" will see (ὄψεσθε) heaven opened (1:51), thus drawing in the audience. See also Moloney, *Belief*, 74.

[23] Reinhartz, *Word in the World*, 110-11. On the OT background of the arrival of Jesus as king in 12:12-15, see B. G. Schuchard, *Scripture within Scripture: The Interrelationship of Form and Function in the Explicit Old Testament Citations in the Gospel of John* (SBLDS 133; Atlanta: Scholars, 1992) 71-84.

[24] Our translation attempts to preserve the emphatic contrast between the "you" (Pilate) and the "I" (Jesus); see also de la Potterie, *La vérité*, 100 n. 56.

logue to the narrative (1:1-18).[25] As "the Word" that was with God in the beginning (1:1-2), Jesus was born and "became flesh" as the "only begotten one
coming from the Father, full of the gift of truth (ἀληθείας)" (1:14), the divine
revelation that became a reality through his very person (1:17).[26] He "came
into the world" as the revelatory "Light" that gives light to every human being
(1:9). John came for testimony to testify (μαρτυρήσῃ) about the "Light" so that
all might believe through him (1:7-8). Jesus reminded his Jewish enemies that
they sent messengers to John (1:19-34), and he has testified (μεμαρτύρηκεν)
to the truth (ἀληθείᾳ) of Jesus (5:33). But Jesus has a testimony greater than
John: The revelatory works that the Father gave him to complete testify (μαρτυρεῖ) that the Father sent him and the Father himself has testified (μεμαρτυ-
΄ρηκεν) about him. Nevertheless, the Jewish opponents have failed to believe
(5:36-38; see also 3:11-12, 26-28, 32-33; 8:13-18; 10:25-26).

The implication that "testifying to the truth" is meant to arouse faith
becomes more explicit with Jesus' universal appeal: "All who are of the truth
hear my voice" (18:37). Those who are "of" (ἐκ) the truth, in contrast to those
who are "of" (ἐκ) this world and know only the kingship of this world, are dis-
posed to believe in Jesus and experience his kingship that is not of this world
(18:36). That they hear (ἀκούει) the voice (φωνῆς) of Jesus establishes them as
"sheep" (disciples), who hear (ἀκούει) the voice (φωνῆς) of the "shepherd"
(Jesus) (10:3), who is also their king.[27] Others will hear (ἀκούσουσιν) his voice
(φωνῆς) so that there will be one flock and one shepherd (10:16). To those who
become the sheep, who hear (ἀκούουσιν) his voice (φωνῆς) and follow him
with faith, the shepherd-king gives eternal life (10:26-28) by laying down his
own life (10:11, 17-18).

[25] For recent discussions of the Johannine prologue, see W. Carter, "The Prologue and John's
Gospel: Function, Symbol and the Definitive Word," *JSNT* 39 (1990) 35-58; M. Cholin, "Le
Prologue de l'Évangile selon Jean: Structure et formation," *ScEs* 41 (1989) 189-205, 343-362; I. de
la Potterie, "Structure du Prologue de Saint Jean," *NTS* 30 (1984) 354-81; R. Meynet, "Analyse
rhétorique du Prologue de Jean," *RB* 96 (1989) 481-510; J. L. Staley, "The Structure of John's
Prologue: Its Implications for the Gospel's Narrative Structure," *CBQ* 48 (1986) 241-64; T. H.
Tobin, "The Prologue of John and Hellenistic Jewish Speculation," *CBQ* 52 (1990) 252-69; W.
H. Kelber, "The Birth of a Beginning: John 1:1- 18," *How Gospels Begin* (*Semeia* 52; ed. D. E.
Smith; Atlanta: Scholars, 1991) 121-44.

[26] The words "grace and truth" in 1:14 as well as in 1:17 function as a hendiadys, "gift of truth."
See de la Potterie, *La vérité*, 76-78, 169-212; idem, "Jésus Christ, plénitude de la vérité, lumière du
monde et sommet de la révélation d'après saint Jean," *Studia Missionalia* 33 (1984) 305-24.

[27] On the close relation between Jesus as shepherd and king, see Reinhartz, *Word in the
World,* 110-12.

The formula of Jesus' universal appeal for "all who are of the truth" (πᾶς + participle) continues his previous appeals that use this formula to invite all to believe in order to have eternal life:[28]

all who are born of the Spirit (3:8)
all who believe may have eternal life in him (3:15)
all who believe in him may not die but have eternal life (3:16)
all who drink . . . the water I give will never thirst (4:13-14)
all who see the Son and believe in him have eternal life (6:40)
all who hear from the Father and learn come to me (6:45)
all who live and believe in him may not die forever (11:26)
all who believe in me may not remain in darkness (12:46)

The appeals that "all who are of the truth hear my voice" (18:37) and "all who hear from the Father and learn come to me" (6:45) indicate how a proper and attentive "hearing" from God of the voice of Jesus disposes one to believe.[29]

The Pilate who summoned (ἐφώνησεν) Jesus at the beginning of this scene (18:33) is now invited to be of the truth and hear the voice (φωνῆς) of Jesus in order to believe and experience the kingship that is not of this world (18:36). But in apparent exasperation by the proceedings Pilate mutters an ironic "What is truth?" (18:38a).[30] Pilate thus raises a question for the reader to answer. The reader knows that Pilate's question, "What is truth?" (Τί ἐστιν ἀλήθεια), is ironically answered by the answer to his previous, parallel question, "What have you done?" (τί ἐποίησας) (18:35). The revelatory works that Jesus has "done" are "truth" (5:31-36). And the revelatory words that Jesus has spoken, precisely and ironically those just spoken to Pilate (18:36), are "truth" (8:40-47; 17:17). But ultimately the very person whom Pilate is questioning embodies the divine revelation that is "truth." As Jesus revealed to Thomas, "I am the way and the truth (ἀλήθεια) and the life. No one comes to the Father except through me" (14:6). The "truth" that is Jesus provides the revelation that leads to eternal life with God for all who believe.[31]

---

[28] This same formula is used in a negative sense in 3:20; 8:34; 16:2; 19:12. See de la Potterie, *La vérité*, 101 n. 57, 626.

[29] Ibid., 627-31.

[30] According to Stibbe, *John as Storyteller*, 107, Pilate's question is "not a cruel taunt, or philosophical playfulness, or even melancholic scepticism, but the frustrated exclamation of a man who has expended time and energy trying to get at the truth through a questioning of both accusers and defendants, but with absolutely no success. Truth for Pilate means 'the facts of the case'."

[31] de la Potterie, *La vérité*, 241-78.

In contrast to the previous scene in which the Jews refuse not only to enter into the praetorium but to take back Jesus and judge him themselves (18:28-32), in this scene Pilate enters into the praetorium and interrogates Jesus himself (18:33-38a). To Pilate Jesus reveals that his kingship is not of this world and invites Pilate, the audience, and all others to experience his kingship by hearing the voice of the shepherd/king who testifies to the truth that his death offers eternal life for all who believe and follow him.[32]

Outside the Jews Reject Pilate's Offer To Release Jesus as Their King (A² 18:38b-40)

38b And having said this, he again came out to the Jews and said to them, "I find no case against him. 39 But you have a custom that I release someone to you at Passover. Do you want me to release to you the King of the Jews?" 40 They then cried out again saying, "Not this one but Barabbas!" Now Barabbas was a bandit.

Pilate offers to release Jesus as King to the Jews (18:38b-39)

This third scene forms an A-B-A sandwich with the two previous scenes. As an A scene in which the Jews outside the praetorium reject Pilate's offer to release Jesus as their King (18:38b-40), it contrasts with the previous B scene in which Jesus inside the praetorium revealed his kingship to Pilate (18:33-38a). But it also develops Pilate's encounter with the Jews outside the praetorium in the first A scene (18:28-32).

In the first A scene Pilate came out (ἐξῆλθεν) of the praetorium to the Jews and asked, "What charge do you bring against this man?" (18:29). Now Pilate again came out (ἐξῆλθεν) to the Jews and declares Jesus innocent: "I find no case against him" (18:38b). Although the Jews claimed that Jesus was a serious evildoer (18:30) deserving the death penalty (18:31), Pilate contradicts them by finding nothing with which to charge Jesus. The theme of the Jews' attempt to put Jesus to death thus reaches a critical point.

That Pilate finds no "case" (αἰτίαν) with Jesus has a double meaning. While the Greek word αἰτία in a judicial context means "case," "charge," or "accusation" against someone, it can also mean simply "cause" or "reason" with regard

---

[32] For possible background for the combination of kingship and testifying, see J. D. M. Derrett, "Christ, King and Witness (John 18,37)," *BeO* 31 (1989) 189-98.

to someone.³³ In contrast to Jesus' declaration in the previous B scene that he has a kingship not of this world (18:36) and that he is the divine revealer who testifies to the truth (18:37), Pilate declares that he finds no significant "cause" or "reason" in Jesus. He finds no reason to become a believing disciple of Jesus by "hearing his voice" (18:37).

Pilate's offer to release Jesus to the Jews at the Passover (18:39) continues the theme, present in the previous A scene, of putting Jesus to death in conjunction with the Passover (18:28). The offer to release Jesus at the Passover corresponds to the liberation this feast commemorates. At the same time, however, it subtly underlines the current subjugation of the Jewish people to the Roman regime. The Jews lack not only national independence but more importantly the true freedom as a people that can only come from believing in the Jesus (8:31-38) that the Roman governor is ironically offering them at the Passover.

The taunting offer of Pilate to release to the Jews the Jesus he derisively calls "the King of the Jews" (18:39) continues his contempt for them and the insignificant "this man" (18:29) they have brought him in the first A scene. Pilate thus pompously mocks their claim that Jesus is a serious criminal (18:30) deserving death at the hands of the Romans (18:31) with what he intends to be an ironic overstatement, that Jesus is their "King." But with the contrast to the previous B scene in which Jesus revealed that his kingship embraces yet transcends that of this world (18:36), Pilate's ridiculing reference to Jesus as "the King of the Jews" actually functions for the audience as an ironic understatement.³⁴

The Jews reject Jesus in favor of the bandit Barabbas (18:40)

In development of the previous A scene the Jews take up Pilate's own contempt for Jesus as merely "this" (τούτου) man (18:29) and again reject the Jesus Pilate wants them to take back (18:31): "Not this one (τούτου) but Barabbas!" (18:40). The narrator's comment that Barabbas was a bandit creates the irony of the Jews preferring a real, guilty criminal to the innocent Jesus who is truly their King. In contrast to the previous B scene and in accord with the "good shepherd" metaphor (10:1-18), the Jews choose in Barabbas a "bandit" or

³³ BAGD, 26; W. Radl, "αἰτία," *EDNT* 1. 43.

³⁴ With regard to Pilate's reference to Jesus as "King of the Jews," Duke, *Irony,* 89, states: "Pilate means the title as a jibe at 'the Jews,' but is even more correct than he knows."

"robber" (ληστής), one of the false leaders who came before the good shepherd (10:1, 8), rather than "hearing the voice" (18:37; 10:3, 16, 27) of Jesus, their good shepherd-king and true leader.[35]

Inside Pilate's Soldiers Mock Jesus' Kingship (B² 19:1-3)

1 Then Pilate took Jesus and had him scourged. 2 And the soldiers, having woven a crown out of thorns, placed it on his head, and they dressed him in a purple robe. 3 They kept coming up to him, saying, "Hail, King of the Jews!," as they were giving him slaps.

Pilate punishes the innocent Jesus (19:1)

Forming a B-A-B intercalation with the two previous scenes, the punishing and mocking of Jesus as King of the Jews by the Romans inside the praetorium (19:1-3) contrasts with the Roman governor's offer to release an innocent Jesus to the Jews as their King outside the praetorium (18:38b-40). It also develops the revelation of Jesus' true kingship to Pilate inside the praetorium (18:33-38a).

In direct contradiction to his proclamation of Jesus' innocence (18:38b) in the previous A scene, Pilate has the Jesus he offered to release (18:39) scourged (19:1)! He thus took (ἔλαβεν) the Jesus he ordered the Jews to take (Λάβετε) and judge according to their own law (18:31) in the first A scene, and incongruously punishes him whom he himself has judged to be innocent.[36]

In development of the first B scene, the Pilate who failed to answer the challenge of Jesus to hear his voice as *the* divine revealer who testifies to the truth

---

[35] Duke, *Irony*, 131

[36] H. Balz, "μαστιγόω," *EDNT* 2. 395: "The flogging of Jesus in John 19:1; Mark 10:34 par. corresponds to the Roman punishment of scourging (*verberatio*), which was done as chastisement or torture (not to Roman citizens; cf. Acts 16:37; 22:24ff.), esp. as a punishment accompanying other humiliating punishments and the sentence of death—above all, crucifixion, which it almost always preceded. . . . In John 19:1 a separate flogging may be in view, perhaps in the sense of a torturing, in order to coerce a confession (cf. vv. 4f.)." According to Brown, *Death*, 852, it is difficult to classify the scourging of Jesus in John 19:1. "Pilate's motive seems to be to make Jesus look wretched so that 'the Jews' will be satisfied and accept his release." According to Rensberger, *Johannine Faith*, 93, the scourging of Jesus here is "a procedure that should not properly be used on a guilty man until he has been formally condemned, let alone on one who has just been declared innocent."

(18:37) now intensifies his lack of faith by inflicting bodily harm upon the one who offers eternal life to all who believe. He "took" (ἔλαβεν) Jesus, and instead of "taking" or "receiving" him with faith, the most appropriate object of this Johannine verb (see above on 18:31), he "took" and had the innocent Jesus scourged.

Roman soldiers mock the Jewish kingship of Jesus (19:2-3)

The Roman soldiers' mocking acknowledgment of the Jewish kingship of Jesus (19:2-3) contrasts the Jews' refusal to accept Jesus as their King in the previous A scene (18:39-40). In a cruel parody of a royal Roman coronation and investiture they place a crown made of thorns on Jesus' head and clothe him with an imperial purple robe (19:2).[37] They pay him mock homage by hailing him as the King of the Jews (19:3) in the same way they would hail their own Roman king or emperor.[38] But at the same time they are coming up to him and giving him not honor but slaps (ῥαπίσματα) (19:3), mistreating him in the same way as the Jewish officer of the high priest, who likewise gave Jesus an undeserved slap (ῥάπισμα) (18:22). As Romans ridiculing Jesus as King of the Jews in a Roman way, they are illustrating on a deeper, ironic, and paradoxical level for the audience that Jesus is King not only of the Jews but of Gentiles as well.

The Roman ridicule of Jesus as the King of the Jews also develops Jesus' revelation of his true kingship in the first B scene (18:33-38a). The mock crown, clothing, and cruel obeisance merely confirm for the reader what Jesus has already declared—that his kingdom is not of this world (18:36). He is not a king who revels in the trappings of worldly royalty and power, but one who testifies to the truth God reveals in and through him. He is the king of those who are "of the truth" rather than "of the world," those who hear his voice and become his believing followers (18:37). He establishes his kingship not by administering violence to others but by becoming a victim of imperial violence and laying

---

[37] H. Kraft, "στέφανος," *EDNT* 3. 273-74: "Στέφανος encompasses the meanings of both "wreath" and "crown," though the latter also corresponds to διάδημα, the bejeweled diadem. ... The most significant uses of the wreath in the public life of antiquity were the Olympic laurel and the victory wreath of the Roman conqueror." Brown, *John*, 874-75: "The mockery is probably based on the crown as generally representative of kingship, although some have thought more specifically of a mockery of the laurel wreath worn by the Emperor."

[38] Ibid., 875: "The soldiers mimic the '*Ave Caesar*' greeting given the Emperor."

down his own life as the good shepherd-king who leads his believing subjects to eternal life with the Father (10:11, 17-18, 27-29).[39]

The followers of the kingship not of this world can expect similar hatred, suffering, and persecution from the world. In his farewell discourse Jesus warned his disciples: "If the world hates you, know that it hated me before you. If you were of the world, the world would love its own; but because you are not of the world, but I have chosen you out of the world, therefore the world hates you . . . If they persecuted me, they will also persecute you (15:18-20) . . . An hour is coming when everyone who kills you will think he is offering worship to God" (16:2). And in Jesus' farewell prayer to the Father: "The world hated them, because they are not of the world just as I am not of the world" (17:14).

Outside the Jews Reject Pilate's Offer of the Innocent Jesus, God's Son (A³ 19:4-7)

4 Then Pilate again came outside and said to them, "Behold, I am leading him out to you, so that you may know that I find no case against him." 5 Jesus then came outside, wearing the thorny crown and the purple robe. And he said to them, "Behold the man!" 6 When the chief priests and the officers saw him, they cried out saying, "Crucify him, crucify him!" Pilate said to them, "Take him yourselves and crucify him, for I do not find a case against him." 7 The Jews answered him, "We have a law, and according to that law he ought to die, because he made himself Son of God."

Pilate presents the innocent "man" Jesus to the Jews (19:4-5)

Functioning as an A-B-A intercalation in conjunction with the two previous scenes, the Jews' rejection of Pilate's offer of the innocent "man" Jesus, the Son of God, outside the praetorium (19:4-7) contrasts with the Roman soldiers' mockery of Jesus as the King of the Jews inside the praetorium (19:1-3). At the same time it develops Pilate's offer to release the innocent Jesus to the Jews as their King outside the praetorium (18:38b-40).

In contrast to the previous B scene (19:1-3) that implicitly takes place in the more private domain inside the praetorium, this third A scene explicitly takes

---

[39] As Senior, *John*, 85, perceptively notes: "The reader, of course, knows that Jesus *is* a 'king' and that through him the divine source of all genuine power is revealed. From the perspective of the Gospel, therefore, the mockery turns back upon itself. It is not Jesus who is derided in this scene but the trappings of human sovereignty: the crown, the royal robe, the acclamations and rituals of homage. True dignity and power are now expressed in the anti-signs of seeming powerlessness born by this prisoner."

place in the more public domain outside the praetorium. In development of the previous A scenes (18:28-32, 38b-40), in which Pilate alone "came out" (ἐξ-ῆλθεν) to the Jews (18:29, 38b), now both Pilate and Jesus "came out" of the praetorium (19:4, 5). The Jesus that the Jews led (ἄγουσιν) to Pilate in the praetorium (18:28) as an evildoer (18:30) deserving of death (18:31) in the first A scene Pilate now leads (ἄγω) back to the Jews outside the praetorium as one with whom he finds no case or cause (19:4). The Jesus whom Pilate derisively offered to release to the Jews as their supposed King (18:39) in the second A scene he now publicly presents to them as their innocent yet scourged, mockingly crowned and clothed, King. Indeed, the exaggerated emphasis on coming outside of the praetorium—Pilate came out (ἐξῆλθεν) outside (ἔξω), leads Jesus outside (ἔξω), and Jesus came out (ἐξῆλθεν) outside (ἔξω)—underlines this as the mock but ironically true public epiphany of Jesus as King (19:4-5).[40]

In the previous A scene Pilate reported to the Jews that he finds no judicial "case" (αἰτίαν) against the innocent Jesus, and, through the double meaning, no "cause" to take him seriously and believe in him (18:38b). Now Pilate leads Jesus outside the praetorium so that the Jews can "behold" ("Ἴδε) and know for themselves that Pilate finds no case or cause (αἰτίαν) with him (19:4). But that Pilate finds no "case" against the innocent Jesus contradicts his punishing him by scourging in the previous B scene (19:1). And that Pilate finds no "cause" or "reason" to take Jesus seriously conflicts with the Roman soldiers' ironic acknowledgment of Jesus in that same B scene as the King of the Jews, who is also their own King (19:2-3).

In the previous B scene Jesus was a totally passive victim: He was scourged by Pilate (19:1), and mockingly crowned, clothed, and slapped by the Roman soldiers (19:2-3). In contrast, he now "came outside" on his own rather than being led out, actively "wearing" rather than passively clothed with the thorny crown and royal purple robe (19:5).[41] This accords with Jesus not only laying down his own life as the good shepherd-king (10:11, 17-18), but also testifying to the truth that, although his kingship is not of this world (18:36-37), as revealed in the first B scene, he is nevertheless the true King of both Jews and Gentiles. In development of the previous A scene, the Jesus whom Pilate derisively offered to release as "the King of the Jews" (18:39) now comes out of the Roman praetorium actively "wearing" the mock Roman imperial crown and clothing that ironically establish him as King also of the gentile Romans.

---

[40] Duke, *Irony*, 132.
[41] Ibid.

In correspondence to Pilate's invitation for the Jews to "behold" ("Ἴδε) that he finds no case or cause with Jesus (19:4), he now invites them to "Behold ('Ιδοὺ) the man!" (19:5). The Jesus whom Pilate contemptuously referred to as "this man" (ἀνθρώπου τούτου) in the first A scene (18:29) and ridiculed as "King of the Jews" in the second A scene (18:39) he now derides as merely "the man" (ὁ ἄνθρωπος). In contrastive correspondence to Pilate's saying that Jesus is a king in the first B scene (18:37) and to the Roman soldiers' mock acclamation of Jesus in the second B scene, "Hail, King of the Jews!" (19:3), Pilate exclaims, "Behold the man!," denigrating the royally crowned and clothed Jesus as only a man not a king.

Pilate's disdaining of Jesus as merely a "man" confirms, by way of ironic contrast with the first B scene, what Jesus declared to Pilate about his revelatory mission. Jesus explained that the reason he was born and came into the world, that is, the reason he, as the Word that pre-existed with God (1:1-2), became flesh (1:14), a human being, a "man," was to testify to the truth as the divine revealer (18:37). Pilate's jeering, "Behold the man!," as Jesus came out wearing the mock royal robes that ironically reveal his true kingship (19:5), brings to a climax the narrative's various references to Jesus as the "man" who "speaks" and "does" the truth that is divine revelation:

> Come see a *man* who told me everything I have done (4:29)
> No one has ever spoken like this *man* (7:46)
> But now you are trying to kill me, a *man* who spoke to you the truth
>   that I heard from God (8:40)
> How can a sinful *man* do such signs? (9:16)
> This *man* does many signs (11:47)[42]

By contemptuously inviting the Jews to behold Jesus as "the man" (ὁ ἄνθρωπος), Pilate is unwittingly confirming what the Jews have already determined about Jesus, namely, that he is *the* one "man" whose death can save the people from dying at the hands of the Romans. Caiaphas had advised the Jews that it was better for "one man (ἄνθρωπος)" to die for the people, so that the whole nation may not perish (11:48-51; 18:14). That the royally crowned and robed Jesus is revealing himself as "the man" who is the true King of both Jews

---

[42] Panackel, *ΙΔΟΥ Ο ΑΝΘΡΩΠΟΣ (Jn 19,5b)*, 334-35. Although he presents the many different references and rich nuances Pilate's laconic exclamation, "Behold the man!," can have in the narrative, Panackel limits his interpretation to an emphasis on the humanity of Jesus, who is also the Son of God (pp. 336-38).

and Romans (19:5) deepens the irony. While Pilate is unknowingly reminding the Jews that Jesus is "the man" who can save them from the Romans, the audience hears Pilate pointing out "the man" who, as the shepherd-king whose death effects eternal life (10:11, 28), can save both Jews and Romans from perishing eternally.

Pilate's scornful, "Behold the man!" (19:5), ironically echoes what Jesus predicted about himself as the Son of Man.[43] Jesus predicted his death by crucifixion in terms of his "lifting up" or "exaltation" as the Son of Man (3:14; 8:28; 12:32-34) that would also be his "glorification" by God.[44] After some Greeks who had come up to worship at the Passover feast asked to "see" him (12:20-22), Jesus announced, "The hour has come for the Son of Man to be glorified" (12:23), and then spoke about his upcoming death (12:24-25). Once Judas went out to betray him to be put to death, Jesus declared, "Now is the Son of Man glorified, and God is glorified in him. If God is glorified in him, God will also glorify him in himself, and he will glorify him at once" (13:31-32). The Roman soldiers have derisively "glorified" with the mock accoutrements of kingship (19:5) the Jesus who is laying down his life as the shepherd-king. Consequently, Pilate, by proclaiming, "Behold the *man!*," instead of the expected, "Behold the king!," is ironically confirming for the reader that Jesus, in and through his dying, is being "glorified" as the Son of Man.[45]

The Jews claim that Jesus made himself Son of God (19:6 7)

In the previous A scene the Jews rejected Pilate's invitation to release Jesus and chose instead the bandit Barabbas, as they cried out (ἐκραύγασαν), saying

[43] Duke, *Irony,* 107: "Pilate, the Gentile, cannot be made to say *Son of man* outright, for that would not only be historically implausible but violate the sanctity of that title as Jesus' own. Pilate can, however, be permitted to say with plausibility and great sarcasm, 'Behold the man!'—not only a majestic title itself, but one that evokes for perceptive readers a vision of 'heaven opened, and the angels of God ascending and descending upon the Son of man' (1:51)."

[44] The suffering Servant of Yahweh is "lifted up" and "glorified" through death in LXX Isa 52:13; see D. Burkett, *The Son of the Man in the Gospel of John* (JSNTSup 56; Sheffield: JSOT, 1991) 127.

[45] For those who hold to a reference to the Son of Man in 19:5, see Panackel, *ΙΔΟΥ Ο ΑΝΘΡΩΠΟΣ (Jn 19,5b),* 315-18. On the Johannine Son of Man in general, see F. J. Moloney, *The Johannine Son of Man* (2d ed.; Biblioteca di Scienze Religiose 14; Rome: Libreria Ateneo Salesiano, 1978); R. Rhea, *The Johannine Son of Man* (ATANT 76; Zürich: Theologischer Verlag, 1990); M. M. Pazdan, *The Son of Man: A Metaphor for Jesus in the Fourth Gospel* (Collegeville: Liturgical Press, 1991); J. W. Pryor, "The Johannine Son of Man and the Descent-Ascent Motif," *JETS* 34 (1991) 341-51; Burkett, *Son of the Man.*

(λέγοντες), "Not this one but Barabbas!" (18:40). In development, the chief priests and the officers, the Jewish leaders perpetrating the demise of Jesus (18:3, 12, 18, 22, 35), have "seen" what Pilate invited them to "behold" (19:4-5), and they again cried out (ἐκραύγασαν), this time directly demanding his death, saying (λέγοντες), "Crucify him, crucify him!" (19:6). They are thus ironically calling for Jesus to be "lifted up" (3:14; 8:28; 12:32-34) by crucifixion and "glorified" as the Son of Man (12:23; 13:31-32). In contrast to the previous B scene, the Jewish leaders are calling for the Romans to crucify the Jesus they have ironically installed as King of both Jews and Romans (19:2-3).

In the first A scene Pilate directed the Jews to take back Jesus, "Take him yourselves" (Λάβετε αὐτὸν ὑμεῖς), and judge him according to their own law (18:31)—a "taking" that could lead them to faith (see above). In the second A scene Pilate taunted the Jews by offering to release as their "King" (18:39) the Jesus he knows they want to put to death (18:31), but the Jesus who is the true King of those who believe (18:37). In this third A scene Pilate intensifies his taunt as he again directs the Jews to "take him yourselves" (Λάβετε αὐτὸν ὑμεῖς) and crucify him (19:6), although he knows they cannot put anyone to death (18:31).[46] While contemptuously reminding the Jews of their subjugation to the Romans, Pilate, on the deeper, ironic level, is offering them again a "taking" that could lead them and others to faith. The crucifixion of Jesus is his "lifting up" or "exaltation" as the Son of Man, the ultimate demonstration that he is the Father's divine revealer (8:28), who draws all to himself (12:32) and grants eternal life to those who believe (3:14).

That Pilate orders the Jews to take (Λάβετε) Jesus and crucify him themselves because he finds no case or cause with him (19:6) contradicts Pilate's own taking (ἔλαβεν) of the innocent Jesus and having him scourged (19:1) in the previous B scene. Whereas the Romans scourged, mockingly crowned, clothed, and slapped Jesus as the King of the Jews (19:2-3), Pilate taunts the humiliated and powerless Jews to be the ones to crucify their own disgraced King.

This is the third time Pilate contemptuously claims that he finds no case or cause (αἰτίαν) with Jesus. All three are contradictory and their progression heightens the dramatic irony of the proceedings. In the previous A scene Pilate announced no significant case or cause with Jesus yet offered to release him to

---

[46] Duke, *Irony,* 133; Rensberger, *Johannine Faith,* 94; Cassidy, *John's Gospel,* 46: "In context, Pilate's statement to the chief priests that they should take and crucify Jesus themselves essentially emphasizes his own position as *the only one* possessing authority and power for crucifixion."

the Jews as their King (18:38b-39). In this third A scene he again declared no significant case or cause with Jesus yet had him scourged (19:1) and led out of the praetorium dressed by Romans as King of the Jews (19:4-5). Now he again claims no significant case or cause with Jesus yet taunts the Jews to crucify him (19:6). Pilate's mocking claims that he finds nothing significant in Jesus ironically show how profoundly significant Jesus is for Jews, Romans, and all readers.

Defending their honor and integrity, the Jews cleverly counter Pilate's ruthless exploitation of Jesus to belittle them. Although Pilate has relentlessly ridiculed their national sovereignty, the Jews insist that "We have a law" (19:7).[47] And according to that law, the very law that Pilate himself invoked for them to judge Jesus (18:31) in the first A scene, he ought to die (19:7). To Pilate's degrading of Jesus from the supposed King of the Jews (18:39) in the second A scene to merely a "man" (19:5) in this third A scene, the Jews counter with the new charge that the reason he should die is that, although he is indeed merely a "man," as Pilate derisively asserts, "he made himself Son of God" (19:7).

After Jesus healed the lame man on the sabbath and told the incensed Jews that he was merely doing the saving work of his Father (5:1-17), the Jews sought to kill him because he not only broke the sabbath but called God his own Father, making ($\pi o \iota \tilde{\omega} \nu$) himself equal to God (5:18). After Jesus told the Jews that "I and the Father are one" (10:30), they wanted to stone him for blasphemy, telling him that "you being a man are making ($\pi o \iota \varepsilon \tilde{\iota} \varsigma$) yourself God" (10:31-33). Whereas the Jews claim that their "law" demands his death (19:7), Jesus had explained how their "law" points to his divine sonship: "Is it not written in your law, 'I said, "You are gods"' (Ps 82:6)?[48] If it calls them gods to whom the word of God came, and the scripture cannot be annulled, can you say that the one whom the Father has sanctified and sent into the world blas-

---

47 Rensberger, *Johannine Faith,* 94.

48 Note that "law" here refers to the whole OT in general and not just to the Torah, since a psalm is quoted. As Brown, *John,* 409, points out: "The whole verse reads: 'I say, "You are gods, sons of the Most High, all of you."' Jesus is interested not only in the use of the term 'gods' but also in the synonymous expression 'sons of the Most High,' for he refers to himself as Son of God in vs. 36." According to Schuchard, *Scripture,* 70: "The psalm is recalled in order to facilitate an argument in which John apparently wishes to establish the following: (1) The psalm addresses Israel's judges who, because they possess an identity and authority derived from Moses (who is himself 'like God'), are referred to as 'gods.' (2) Because Moses' identity surpasses that of the 'gods,' and Jesus' identity surpasses that of Moses (1:17), Jesus is able to speak as he does of his unity with the Father and is worthy of the title 'Son of God.'"

phemes because I said, 'I am Son of God'?" (10:34-36). It is not that Jesus "made" (ἐποίησεν) himself the Son of God (19:7), but that he "does" the revelatory works of the Father. As he told the Jews, "If I am not doing (ποιῶ) the works of my Father, do not believe me; but if I am doing (ποιῶ) them, even though you do not believe me, believe the works, so that you may know and understand that the Father is in me and I am in the Father" (10:37-38).

In the first B scene Pilate inquired whether Jesus was the King of the Jews (18:33, 37) and in the second B scene Pilate's soldiers ridiculed Jesus as the King of the Jews (19:3). In contrast, the Jews, in this third A scene, force Pilate to deal with Jesus as one who, although only a "man" (19:5), made himself Son of God (19:7). Their new charge contains two ironic half truths for the audience. While it is true that Jesus must die, it is not according to the Jewish law that he ought to die (19:7), but he must die in accord with God's saving plan (18:11; 12:27-28; 10:11-18). And while it is true that Jesus is Son of God, it is not that he made himself Son of God (19:7), but that God made him his Son, sending him into the world: "For God so loved the world that he gave his only Son, so that all who believe in him may not perish but have eternal life. For God did not send his Son into the world to condemn the world, but that the world might be saved through him" (3:16-17).

Inside Jesus Reveals His Divine Origin to Pilate (B³ 19:8-11)

8 Now when Pilate heard this statement, he became very much afraid, 9 and entered into the praetorium again and said to Jesus, "Where are you from?" But Jesus gave him no answer. 10 So Pilate said to him, "To me you do not speak? Do you not know that I have authority to release you and I have authority to crucify you?" 11 Jesus answered him, "You would not have any authority over me unless it had been given you from above. Therefore the one who handed me over to you has a greater sin."

A fearful Pilate inquires about Jesus' origin (19:8-9)

Completing a B-A-B sandwich with the two previous scenes, Jesus' revelation of his divine origin to Pilate inside the praetorium (19:8-11) contrasts with the Jews' rejection of Pilate's offer of the innocent "man" Jesus outside the praetorium (19:4-7). It also develops Jesus' revelation of his kingship through the Roman soldiers' mockery of him as the King of the Jews inside the praetorium (19:1-3).

In each of the three previous A scenes (18:28-32; 38b-40; 19:4-7) Pilate brashly ridiculed, taunted, and humiliated the Jews as they brought him an apparently innocent and insignificant man. In contrast, after hearing the Jews' statement that according to their law Jesus ought to die because he made himself Son of God (19:7), Pilate becomes "very much afraid" in this third B scene (19:8).[49] With this new claim of a supernatural status the case of Jesus is more serious and significant than Pilate thought.

In the first B scene (18:33-38a) Pilate entered (εἰσῆλθεν) into (εἰς) the praetorium (18:33) and had a revelatory encounter with Jesus, after the Jews outside the praetorium suggested that he deserved the death penalty (18:31). In the second B scene (19:1-3) Pilate's scourging and the Roman soldiers' mockery ironically revealed Jesus as King of the Jews and of the Romans inside the praetorium, after the Jews outside the praetorium chose the bandit Barabbas instead of Jesus (18:40). In this third B scene Pilate again entered (εἰσῆλθεν) into (εἰς) the praetorium (19:9) for another encounter with Jesus, after the Jews outside the praetorium raised the issue of his divine sonship (19:7).

The fearful Pilate initiates the encounter by asking about the origin of the Jesus who claims to be Son of God, "Where are you from?" (19:9). Continuing the confrontation that began in the first B scene, Pilate's inquiry is ironically more profound than he realizes. He adds another to a series of provocative questions about Jesus' divine revelatory identity, origin, and mission whose answers could lead him to faith:

You are the King of the Jews? (18:33)
What have you done? (18:35)
So you are a king? (18:37)
What is truth? (18:38a)
Where are you from? (19:9)

Pilate's question of where (πόθεν) Jesus is from climaxes similar ironically profound questions that indicate the divine origin of Jesus' revelatory mission and activity. Nathanael is subtly pointing the audience to Jesus' divine origin when he asks, "From where (πόθεν) do you know me?" (1:48). The headwaiter who tasted the water become wine at the wedding in Cana, Jesus' first revela-

---

[49] It is appropriate to translate μᾶλλον ἐφοβήθη in 19:8 as "he became very much afraid" rather than "he became even more afraid," since Pilate has exhibited no fear to this point. See Rensberger, *Johannine Faith*, 94; Carson, *John*, 599-600; Barrett, *John*, 542; Brown, *John*, 877; B. Lindars, *The Gospel of John* (NCB; London: Oliphants, 1972) 567.

tory "sign" (2:11), did not know where (πόθεν) it was from (2:9)—its divine origin. Nicodemus does not know the divine origin and goal of the Spirit— from where (πόθεν) it comes and where it goes (3:8). The Samaritan woman does not know from where (πόθεν), the divine origin, Jesus has the living water he will give her (4:11). Before Jesus miraculously multiplied bread (6:1-15) as a sign of his heavenly origin (6:31-33, 38, 41-42, 50-51, 58), Philip does not know from where (πόθεν) they will buy bread for the crowd to eat (6:5).

Since Jesus came from Nazareth in Galilee, some in Jerusalem think he cannot be the Christ because they know where (πόθεν) he is from. They ironically confirm their own prediction that when the Christ comes no one will know where (πόθεν) he is from (7:27).[50] Jesus, however, chides them on not knowing his divine origin and mission: "You know me and you know where (πόθεν) I am from? Yet I did not come on my own, but the one who sent me, whom you do not know, is true. I know him, because I am from him, and he sent me" (7:28-29).

After the Pharisees accused Jesus of bearing false testimony about himself (8:13), Jesus indicated that they did not know the divine origin and purpose of his revelatory mission: "Even if I testify about myself, my testimony is true, because I know from where (πόθεν) I have come and where I am going. You do not know from where (πόθεν) I come and where I am going" (8:14). After Jesus opened the eyes of the man born blind, the Pharisees again indict themselves of not knowing Jesus' heavenly origin: "We know that God has spoken to Moses, but as for this one, we do not know where (πόθεν) he is from" (9:29). But the man born blind rebuked them: "Now this is what is so amazing, that you do not know where (πόθεν) he is from, yet he opened my eyes (9:30) . . . If this man were not from God, he would not be able to do anything" (9:33). In asking Jesus, "Where (πόθεν) are you from?" (19:9), Pilate is unwittingly opening himself and the audience up to another revelatory encounter involving Jesus' heavenly origin.[51]

Jesus' defiant refusal to give Pilate an answer (19:9) develops the previous B scenes in a triple way. First, Jesus remains silent because he has already indirectly revealed his divine origin to Pilate in the first B scene. He indicated that his kingship was "not of this world" (18:36) and that from his implied heavenly origin he was born and came into the world to testify to the truth (18:37). Second, Jesus' reticence furthers the powerful passivity that demonstrates his

---

[50] Duke, *Irony*, 65-66.

[51] L. M. Dewailly, "'D'où es tu?' (Jean 19,9)," *RB* 92 (1985) 481-96; D. Zeller, "Jesus und die Philosophen vor dem Richter (zu Joh 19,8-11)," *BZ* 37 (1993) 88-92.

superior status. By being scourged and mocked as King of the Jews in the second B scene (19:1-3), Jesus, through his silence and passivity, ironically testified that he is a king transcendent to any of this world. In contrast to the Jews, who continually "answered" Pilate's humiliating questions and statements that underlined their inferiority in the previous A scenes (18:30, 31, 40; 19:6, 7), Jesus stands silently superior to the Roman governor. Third, Jesus refuses to answer Pilate because Pilate, like the reader, must make his own decision about Jesus' divine origin. Jesus' poignant silence, then, continues his appeal of the first B scene, that "all who are of the truth hear my voice" (18:37). The question of Jesus' heavenly origin can be answered only by those who believe.

Jesus reveals an authority superior to Pilate (19:10-11)

With emphatic reference to his elevated status Pilate arrogantly asks the silent Jesus, "*To me* you do not speak?" (19:10).[52] Pilate's use of the favorite Johannine word for the revelatory "speaking" (λαλεῖς) of Jesus develops the irony of Jesus' revelation to the Roman governor in the B scenes.[53] Jesus "spoke" revelatory words to Pilate in the first B scene, when he testified to the truth that his kingship is not of this world (18:36-37). Indeed, in contrast to the A scenes, in which Pilate and the Jews jostle over Jesus outside the praetorium, Jesus inside the praetorium privately "speaks" revelation to the Roman governor in the B scenes. Privileged with Jesus' revelation, Pilate is unwittingly in a position superior not to Jesus but to the Jews at this point. He, and the reader for whom he is transparent, will prove to be truly "superior" only if they believe in the Jesus the Jews have rejected.

Pilate's pompous pronouncement that he possesses imperial authority to release or to crucify Jesus (19:10) contradicts what has transpired between Pilate and the Jews in the previous A scenes, and thus functions as an ironic overstatement. When Pilate teased the Jews by offering to release Jesus, they thwarted him by choosing Barabbas instead in the second A scene (18:39-40). And when the Jews demanded that Pilate crucify Jesus, he declined and derisively directed them to crucify Jesus themselves in the third A scene (19:6).

With a counter pronouncement Jesus deflates Pilate's puffy pomposity: "You would not have any authority over me unless it had been given you from above" (19:11).[54] Pilate is only a pawn in God's plan. The authority he exercises

---

[52] Note the emphatic position of "to me" (Ἐμοὶ) in Pilate's question.

[53] On Jesus' revelatory "speaking" expressed by λαλεῖν, see above on 18:10 in chapter 2.

[54] Because the verbal form "it had been given" (ἦν δεδομένον) is neuter, Cassidy, *John's*

over Jesus in this situation "has been given" (divine passive) to him by God "from above" (ἄνωθεν)—the heavenly, transcendent realm (3:3, 7, 31). Jesus again indirectly indicates the answer to Pilate's question about his origin, "Where are you from?" (19:9). That Jesus is "from above," the same place from where Pilate's authority over him derives, confirms Jesus' superiority to Pilate.[55] That Pilate's authority and Jesus' origin are "from above" develops Jesus' revelation that his kingship is not of this world in the first B scene (18:36). And it further explains why Jesus passively endured scourging and mockery in the second B scene (19:1-3).

Jesus' allusion to the "authority" or "power" (ἐξουσίαν) that comes from above (19:11) contributes to the Johannine theme of the authority given to Jesus and those who believe in him. Jesus previously prayed, "Father, the hour has come. Glorify your Son, so that the Son may glorify you, just as you have given him authority (ἐξουσίαν) over all people, so that he may give eternal life to all whom you have given him" (17:1-2). As the good shepherd who lays down his life for the sheep (10:11, 17), Jesus' obedience to the command he received from his Father, giving him authority over his life (10:18):

"I have authority (ἐξουσίαν ἔχω) to lay it down,
and I have authority (ἐξουσίαν ἔχω) to take it up again,"

overshadows Pilate's vain assertion of his imperial authority over Jesus' life (19:10):

"I have authority (ἐξουσίαν ἔχω) to release you
and I have authority (ἐξουσίαν ἔχω) to crucify you."

As the Father has Life in himself, so he granted the Son to have Life in himself; and he gave him authority (ἐξουσίαν) to exercise judgment (5:26-27). But all who believe in the Son in order to have eternal life avoid the condemnation

---

Gospel, 49-50, following Carson, *John*, 601-2, thinks that it refers not to the feminine "authority" (ἐξουσίαν) but to "this framework of events," more specifically, the event of Jesus' betrayal to Pilate. But the verbal form "it had been given" can refer to the broader verbal expression, "you would not have authority." The more precise meaning, then, is "You would not have any authority over me unless it (your having authority) had been given you from above" (19:11). See M. Zerwick and M. Grosvener, *A Grammatical Analysis of the Greek New Testament* (2 vols.; Rome: Biblical Institute, 1974, 1979) I. 341.

55 On "from above" Rensberger, *Johannine Faith*, 98, states: "It characterizes Pilate's authority *over Jesus* (not the state's authority in general!) as coming in fact from the same place as Jesus himself. The authority thus does not originate with Pilate or the world in which he governs, and Pilate's ignorance only confirms the fact that Jesus, as 'from above,' is totally superior to him."

of judgment (3:16-18). Whereas his own people rejected him, Jesus gives those who believe in him the authority (ἐξουσίαν) to become children of God (1:11-12). The pointing of Pilate by Jesus to the authority from above (19:11), then, functions as an appeal for the audience to believe in the Jesus who has divine authority to grant them eternal life as God's children.

Jesus' mention of the one who handed over or betrayed (παραδούς) him to Pilate (19:11) serves as a global reference to all those responsible for his betrayal. It includes Judas, the disciple who betrayed Jesus to the Jews (6:64, 71; 12:4; 13:2, 11, 21; 18:2, 5); Caiaphas, the high priest who allowed Jesus to be delivered to Pilate as the one man to die for the people (11:49-50; 18:14, 28); and the chief priests and Jews who brought Jesus to the praetorium and handed him over to Pilate (18:30, 35). The use of the singular, "the one who handed me over," to embrace all those involved accentuates their personal decision and individual guilt.[56]

In contrast to Pilate exerting his imperial dominance over the Jews by haughtily humiliating them in each of the previous three A scenes (18:28-32; 38b-40; 19:4-7), the Jews who have handed Jesus over to Pilate "have a greater sin (ἁμαρτίαν)" against the higher, divine authority, and therefore hold a certain, albeit dubious, superiority to Pilate in these events (19:11).[57] This has both a negative and a positive aspect with regard to Pilate. On the negative side, it adds to Jesus' denigration of Pilate's authority and supposed superiority. But on the positive side, since the fundamental "sin" (ἁμαρτία) in John's Gospel is failure to believe, it presents Pilate and thus the reader with an opportunity to believe in Jesus.[58]

Jesus warned the Jews that they would "die," that is, not attain eternal life, because of their "sin" of unbelief (8:21): "I told you that you will die in your sins, for if you do not believe that I am he, you will die in your sins" (8:24). They cannot convict Jesus of "sin," because he gave them divine revelation by telling them the "truth," so that they should have believed in him (8:46). After the blind man whose eyes Jesus opened confessed his faith (9:35-38), Jesus declared, "For judgment I have come into this world, so that those not seeing may see and those seeing may become blind" (9:39). After the Pharisees asked him, "Surely we are not also blind, are we?" (9:40), Jesus assured them, "If you

---

[56] Schnackenburg, *Johannesevangelium*, 3. 302; Cassidy, *John's Gospel*, 49.

[57] Duke, *Irony*, 134: ". . . for all his blustering about his importance in this affair, the little governor will not even rate the larger share of guilt."

[58] P. Fiedler, "ἁμαρτία," *EDNT* 1. 68.

were blind, you would not have sin; but now that you say, 'We see,' your sin remains" (9:41).[59]

With regard to those of the world who do not believe, Jesus announced that if he had not come and "spoken" revelation to them, they would not have "sin," but now they have no excuse for their "sin" (15:22). If he had not done revelatory works among them that no one else ever did, they would not have "sin," but now that they have seen and hated both him and his Father (15:24), they have sinned against the higher, divine authority (19:11). Nevertheless, the Paraclete whom Jesus will send after he departs (16:7), will convict the world of "sin," because they did not believe in him (16:8-9).

As it concludes this progression of scenes, Jesus' reminder that those who handed him over to Pilate have a greater "sin" (19:11) brings the reader to a climactic moment. The revelation Jesus has been giving Pilate inside the praetorium (B scenes) invites the reader to make a personal decision to avoid the "greater sin," the greater unbelief, of the individuals who are rejecting Jesus outside the praetorium (A scenes). All readers, then, are called to believe in the Jesus who has authority to grant them eternal life as the Lamb of God who takes away the "sin" of the world (1:29).

Summary

John 18:28-19:11 brings the audience through another alternation of contrasting scenes that operate as a dynamic progression of narrative sandwiches. The A scenes unfold the theme of Pilate arrogantly humiliating the Jews outside the praetorium for bringing him an innocent and apparently insignificant Jesus, whom he teases and taunts them to take back, but whom they repeatedly reject with new charges: To Pilate's command that they take the Jesus they claim is an evildoer and judge him according to their own law, the Jews counter that they are not permitted to put anyone to death (A[1] 18:28-32). When Pilate offers to release Jesus as the King of the Jews, the Jews choose the bandit Barabbas instead (A[2] 18:38b-40). After Pilate presents the royally robed and crowned Jesus as only a man, the Jews call for his crucifixion because he made himself Son of God (A[3] 19:4-7).

By way of continual contrast to the A scenes, the B scenes exhibit the theme of Jesus revealing his transcendent identity, origin, and mission to the Roman governor inside the praetorium: To Pilate, who inquires whether he is King of

[59] J. W. Holleran, "Seeing the Light: A Narrative Reading of John 9. I: Background and Presuppositions," *ETL* 69 (1993) 5-26.

the Jews, Jesus reveals that his kingship is not of this world and that he has come to testify to the truth (B¹ 18:33-38a). Scourged and mocked as King of the Jews by Romans, Jesus demonstrates that he is true King of both Jews and Gentiles (B² 19:1-3). To a fearful yet imperious Pilate Jesus discloses his divine origin and superior authority (B³ 19:8-11).

The implied reader/audience experiences this sequence of contrasting scenes as follows:

1) The Jews' inability and Pilate's apparent unwillingness to put Jesus to death in the first A scene outside the praetorium (18:28-32) assures the reader that Jesus, the good shepherd, is laying down his own life as a "lifting up" in crucifixion that will serve as his final revelatory sign and draw all people to himself (12:32).

2) In contrast to his rejection by the Jews outside the praetorium, inside the praetorium Jesus challenges Pilate and thus the reader in the first B scene (18:33-38a) to experience his kingship that is not of this world by hearing his voice as the shepherd/king who testifies to the truth that his death offers eternal life for all who believe and follow him.

3) In contrast to Jesus' revelation of his true kingship inside the praetorium, Pilate's ironic presentation of the innocent Jesus as King of the Jews and the Jews' choice of Barabbas, a bandit and false leader, instead of Jesus in the second A scene outside the praetorium (18:38b-40) advances the theme of his rejection outside the praetorium. It propels the reader to follow Jesus as the true leader, the good shepherd-king, whose kingship embraces yet transcends this world.

4) In contrast to the Jews' rejection of his kingship outside the praetorium, but advancing the theme of his revelation inside the praetorium, the scourging and mockery of Jesus as King of the Jews by Pilate and the Roman soldiers in the second B scene inside the praetorium (19:1-3) ironically establishes him as the transcendent King. His kingship embraces both Jews and Gentiles, and it serves as a model for the reader who can expect similar suffering and persecution from the world (15:18-20; 16:1-4; 17:14).

5) In contrast to the gentile soldiers' mockery of Jesus' kingship inside the praetorium, Pilate's denigration of the true King, Jesus, as only a man and the Jews' demand for the crucifixion of the Jesus who made himself Son of God in the third A scene outside the praetorium (19:4-7) advances the theme of his rejection outside the praetorium. It reveals to the audience Jesus' profound identity as the one human being whose death can

save the world. Jesus can save the world as both the Son of Man to be glorified in death and the Son of God whose crucifixion will offer eternal life to all who believe.

6) In contrast to those individuals who have demonstrated a "greater sin" of unbelief outside the praetorium, Jesus' disclosure to Pilate of his heavenly origin and superior authority in the third B scene inside the praetorium (19:8-11) advances the theme of his revelation inside the praetorium. It arouses the reader to a personal decision of greater faith in the Jesus who has the divine authority to grant eternal life to those who become God's children through their faith (1:11-12).

CHAPTER 4

The Revelatory Death and Burial
of Jesus (19:12-42)

Pilate Invites the Jews To See and Accept
Jesus as King (A[1] 19:12-22)

12 At this Pilate tried to release him, but the Jews cried out, saying, "If you release this one, you are not a friend of Caesar. Everyone who makes himself a king opposes Caesar." 13 Having heard these words, Pilate then led Jesus out and sat (him) on the judicial bench at a place called Stone Pavement, in Hebrew, Gabbatha. 14 It was preparation day for the Passover, the hour was about the sixth (noon), and he said to the Jews, "Behold your King!" 15 They cried out, "Away with him, away with him! Crucify him!" Pilate said to them, "Shall I crucify your King?" The chief priests answered, "We have no king but Caesar."

16 He then handed him over to them to be crucified. So they took Jesus, 17 and carrying the cross for himself, he came out to what is called Place of the Skull, which in Hebrew is called Golgotha. 18 There they crucified him, and with him two others, one on either side, with Jesus in the middle.

19 Pilate, on the other hand, also wrote an inscription and placed it on the cross. There was written, "Jesus the Nazorean, the King of the Jews." 20 Now many of the Jews read this inscription, because the place where Jesus was crucified was near the city. And it was written in Hebrew, Latin, and Greek. 21 Then the chief priests of the Jews said to Pilate, "Do not write, 'The King of the Jews,' but, 'This one said, I am King of the Jews.'" 22 Pilate answered, "What I have written, I have written."[1]

---

[1] The literary criterion of inclusion divides this passage into three sub-units: The first, 19:12-15, begins and ends with references to Caesar; the second, 19:16-18, begins and ends with refer-

77

The Jews choose Caesar over Jesus as their King (19:12-15)

At the same time that this first A scene (19:12-22) commences a new sequence of contrasting scenes (19:12-42), as the final scene "outside" the praetorium, it climactically concludes the alternation of scenes "inside" and "outside" the praetorium (18:28-19:11).[2] Completing an A-B-A intercalation with the two previous scenes, Pilate's handing over of Jesus to the Jews outside the praetorium to be crucified as their King (19:12-22) contrasts with Jesus' revelation of his divine origin to Pilate inside the praetorium (19:8-11). It also develops the Jews' rejection of Pilate's offer of the innocent "man" Jesus outside the praetorium (19:4-7).

A notable change has come over Pilate. Earlier he mocked and taunted the Jews with a devious offer to release to them as their "King" the innocent and insignificant Jesus (18:38b-39) he knows they want to put to death (18:31). But now a fearful Pilate (19:8), having been reminded by Jesus that he is responsible to a higher authority and that betrayal of that authority is a grave offense (19:11), "at this" (ἐκ τούτου), for the first time seriously seeks to release Jesus (19:12).[3]

That the Jews cried out (ἐκραύγασαν) when Pilate decided to release Jesus (19:12) advances their vociferous rejections of Jesus in the previous A scenes outside the praetorium. When Pilate teased them with his offer to release Jesus in accord with the Passover custom, they chose the bandit Barabbas, as they cried out (ἐκραύγασαν) against Jesus "again" (πάλιν) (18:39-40), implying that they had also "cried out" when they accused Jesus of being an evildoer who deserves death (18:30-31). When Pilate presented the regally crowned and robed Jesus outside the praetorium as merely "the man" in the previous A scene, the Jews cried out (ἐκραύγασαν) for his crucifixion (19:5-6). Now, even

---

ences to crucifixion; and the third, 19:19-22, begins and ends with references to what Pilate has written. Occurrences of the term "king" in the first and last sub-unit (19:12, 14, 15 [*bis*], 19, 21 [*bis*]) secure the overall unity of the scene.

[2] As we noted in chapter 1, this first A scene (19:12-22) initiates a new section because (1) as the Jews' objection to Pilate's decision to release Jesus is now heard by Pilate inside the praetorium (19:13), it breaks the pattern of the previous section in which the words of the Jews to Pilate were heard only outside the praetorium (18:28-32, 38b-40; 19:4-7), and (2) it moves the action to new locations—the judicial bench at a place called Stone Pavement (19:13) and the Place of the Skull, where Jesus was crucified (19:17-18).

[3] Rensberger, *Johannine Faith,* 94: ". . . for the first and only time, Pilate seriously tries to release Jesus. Again, the wording is noteworthy: ἐκ τούτου, 'at this'—but *only* at this—ἐζήτει ἀπολῦσαι αὐτόν, 'he began seeking to release him' (19:12)."

while Pilate is still inside the praetorium, the Jews "cried out" again, warning him not to release Jesus.

In the previous B scene Jesus reminded the haughty Pilate of his subordination to the divine authority "from above" (19:11), which prompted Pilate's decision to release him (19:12). In contrast, the Jews now cleverly counter by reminding Pilate of his subordination to the higher authority of the Roman emperor. If Pilate releases "this one," an evildoer deserving death (18:30-31, 40), he will, the Jews insinuate, risk betrayal of his allegiance to Rome and the loss of his status as a "friend of Caesar" (19:12).[4]

The Jews' further accusation with regard to Jesus, "Everyone who makes himself a king opposes Caesar" (19:12), contains a couple of ironic half truths. In advancement of their strategy in the previous A scene, where the Jews charged that Jesus "made himself (ἑαυτὸν ἐποίησεν) Son of God" (19:7), they now intimate that he "makes himself (ἑαυτὸν ποιῶν) a king." While it is true that Jesus is a king, he has not "made himself" a king. Others have acclaimed (1:49; 12:13-15) and unsuccessfully attempted to "make (ποιήσωσιν) him a king," forcing their own kingship upon him by "seizing" him (6:15). But those who hear with faith the voice of the Jesus who testifies to the truth (18:37) recognize that Jesus' kingship is not of this world (18:36). And it is not so much that the kingship of Jesus "opposes" Caesar as that it totally transcends the pretensions of worldly power with an authority that comes "from above" (19:11).[5]

By invoking loyalty to Rome, the Jews promote the ironic reversal of roles that has emerged in their contest with Pilate. On the ironic level Pilate becomes increasingly Jewish, while the Jews become more and more Roman. By addressing the Jews outside the praetorium, Pilate honored the Jewish concern not to enter the praetorium in order to avoid ritual defilement for the Passover celebration (18:28-29). Although derisively, he directed the Jews to judge Jesus according to their own Jewish law (18:31). He mockingly observed the custom of releasing a prisoner during the Jewish feast of Passover (18:39). He, not the Jews, is the one who has suggested that Jesus is King of the Jews (18:33, 37, 39; 19:3, 5). His question, "I am not a Jew, am I (Μήτι ἐγὼ Ἰουδαῖός εἰμι)?" (18:35), on the surface expects an obvious negative answer

---

4 On whether "friend of Caesar" was a special honorific title granted to Pilate or merely a general expression of loyalty to the Roman emperor, see Brown, *John*, 879-80; idem, *Death*, 843-44; Barrett, *John*, 543; Carson, *John*, 607

5 Senior, *John*, 94: "It is true that anyone who claims to be a king challenges Caesar's power, and no greater challenge is possible than the kingship of Jesus whose God-given power eclipses by an infinite degree the pretensions of secular power."

but is open to a positive answer on a deeper, ironic level. The Jews, on the other hand, seek the death of Jesus in order to avoid the destruction of their nation by the Romans (11:48). While they are concerned to celebrate their national liberation in the Passover (18:28), however, they ironically appeal for loyalty to the Roman emperor (19:12)![6]

In the previous A scene Pilate again came outside (ἔξω) of the praetorium and told the Jews he was leading (ἄγω) the innocent Jesus out to them, and then humiliated them by scorning the royally robed Jesus as only a "man" (19:4-5). Having heard the warning of the Jews, Pilate again led (ἤγαγεν) Jesus outside (ἔξω) the praetorium (19:13). Then, in an exquisite example of Johannine double meaning with purposeful ambiguity, either he himself sat (intransitive meaning of ἐκάθισεν, see 12:14) or he made Jesus sit (transitive meaning of ἐκάθισεν) on the judicial bench (19:13).[7] On the most obvious and historically accurate level Pilate himself sat on the judicial bench (βήματος) in order to humiliate further the Jews by judging Jesus to be their King.[8] But on the deeper, ironic, and theologically accurate level the perceptive reader realizes that Jesus sat on the judicial bench as *the* judge.[9] This accords with the Johannine view

[6] As Senior, *John,* 94, remarks, ". . . it is another example of biting Johannine irony. It is the Jewish leaders—not the Roman—who introduce the issue of loyalty to Caesar." See also Duke, *Irony,* 134.

[7] For another example of syntactical double meaning in John, see 7:37-38, where it is ambiguous whether the rivers of living water will flow from Jesus or the believer.

[8] According to B. Schaller, "βῆμα," *EDNT* 1. 215, the common use of βῆμα in the Hellenistic official and legal language is as a technical term for public seats or stands. "In Matt 27:19 and John 19:13, just as in Acts 18:12, 16f.; 25:6, 10, 17, βῆμα indicates the portable *official seat (sella curulis)* on which the higher Roman officials sat in their function as judge."

[9] Many feel obliged to choose only one of the meanings (transitive or intransitive), thus repressing the richness of the purposefully ambiguous double meaning. For various opinions, see I. de la Potterie, "Jésus roi et juge d'après Jn 19,13," *Bib* 41 (1960) 217-47; R. Robert, "Pilate a-t-il fait de Jésus un juge? *ekathisen epi bematos* (Jean, xix, 13)," *RevThom* 83 (1983) 275-87; Brown, *John,* 880-81; idem, *Death,* 1388-93; Senior, *John,* 95-96; Carson, *John,* 607-8. Barrett, *John,* 544, and Duke, *Irony,* 134-35, allow for the double meaning. According to Duke, "It is not impossible that the author is deliberately ambiguous, honoring both the historical probability that Pilate sat and the suggestive possibility for perceptive readers that Jesus sat." According to Barrett, "Probably John was conscious of both meanings of ἐκάθισεν. We may compare his habit of playing on words of double meaning (see on 3.3) and also his subtle presentation of the investigation in ch. 9, where ostensibly the blind man is examined while through him Jesus himself is being tried, only to turn the tables on his accusers by judging them. We may suppose then that John meant that Pilate did in fact sit on the βῆμα, but that for those with eyes to see behind this human scene appeared the Son of man, to whom all judgement has been committed (5.22), seated upon his throne."

that the Father has given all judgment to the Son (5:22), because he is the Son of Man (5:27). But Jesus is *the* judge in the sense that he compels a faith decision. God sent the Son into the world not to judge/condemn (κρίνῃ) the world, but that the world might be saved through him. Whoever believes in him is not judged/condemned (κρίνεται), but whoever does not believe has already been judged/condemned (κέκριται) (3:17-18).

That Pilate or Jesus sat on the judicial bench "at a place called Stone Pavement, in Hebrew, Gabbatha" (19:13) signals a new location, and therefore the beginning of a new section of scenes after the focus on the alternation "inside" and "outside" the praetorium (18:28-19:11). That both the Greek and Hebrew names are given for this new setting underlines the significance of what is happening for both Jews and non-Jews.

The narrator's temporal notice that "it was preparation day for the Passover, the hour was about the sixth (noon)" (19:14) advances the Johannine theme, present in previous A scenes (18:28, 39), of Jesus' death during the Passover as the true Passover Lamb of God. The decisive Passover of Jesus' death that has been "near" throughout the narrative (2:13; 6:4; 11:55; 12:1; 13:1) has finally arrived.[10] About the sixth hour (noon) on the preparation day before the Passover is the time that the priests in the temple began to slaughter the paschal lambs to be eaten in the Passover meal that evening.[11]

In John specifically numbered hours indicate significant times for faith decisions. The hour was "about the tenth" (1:39) after two disciples of John the Baptist remained with the Jesus whom John had pointed out to them as the Lamb of God (1:36-38). They then brought others to share their faith in Jesus (1:40-51). The hour was "about the sixth" (4:6) when a tired Jesus sat at the well for the revelatory encounter that moved the Samaritan woman to bring many of her people to faith in Jesus as the savior of the world (4:7-42). The "sixth hour" corresponded to the "hour that is now here" (4:23), when true worshippers will no longer worship in Jerusalem or on the Samaritan mountain (4:21), but through Jesus will worship the Father in Spirit and truth (4:23).[12] It

[10] On the narrative theme of the "nearness" of the Passover festival as the time for Jesus' death, see above on 18:28 in chapter 3.

[11] Brown, *John,* 883; idem, *Death,* 847-48; Barrett, *John,* 545; Schnackenburg, *Johannesevangelium,* 3. 307; Senior, *John,* 96.

[12] On John 4, see G. R. O'Day, *Revelation in the Fourth Gospel: Narrative Mode and Theological Claim* (Philadelphia: Fortress, 1986) 49-92; L. Eslinger, "The Wooing of the Woman at the Well: Jesus, the Reader and Reader-Response Criticism," *Literature & Theology* 1 (1987) 167-83; T. Okure, *The Johannine Approach to Mission: A Contextual Study of John 4:1-42* (WUNT 2/31; Tübingen: Mohr, 1988); H. Boers, *Neither on this Mountain Nor in Jerusalem:*

was the "seventh hour" when the fever left the son of the royal official who, along with his whole household, believed in the Jesus who at that same hour had said, "Your son lives" (4:52-53). Jesus' revelatory "sign" (4:54) of saving this boy from death confirmed his pronouncement that the "hour is now here" when those who are spiritually "dead" will hear with faith the voice of the Son of God and "live" eternal life (5:25). That it is "about the sixth hour" on the preparation day for Passover (19:14), during the more general "hour" when Jesus will be glorified through death (2:4; 7:30; 8:20; 12:23, 27; 13:1; 17:1), signals another important moment for a faith decision.

That moment arrives when, with either Pilate or Jesus sitting on the judicial bench (19:13), Pilate presents the Jews with his mock but ironically definitive judicial decision, "Behold your King!" (19:14). Pilate is officially establishing as King the Jesus whom the Jews claimed "made himself" king (19:12). In development of the previous A scene Pilate now pronounces the expected "Behold your King!" instead of the denigrating "Behold the man!" (19:5), when he first presented the royally crowned and clothed Jesus to the Jews. Pilate's "Behold ("Ἴδε) your King!" recalls John the Baptist's "Behold ("Ἴδε) the Lamb of God!" (1:29, 36). On the ironic level, while the lambs are being killed for the Passover, Pilate is inviting the Jews and the reader to a faith decision—to behold and believe that Jesus is their true King precisely as the Passover Lamb of God now being put to death.

But in response to Pilate's official presentation of Jesus as their King, the Jews again vehemently "cried out" (ἐκραύγασαν) in rejection of Jesus (19:15; see 18:40; 19:6, 12). With their agitated outburst, "Away with him, away with him! Crucify him!" (19:15), the Jews demand that Pilate take away (ἆρον) and kill the Jesus who, as the Lamb of God who takes away (αἴρων) the sin—the unbelief—of the world (1:29), is their true King. In the previous A scene the Jews called for the crucifixion (σταύρωσον, 19:6) that will elevate and glorify Jesus as *the* one "man" who is the Son of Man (19:5) and Son of God (19:7). Now they demand the crucifixion (σταύρωσον, 19:15) that will enthrone and glorify Jesus as *the* Passover Lamb of God who is truly the King of the Jews (19:14).

A sneering and pernicious Pilate, who in the previous A scene had contemptuously commanded the Jews to crucify the innocent and insignificant

A Study of John 4 (SBLMS 35; Atlanta: Scholars, 1988); C. R. Koester, "'The Savior of the World' (John 4:42)," JBL 109 (1990) 665-80; J. E. Botha, "Reader 'Entrapment' as Literary Device in John 4:1-42," Neot 24 (1990) 37-47; idem, Jesus and the Samaritan Woman: A Speech Act Reading of John 4:1-42 (NovTSup 65; Leiden: Brill, 1991); Moloney, Belief, 132-91.

Jesus themselves (19:6), now teases and taunts the Jews to condemn to death the Jesus he has mockingly judged to be their King, "Shall I crucify your King?" (19:15). Pilate has provoked the Jews to condemn themselves, however, as the chief priests utter the ultimate blasphemy in order to win the death of Jesus, "We have no king but Caesar" (19:15). The Jews who are worried that the Romans may destroy their nation (11:48), and who are preparing to eat the Passover meal (18:28) that celebrates their covenant with the God who liberated and established them as a people with him as their sovereign King, not only reject Jesus as their messianic king (12:12-15) but astoundingly pronounce the sacrilege that their only king is the Roman emperor.[13]

But the Jews' apparent apostasy also acts as a calculated, counter taunt to Pilate, as it continues the ironic reversal of Jewish and Roman roles. The Jews profess to be more Roman than Pilate. They pledge their allegiance to the Roman king (19:15) before a Roman governor whose loyalty to the Roman king they have questioned (19:12). Pilate, on the other hand, is insisting, through a mock judicial decision, that the Jesus they want to kill as the Lamb of God, while the lambs are being killed for the Jewish Passover, is their true King (19:14). But it is only Pilate who is concerned to establish Jesus as the Jewish King; the Jews claim no king but the Roman emperor. This ironic reversal, in which the Roman governor mocks the Jewish kingship the Jews themselves reject in favor of the Roman emperor, underlines for the audience how Jesus' kingship is indeed not of this world (18:36). It is ironically, soberly, and tragically true that for those who do not believe in the kingship not of this world there is indeed "no king but Caesar" (19:15).

Crucifixion enthrones Jesus as King (19:16-18)

In the previous B scene Jesus told Pilate that the Jews who handed over and betrayed (παραδούς) him have a greater sin (19:11). In ironic contrast, Pilate continues to disclose his Jewishness and his own sin of unbelief as he handed over and betrayed (παρέδωκεν) Jesus to the Jews to be crucified (19:16). Despite the revelation to him of Jesus' divine origin and superior authority (19:11), Pilate betrays back to the Jews the Jesus they had betrayed to him (18:30, 35). Although Pilate boasted to Jesus of his power to release or crucify him in the previous B scene (19:10), the Jews have demonstrated otherwise.

[13] Brown, *John*, 894-95; idem, *Death*, 848-49; Barrett, *John*, 546; Duke, *Irony*, 135-36; Senior, *John*, 97; Schnackenburg, *Johannesevangelium*, 3. 308.

They have cleverly constrained Pilate to hand over to be crucified the Jesus Pilate had tried to release (19:12). They finally force the crucifixion for which they have been fiercely clamoring (19:6, 15).

That the Jews then took or received (παρέλαβον) Jesus to crucify him (19:16) ironically underlines their failure to believe, as it recalls the indictment of the Johannine prologue: "To his own he came, and his own did not receive (παρέλαβον) him" (1:11) with faith. In the first A scene of the previous section Pilate urged the Jews to take (Λάβετε) Jesus and judge him according to their own law (18:31), a taking that could lead them to faith. But in advancement of the last A scene of the previous section, the Jews now took (παρέλαβον) for crucifixion, not for faith, the Jesus Pilate had taunted them to take (Λάβετε) and crucify themselves (19:6).

In the previous A scene Jesus actively came outside (ἐξῆλθεν) on his own rather than passively being led out of the praetorium, boldly wearing the thorny crown and the purple robe of his derided kingship (19:5). In development, he now again actively came out (ἐξῆλθεν) on his own to the place of crucifixion, triumphantly carrying the cross of his royal enthronement "for himself" (ἑαυτῷ) (19:17).[14] He thus continues to demonstrate that he is the shepherd-king, who allows no one to take his life from him, but lays down his life "on my own" (ἀπ᾽ ἐμαυτοῦ) (10:18) for the sheep (10:11).

That Jesus carried his cross to a morbid place—"to what is called Place of the Skull, which in Hebrew is called Golgotha" (19:17)—parallels and progresses what happened "at a place called Stone Pavement, in Hebrew, Gabbatha" (19:13).[15] The official judgment on the judicial bench at Gabbatha that Jesus is the King of the Jews (19:14) now becomes his official enthronement as King of the Jews through crucifixion at Golgotha.[16] That both Greek and Hebrew

[14] de la Potterie, *Hour*, 93: "Literally the Greek means: 'He carried the cross for himself' as something that for him had great value. In this way the evangelist wants to show that Jesus did not carry the cross like a man condemned to death, undergoing punishment unwillingly, going to his fate passively, facing torments under compulsion. No. Christ carries the cross 'for himself' as the privileged instrument of his work of salvation, the sign of his triumph and of his sovereignty."

[15] On the progressive parallelism between what happens at "Gabbatha" and what happens at "Golgotha," two three-syllable words related by assonance—each have the same initial consonant and the same final vowel, see de la Potterie, *Hour*, 90-92.

[16] de la Potterie, *Hour*, 92: "The parallelism between Gabbatha and Golgotha is of great importance for a theological interpretation of the facts. We might sum it up by saying that Pilate's proclamation at the praetorium that Jesus was the King of the Jews was the prophecy and the prefiguration of the supreme reality which was to take place on the cross."

names are given for the place of Jesus' crucifixion and enthronement underscores how he is King of both Jews and Gentiles. The Jewish chief priests have insisted they have no king but Caesar (19:15). But by crucifying Jesus in the middle of two others at a place with a Jewish name, like a king elevated and enthroned between his royal attendants (19:18), these Jewish leaders are ironically establishing the Jewish kingship of Jesus that is not of this world (18:36). The Jews, who in earlier A scenes maintained that according to their law Jesus ought to die because he made himself Son of God (19:7), but that they are not allowed to put anyone to death (18:31), now crucify Jesus as their King.

Pilate decisively inscribes Jesus as King of the Jews (19:19-22)

Pilate and the Jews complement one another in ironically installing Jesus as King of the Jews. As Pilate handed over (παρέδωκεν) Jesus to the Jews to be crucified, they correspondingly took or received (παρέλαβον) him (19:16). The Jews crucified him as a king enthroned between royal attendants (19:18). Now Pilate complements them with his part, as he "on the other hand" (δὲ) "also" (καὶ) wrote an inscription and placed it on the cross (19:19). Although the Jews claim they have no king but Caesar (19:15), Pilate continues to humiliate them by insisting Jesus is their King. What was written as the crime for his execution serves also as the definitive proclamation of his Jewish kingship: "Jesus the Nazorean, the King of the Jews" (19:19).

This inscription combines Pilate's two previous abuses of Jesus to degrade the Jews. In the previous A scene Pilate denigrated the royally robed and crowned Jesus as merely a "man" (19:5). At the judicial bench he mocked him as their king (19:14). Now he derisively writes that this mere man from Nazareth is King of the Jews. But that Jesus is only a man from Nazareth stands in ironic contrast to the revelation of his divine origin and superior authority to Pilate in the previous B scene (19:8-11).

Pilate wrote (ἔγραψεν) and it was definitively written (γεγραμμένον, perfect tense) that Jesus the Nazorean is the King of the Jews (19:19). What he "wrote" complements what was "written" in the Jewish scriptures about Jesus. When Philip found Nathanael, he informed him that "Jesus son of Joseph from Nazareth" was the one about whom Moses and the prophets wrote (ἔγραψεν) (1:45). To Nathanael's sarcastic reply, "Can anything good come from Nazareth?" (1:46), Pilate now unwittingly responds that from Nazareth comes the King of the Jews.

Complementing what they read in their scriptures, many of the Jews "read" this inscription, because Jesus was crucified in a public place near the "city" of Jerusalem (19:20). This written (γεγραμμένον) inscription of Jesus' kingship as he is being humiliated by death through crucifixion concurs with Jesus' fulfillment of what was written in the Jewish scriptures regarding his kingship. When he entered the city of Jerusalem for the Passover, the great crowd jubilantly acclaimed him the King of Israel. But Jesus mounted an ass rather than a war horse, in fulfillment of what was written (γεγραμμένον, 12:14) in scripture (Zech 9:9), to indicate how his humble and peaceful kingship differs from that of the kings of this world (12:12-15).

That the inscription was written (γεγραμμένον) in "Hebrew, Latin, and Greek" (19:20) underlines the unifying and universal nature of Jesus' kingship. Although mocked as the Nazorean King of the Jews, Jesus, whose kingship is not of this world (18:36), is King not only of those Jews who read Hebrew/Aramaic ('Εβραϊστί), but also of the Romans who read Latin ('Ρωμαϊστί), and of all those who read Greek ('Ελληνιστί). Jesus' kingship embraces not only those Jews and Romans collaborating in putting him to death as their King, but extends to the whole world—even to the Greeks. The confused Jews earlier wondered whether Jesus intended to go "to the dispersion among the Greeks and teach the Greeks" (7:35). But instead, after Jesus entered Jerusalem and was proclaimed as King (12:12-18), some Greeks came to see Jesus (12:20-21) in ironic response to the Pharisees' exasperation: "Behold, the world has gone after him!" (12:19). This universal inscription thus confirms the unifying kind of death Jesus would die (12:33; 18:32)—a "lifting up" from the earth in crucifixion that will draw all to himself (12:32).[17]

It was the chief priests who insisted that the Jews have no king but the Roman emperor (19:15). Now the chief priests (19:21) continue that insistence as they make explicit the Jews' implication that Jesus made himself a king (19:12). They demand that Pilate not write as the inscription, "The King of the Jews," but rather "This one said, I am King of the Jews" (19:21). But this contradicts the first B scene (18:33-38a) in the previous section. It was Pilate who sarcastically scoffed to Jesus, "You are the King of the Jews?" (18:33). Even after Jesus disclosed that his kingdom is not of this world (18:36), he never claimed to be the King of the Jews. He told Pilate, "It is you who say I am a king," and explained that he was born and came into the world to testify to the

---

[17] Senior, *John*, 104.

truth (18:37), in other words, to be the divinely sent revealer of God's truth. Jesus did not announce, "I am the King of the Jews" (19:21), but when arrested he did declare, "I am he" (18:5-8), that is, that he is the absolute and definitive revealer of God (see also 4:26; 8:18-28; 13:19). The chief priests' charge, then, is not only dismally inaccurate but an ironic understatement for the audience.

To the chief priests' request that he not "write" (γράφε) as the inscription, "The King of the Jews" (19:21), Pilate resolutely replies, "What I have written (γέγραφα), I have written (γέγραφα)" (19:22). In other words, in accord with his emphatic repetition of the Greek perfect tense, what Pilate has written is decisive, definitive, and remains forever written.[18] Pilate thus has the last word in his manipulative contest with the Jews outside the praetorium (18:28-19:22). His determined and conclusive inscription that Jesus is the King of the Jews brings to a climax all of the previous Roman mockeries of that kingship (18:33, 37, 39; 19:3, 5, 14, 15) and reinforces its ironic truth for the reader. Over the Jews' insistence that they have no king but Caesar (19:15) Pilate superimposes his own absolute insistence that Jesus is their King. He thereby completes his role in the Jewish-Roman collaboration that enthrones Jesus through crucifixion as the true King of all.

As the last scene "outside" the praetorium, this opening scene (19:12-22) introduces a new section by moving the action to Gabbatha and Golgotha. The topic of kingship unifies this scene with its three sub-units:

1) Although Pilate has decided to release Jesus, the Jews prevent him by invoking his friendship with the Caesar the kingship of Jesus opposes. On the judicial bench at Gabbatha Pilate derisively invites the Jews to see and accept Jesus as their King, the true Passover Lamb of God. But the Jews convict themselves of unbelief, as they pronounce the astounding blasphemy that their only king is the Roman emperor (19:12-15).

2) After Pilate allows the Jews to crucify him, Jesus, as the good shepherd-king who lays down his own life for his sheep, majestically carries his own cross to Golgotha, where he is ironically enthroned as King by being crucified in the midst of two others, his royal entourage (19:16-18).

3) Pilate conclusively complements the Jewish royal enthronement of Jesus as he adamantly refuses to alter his definitively written inscription that Jesus is indeed the King of the Jews for all peoples (19:19-22).

---

[18] de la Potterie, *Hour,* 96-97.

Soldiers Take Jesus' Clothing and Fulfill Scripture
(B¹ 19:23-24)

23 Then the soldiers, when they crucified Jesus, took his clothes and made four shares, a share for each soldier, and his tunic. But his tunic was seamless, woven from above as a whole. 24 So they said to one another, "Let us not tear it, but cast lots for it to see whose it will be," in order that the scripture might be fulfilled that says:
"They divided my clothes among themselves,
    and for my clothing they cast lots" (Ps 22:19).
The soldiers then did these things.

Four Roman soldiers share the clothes of Jesus (19:23a)

The scene of the Roman soldiers' taking the clothing of the crucified Jesus in fulfillment of the authority of Jewish scripture (19:23-24) forms a B-A-B sandwich with the two previous scenes. It contrasts with the Jews' taking of Jesus to crucify him as their King (19:12-22). It also develops Jesus' revelation of his divine origin and authority to the Roman governor (19:8-11).

Whereas in the previous A scene it is stated that the Jews crucified (ἐσταύρωσαν) Jesus (19:18), now it is reported that the Roman soldiers crucified (ἐσταύρωσαν) him (19:23). That both Jews and Romans crucified Jesus continues to illustrate their collaboration in putting Jesus to death. But in contrast to the Jews, who took (παρέλαβον) Jesus (19:16) and crucified him as the one they rejected but ironically established as their King (19:18), these four Roman soldiers crucified Jesus and took (ἔλαβον) his clothes (19:23), indicative of their unwitting reception of the Life-giving effects of Jesus' death.

Jesus himself took off his clothes (τὰ ἱμάτια) (13:4) when he washed his disciples' feet in order for them to have a share (μέρος) with him (13:8), symbolic of their "share" in, among other things, the eternal life Jesus' death produces.[19] Jesus' clothes represent his life. That Jesus took off or laid down (τίθησιν) his clothes symbolizes how he, as the good shepherd, lays down (τίθησιν) his own life (10:11) to give eternal life to all who become his sheep by hearing, follow-

---

[19] Thomas, *Footwashing*, 93-94: "One of the first things the implied reader must see in μέρος with Jesus is a share in eternal life ... Consequently, the footwashing is a sign which points beyond itself to some deeper meaning. Two things point to the crucifixion-exaltation as essential to that deeper meaning. First, the qualities represented by μέρος (eternal life, identity with Jesus, sharing his destiny, mission, resurrection and martyrdom) are ultimately secured through Jesus' death. Second, Jesus' act of humiliation in washing the disciples' feet foreshadows his ultimate act of humiliation on the cross."

ing, and believing in him (10:27-28).[20] By taking his clothes (τὰ ἱμάτια) and making four shares (μέρη), a share (μέρος) for each soldier (19:23), the Roman soldiers ironically anticipate how Jesus' death will offer a "share" in eternal life to individuals—even gentile individuals.[21]

In the second B scene (19:1-3) of the previous section (18:28-19:11) the Roman soldiers (στρατιῶται) derisively dressed Jesus in a royal purple robe as a mockery that ironically demonstrated the true kingship of Jesus that is not of this world (18:36). Now, by way of development, the Roman soldiers (στρατιῶται) take back to divide individually among themselves not only the kingly purple clothing (ἱμάτιον) they gave Jesus (19:2) but all his clothes (τὰ ἱμάτια), including his tunic (χιτὼν) (19:23).[22] By so doing, they not only ironically indicate how individuals will appropriate the kingship of Jesus for themselves, but also enable Jesus to be the good shepherd-king, who lays down his own clothes/life to give a "share" in eternal life to each individual who believes in his kingship through death by crucifixion.

The soldiers do not tear Jesus' seamless tunic (19:23b-24a)

In the previous A scene, to undermine the establishment of the true Jewish kingship of Jesus that is for all peoples, the chief priests of the Jews implored Pilate not to write (μὴ γράφε) as the inscription on the cross, "The King of the Jews," but, "This one said, I am King of the Jews" (19:20-21). In ironic contrast to the chief priests of the Jews, the gentile soldiers promote the universal and unifying leadership of Jesus as the true King of the Jews. They advise one another that they not tear or divide (μὴ σχίσωμεν) the tunic of Jesus (19:24),

---

[20] Schuchard, *Scripture*, 129: ". . . John would have the reader see in Jesus' crucifixion, in the distribution of his garments among the soldiers, the graphic consummation of that which Jesus anticipated in John 13. In his crucifixion, then, Jesus fulfills his promises by laying down his garments (i.e., his life) so that he might proffer life. Not only this, one sees in the distribution of these garments that this life is given not only to the Jews but also to the Gentiles."

[21] On the biblical background and later eschatological connotations of the term "share" or "heritage" (μέρος) in 13:8, Brown, *John*, 565, states: "Each of the tribes except Levi was to have its 'share' in the Promised Land, and this was its heritage from God (Num 18:20; Deut 12:12; 14:27). When the hopes of Israel turned to an afterlife, the 'share' or 'heritage' of God's people was pictured in heavenly terms."

[22] The χιτών (tunic or undergarment) and ἱμάτιον (outer garment) together constituted one's clothing. According to W. Rebell, "χιτών," *EDNT* 3.468, the tunic was "worn either against the bare skin or over a linen shirt. The χιτών was made of linen or wool, reached to the ankles or knees, had long or half-sleeves, and was worn by both rich and poor. . . . According to Roman privilege of spoils the soldiers performing the execution were given the condemned's clothing."

which symbolizes the divinely profound unity his crucifixion as the true Jewish King and unique high priest preserves for all who believe in him.

The Roman soldiers' concern not to divide Jesus' tunic that was "seamless, woven from above as a whole" (19:23b) alludes to a rich biblical background in which the divinely determined and unified clothing of the high priest represents the people of Israel. The construction of Jesus' tunic is elaborately described in a careful chiasm:

(a) seamless (unity)
(b) woven from above (divine origin)
(a) as a whole (unity)

Two expressions of unity surround a statement of divine origin. Just as divine authority comes "from above" (ἄνωθεν) in the previous B scene (19:11), that Jesus' seamless tunic is woven "from the top" or "from above" (ἐκ τῶν ἄνωθεν) indicates that its emphasized unity has a divine origin. Similarly, the intricate descriptions of the sacred vestments of the high priest underline their unified construction in accord with the command of God.

As Jesus' tunic was woven (ὑφαντὸς), so each of the various vestments of the high priest, according to the detailed descriptions in LXX Exod 28 and 36, was a "woven work" (ἔργον ὑφαντὸν)–the ephod (Exod 28:6; 36:10, 12), the breastpiece (Exod 36:15), the robe (Exod 28:32; 36:29), and the tunic (Exod 36:34). As Jesus' seamless tunic was woven as a whole (δι' ὅλου), so that the soldiers did not want to "tear" it (19:24), so the robe of the ephod was uniformly woven "all" or as a "whole" (ὅλον) of blue (Exod 28:31; 36:29), and it is so constructed "that it might not be torn" (ἵνα μὴ ῥαγῇ, Exod 28:32; ἀδιάλυτον, 36:30). Thus, Jesus' "tunic," the undergarment worn under "the clothes" that the soldiers divided (19:23a), corresponds to the high priestly "robe," described as the undergarment (ὑποδύτην, Exod 28:31; 36:29) worn under (ὑπὸ) the ephod (Exod 36:29).[23] And just as Jesus' unified tunic was woven

---

[23] I. de la Potterie, "La tunique sans couture, symbole du Christ grand prêtre?" *Bib* 60 (1979) 255-69; *Hour*, 99, followed by Senior, *John,* 106-7, and Schuchard, *Scripture,* 128, fail to recognize this correspondence because Jesus' undergarment is a "tunic" and the high priestly robe of the ephod is not a tunic. LXX Exodus 28 and 36, however, describe the robe, although not a tunic, as an "undergarment" worn "under" the ephod and this allows for the symbolic correspondence. Thus, as we have demonstrated above on John 18:1-27, the Gospel of John does present Jesus as a high priest, although on a deeper, ironic level and not in the same sense as in the Letter to the Hebrews. Furthermore, we maintain that the symbolism of the seamless tunic embraces both Jesus' death as a unique high priest and the unity it effects among people; see I. de la Potterie, "La

"from above," that is, from the heavenly realm of divine authority, so it is repeatedly reinforced that the unified high priestly vestments were designed by God's decree—"as the Lord commanded Moses" (Exod 36:12, 14, 28, 33, 36, 38).

The high priestly vestments were representative of the whole people of Israel. Two onyx stones engraved with the names of the sons of Israel—the names of six tribes on one stone and the names of the remaining six tribes on the other stone, thus the names of the twelve tribes constituting the whole people—were to be attached to the shoulder straps of the ephod (Exod 28:9-12; 36:13-14). As part of the high priest's clothing, these stones functioned "as stones of remembrance for the sons of Israel; and Aaron shall bear the names of the sons of Israel before the Lord on his shoulders, a remembrance for them" (Exod 28:12). In addition, twelve stones inscribed with the names of the twelve tribes of Israel were to be affixed to the breastpiece of judgment (Exod 28:21; 36:21). They symbolized the whole people of Israel that the high priest Aaron represented in remembrance before the Lord when he wore the breastpiece into the sanctuary (Exod 28:29).

The prophet Ahijah dramatically illustrated how the tearing of a new garment representative of the whole people of Israel indicates division and destruction of unity. He took hold of the new garment he was wearing and tore it into twelve pieces, symbolic of the twelve tribes of Israel. Then he indicated to Jeroboam the destruction of unity that would occur after the death of Solomon: "Take for yourself ten pieces; for thus says the Lord, the God of Israel, 'See, I am about to tear the kingdom from the hand of Solomon, and will give you ten tribes'" (1 Kgs 11:29-31).[24]

Although there has been division (σχίσμα) among the Jewish people with regard to Jesus (7:43; 9:16; 10:19), by deciding not to tear or divide (μὴ σχίσωμεν) Jesus' tunic, the gentile soldiers are symbolically yet unwittingly promoting the communal unity that Jesus' death as the shepherd-king and unique high priest will effect (19:24a). The Roman soldiers' desire not to divide the dying Jesus' seamless tunic woven from above as a whole (δι' ὅλου), a symbol of unity, corresponds to the high priest Caiaphas' advice to preserve the unity of the whole (ὅλον) Jewish nation by putting the one man Jesus to death (11:50). Indeed, as the unique high priest who transcends the Jewish high priest, Jesus dies not just for the unity of the nation, but to gather the scat-

---

tunique 'non divisée' de Jésus, symbole de l'unité messianique," *The New Testament Age: Essays in Honor of Bo Reicke* (ed. W. C. Weinrich; Macon, GA: Mercer, 1984) 1. 127-38.

[24] de la Potterie, *Hour,* 101; Brown, *John,* 921; idem, *Death,* 955-58.

tered children of God into a unity (11:52).[25] By not tearing his unified tunic, the soldiers advance the goal of Jesus as the good shepherd-king to unify all sheep/people into a believing community, so that there will be one flock and one shepherd (10:15-16).

By preserving the seamless tunic that symbolizes the unity that comes "from above," from God, the gentile soldiers enable Jesus, lifted up in death by crucifixion, to unify all by drawing them to himself (12:32). All who are drawn to the crucified Jesus and believe in him may then be profoundly "one" and participate in the intimate, divine unity "from above" that Jesus enjoys with his Father (17:20-21). That the Roman soldiers want to "cast lots" (19:24a) for their possession of the seamless tunic indicates that the Gentiles' share or allotment in this unity is determined "from above" by God.[26]

The Roman soldiers fulfill Jewish scripture (19:24b)

In the previous A scene the Jewish chief priests protested the written (γεγραμμένον) inscription that Pilate wrote (ἔγραψεν) (19:19), requesting that he not write (μὴ γράφε) that Jesus is the King of the Jews (19:21). Refusing their request, the gentile governor established the Jewish kingship of Jesus for all peoples (19:20) by his authoritative scripture: "What I have written (γέγραφα), I have written" (γέγραφα) (19:22). In ironic contrast, the gentile soldiers, by unknowingly fulfilling the authoritative Jewish scripture (γραφή), demonstrate the Life-giving and unifying effects of Jesus' death as the good shepherd-king and unique Jewish high priest (19:24b). The chief priests want Pilate to write not that Jesus really is the King of the Jews, but only their false assertion that "he said" he was the King of Jews (19:21). The Jewish scripture, however, allows Jesus to state the truth about himself. As the speaker of God's authoritative word from Ps 22:19, a lament of the suffering just one, Jesus himself pronounces the revelatory significance of his disrobing as the shepherd-king and high priest: "They divided my clothes among themselves, and for my clothing they cast lots" (19:24b).[27]

In the previous B scene Jesus reminded Pilate that he would not have any authority over him unless it had been given him from above. It is ultimately

---

[25] de la Potterie, *Hour,* 102; Schuchard, *Scripture,* 130.

[26] On casting lots to allow God to decide, see Acts 1:24-26; see also BAGD, 462; Schuchard, *Scripture,* 128.

[27] John 19:24b reproduces the LXX version of the Ps 22:19 quote; see Schuchard, *Scripture,* 125-32.

because of God's authoritative plan that the Jews have delivered Jesus to the Roman governor (19:11). In development, Jesus, as the speaker of Ps 22:19, proclaims that the superior authority of God is prevailing in what Pilate's soldiers did when they crucified him. What the gentile soldiers did with the clothing of Jesus ironically advances God's authoritative plan as recorded in Jewish scripture. They shared the clothes of Jesus among themselves, enabling them as gentile individuals to appropriate the eternal life Jesus effects by laying down his own life as the good shepherd-king. And they cast lots for his seamless tunic, enabling Gentiles to preserve and participate in the divinely determined and divinely intimate unity "from above" of all believers accomplished through Jesus' death by crucifixion as the unique high priest (19:24b).

Jesus Invites the Beloved Disciple To See and Accept His Mother (A² 19:25-27)

25 Meanwhile, standing by the cross of Jesus were his mother and his mother's sister, Mary the wife of Clopas, and Mary Magdalene. 26 When Jesus saw the mother and the disciple whom he loved standing beside her, he said to the mother, "Woman, behold your son!" 27 Then he said to the disciple, "Behold your mother!" And from that hour the disciple took her to his own.

Four women stand by the cross of Jesus (19:25)

Generating an A-B-A intercalation with the two previous scenes, Jesus' invitation for the beloved disciple to see and accept his mother (19:25-27) contrasts with the Roman soldiers' taking the clothing of the crucified Jesus in the first B scene (19:23-24). It also develops Pilate's invitation for the Jews to see and accept Jesus as their King in the first A scene (19:12-22).

Whereas, "on the one hand" (μὲν), the four soldiers "then did these things" with the clothing of Jesus (19:24b) in the previous B scene, in contrast, "meanwhile" or "on the other hand" (δὲ), there were four women standing by the cross of Jesus (19:25).[28] The four Roman soldiers relate to Jesus in a rather hostile way, taking for themselves the clothing of the one they crucified (19:23). In contrast, the four Jewish women relate to Jesus in a more sympathetic way,

---

[28] As noted in chapter 1 above, the Greek μὲν . . . δὲ construction enhances the contrast between the second A scene (19:25-27) and the first B scene (19:23-24) of this section. See Janssens de Varebeke, "La structure," 512; BAGD, 502; Carson, *John*, 615 n. 1.

simply standing by his cross. The anonymous soldiers share the clothes of Jesus and vie for his tunic ("whose it will be") as separate, impersonal individuals (19:24a). But the women are interpersonally and communally designated in relation to Jesus and other people. The first two are familially related to Jesus and to one another as his mother and his mother's sister. The third and fourth are both specifically named Mary—one defined in relation to Clopas as his wife, and the other, Mary Magdalene, defined in relation to the people of Magdala, a town on the Sea of Galilee.

That Jewish women were standing at the cross of Jesus develops a more favorable attitude toward the crucified Jesus on the part of Jews. In the previous A scene the Jewish chief priests rejected the Jesus they crucified as the true King of the Jews and tried to prevent the promulgation of that kingship to the Jewish people (19:14-22). Now a group of women, closely related to Jesus and the Jewish people, stand by the cross that enthrones Jesus as the true King of the Jews.

The beloved disciple receives the mother of Jesus (19:26-27)

In the previous A scene Pilate at the judgment seat mockingly yet officially presented Jesus for the Jews to see and accept as their King, "Behold (Ἴδε) your King!" But after blasphemously rejecting his kingship, the unbelieving Jews took (παρέλαβον) Jesus and crucified him, ironically enthroning him as their true King(19:14-18). By way of development, the crucified Jesus now invites his mother and the beloved disciple, two individuals representative of Jews who believe in him, to see and accept one another in a new familial relationship based on his death. He exhorts his mother to see and accept a new maternal relationship with the beloved disciple, "Woman, behold (ἴδε) your son!" (19:26). And he in turn urges the disciple whom he loved to see and accept a new filial relationship with the mother of Jesus, "Behold (Ἴδε) your mother!" (19:27). The one introduced as "his" (Jesus') mother (μήτηρ αὐτοῦ) (19:25), and then referred to more generally as "the" mother (τὴν μητέρα; τῇ μητρί), addressed as "woman" (19:26), now becomes "your" (the beloved disciple's) mother (μήτηρ σου) (19:27).[29] The disciple took (ἔλαβεν) her to his own (19:27),[30] forming a new familial community of believers both originating and

[29] de la Potterie, *Hour,* 114.
[30] Brown, *Death,* 1024: "'His own' is the special discipleship that Jesus loves. The fact that the mother of Jesus is now the disciple's mother and that he has taken her to his own is a symbolic way of describing how one related to Jesus by the flesh (his mother who is part of his natural family) becomes related to him by the Spirit (a member of the ideal discipleship)."

resulting "from" (ἀπ') that "hour," the hour of Jesus' Life-giving death.[31]

In the previous B scene the hostile Roman soldiers rapaciously took (ἔλαβον) for themselves the clothes and tunic of the Jesus they crucified (19:23).[32] In contrast, the beloved disciple, obeying the request of the dying Jesus, graciously took (ἔλαβεν) the mother of Jesus into his own community of people (19:27). Whereas the soldiers unwittingly pointed to the communal unity the death of Jesus will effect when they decided not to tear his seamless tunic (19:24), the beloved disciple and the mother of Jesus now begin to actualize that unity.[33]

The anonymous "mother of Jesus" makes her first appearance in the narrative when she together with Jesus and his disciples are invited to a wedding feast at Cana in Galilee (2:1-2).[34] The story about the wedding possesses a symbolic level based upon the rich biblical imagery of the marital union representing the covenant that unites God, the "bridegroom," with the people of Israel, his "bride" and also communal "mother" of individual Israelites.[35] Against this background the mother of Jesus functions as the real bride and mother, while Jesus represents the real bridegroom of this wedding feast. The mother of Jesus, whom Jesus addresses as "woman" (2:4), is the only woman-bride that appears in the story. And the reader knows that the comment of the surprised chief steward to the bridegroom of this wedding is actually addressed to Jesus, the "bridegroom" who has kept the abundant, choice wine until now (2:9-10).[36]

The statement the mother of Jesus directs to him, "They have no wine" (2:3), applies not only to this particular wedding feast at Cana but also to the "wedding" feast of the Jewish people with their God. They lack the abundant,

---

[31] The Greek preposition ἀπό can indicate both origin and cause, thus facilitating the double meaning; BAGD, 86-87.

[32] Senior, *John*, 109: "The faithful women and the Beloved Disciple are a counterpart to the hostile presence of the soldiers, and Jesus' gracious act of entrusting his mother to the disciple contrasts with the rapacious character of the executioners."

[33] Barrett, *John*, 552: "If we are justified in seeing in John's reference to the indivisible χιτών of Jesus a symbol of the unity of the church gathered together by his death, we may here see an illustration of this unity."

[34] She is referred to as "mother" (2:1, 3, 5, 12; 6:42; 19:25-27) and "woman" (2:4; 19:26), but never called "Mary" in John's Gospel.

[35] Hos 1-3; Isa 26:17-18; 49:20-22; 54:1-8; 60:4; 61:10; 62:1-5; 66:7-13; Jer 2:2; 31:4, 15; Ps 87:5-6. See also de la Potterie, *Hour*, 112-13; Senior, *John*, 111-12.

[36] In 3:29 Jesus is even more explicitly designated as the "bridegroom" who has the "bride" by John the Baptist, the "friend of the bridegroom." See R. Infante, "L'amico dello sposo, figura del ministero di Giovanni Battista nel quarto vangelo," *RivB* 31 (1983) 3-19.

choice wine of the end-time, messianic wedding that can truly unite them with God.[37] Jesus, however, seems to put off his mother as the woman-bride of the wedding, "What concern is that to me and to you, woman? My hour has not yet arrived" (2:4). It is not yet the "hour" of Jesus' glorification through death that will definitively unite and unify people with God. Nevertheless, his mother bids the servants, "Do whatever he tells you" (2:5). Her unconditional faith and commitment to the word of Jesus wins the abundant, new, and choice wine that surpasses the old Jewish ritual cleansings with water (2:6) as a way to union with God. After Jesus has attracted individuals (1:35-51), the model faith of his mother brings about an initial manifestation of Jesus' glory that results in "his disciples" believing in him for the first time as a group (2:1, 11).[38] The faith of the mother and woman-bride has "given birth" to a familial community united with Jesus, the "bridegroom": "After this he went down to Capernaum—he and his mother and his brothers and his disciples—and there they remained a few days" (2:12).[39]

Although his disciples believed in him, their faith at this point remains incomplete. Only later, after the "hour" of his glorification, did the disciples "remember" what Jesus said about his death and resurrection in accord with scripture and come to a more authentic faith (2:17, 22; 12:16).[40] Indeed, once the disciples thought they finally believed in Jesus (16:30), he questioned their faith, "Do you now believe?" (16:31). He then predicted their abandonment of familial union with him once the "hour" has arrived: "Behold, the hour is coming and has arrived when each of you will be scattered to his own and leave me alone" (16:32). This is now confirmed during the "hour" at the cross. Mentioned with the mother of Jesus is no longer the initial familial community of his brothers and his disciples (2:12) but her sister and two other women (19:25).[41]

The only male follower reported to be present at the cross is the anonymous

[37] On abundant, new, and choice wine as a feature of the eschatological age, see Amos 9:13-15; Joel 2:19, 24; 4:18; Jer 31:12; Gen 49:11; *1 Enoch* 10:19.

[38] Moloney, *Belief*, 91-92: "Because the mother of Jesus, despite the rebuke that her son directed toward her, trusted completely in the efficacy of the word of Jesus, the disciples have come to see the sign, the *doxa*, and they have come to faith . . .the first to commit herself totally to the word of Jesus (v. 5) does so that others might believe (v. 11)."

[39] Note how the anonymous Samaritan woman-wife similarly represents the Samaritan people (4:20). Through her encounter with Jesus, who "told her everything she did," she led her people to faith in Jesus as the savior of the world (4:29-30, 39-42).

[40] Moloney, *Belief*, 102-3.

[41] Note that "his brothers" did not believe in Jesus (7:3, 5, 10).

disciple whom Jesus loved (19:26).[42] He portrays the ideal disciple, who appeared in the narrative as the disciple closest to Jesus (13:23) only after the arrival of the "hour" (13:1). As the disciple whom Jesus loved, he embodies those for whom Jesus demonstrates his great love by laying down his life for them as his friends (13:1, 34; 15:12-13). He is closely associated, if not identical with, the anonymous "other disciple" known to the "high priest" Jesus, the good shepherd who is laying down his life for his sheep/disciples (18:15-16).[43] His taking of the woman who is the mother of Jesus into his own forms a new familial community of complete and authentic faith flowing from the "hour" and embracing the significance of Jesus' death (19:27).

That the beloved disciple takes the mother of Jesus to his own (εἰς τὰ ἴδια) (19:27) to give birth to a new family of faith reverses the inadequate faith of each of the other disciples who scattered to his own (εἰς τὰ ἴδια) (16:32).[44] Although Jesus came to his own (εἰς τὰ ἴδια) people who did not receive (παρέλαβον) him with faith (1:11), the beloved disciple took (ἔλαβεν) the mother of Jesus, the model of authentic faith, to his own (εἰς τὰ ἴδια) people. The "hour" of the "woman" whose sorrow turns to joy when she gives birth to

---

[42] On the Johannine "beloved disciple," see B. Byrne, "The Faith of the Beloved Disciple and the Community in John 20," *JSNT* 23 (1985) 83-97; I. de la Potterie, "Le témoin qui demeure: le disciple que Jésus amait," *Bib* 67 (1986) 343-59; H.-M. Schencke, "The Function and Background of the Beloved Disciple in the Gospel of John," *Nag Hammadi, Gnosticism & Early Christianity* (ed. C. H. Hedrick and R. Hodgson; Peabody, MA: Hendrickson, 1986) 111-25; J. Kügler, *Der Jünger, den Jesus liebte: Literarische, theologische und historische Untersuchungen zu einer Schlüsselgestalt johanneischer Theologie und Geschichte. Mit einem Exkurs über die Brotrede in Joh 6* (SBB 16; Stuttgart: Katholisches Bibelwerk, 1988); W. S. Kurz, "The Beloved Disciple and Implied Readers," *BTB* 19 (1989) 100-107; G. Segalla, "'Il discepolo che Gesù amava' e la tradizione giovannea," *Teologia* 14 (1989) 217-44; G. M. Napole, "Pedro y el discipulo amado en Juan 21,1-25," *RevistB* 52 (1990) 153-77; J. A. Grassi, *The Secret Identity of the Beloved Disciple* (Mahwah, NJ: Paulist, 1992); R. Bauckham, "The Beloved Disciple as Ideal Author," *JSNT* 49 (1993) 21-44; Beck, "Anonymity," 143-58.

[43] See chapter 2 on 18:15-16.

[44] F. J. Moloney, "Mary in the Fourth Gospel: Woman and Mother," *Salesianum* 51 (1989) 439: "The scattering of 16:32 has been reversed through the 'gathering' which takes place around the crucified, symbolised by the union of the Mother and the Disciple in 19:27. The mother of Jesus, 'the woman' who now becomes a 'mother' in this new situation, will lead the way in that process. She is the woman whose pain of 'the hour' of giving birth now brings joy (see 16:21)." See also F. Neirynck, "*EIS TA IDIA*: Jn 19,27 (et 16,32)," *ETL* 55 (1979) 357-65; idem, "La traduction d'un verset johannique: Jn 19,27b," *ETL* 57 (1981) 83-106; M. Gourgues, "Marie, la 'femme' et la 'mère' en Jean," *NRT* 108 (1986) 174-91; J. A. Grassi, "The Role of Jesus' Mother in John's Gospel: A Reappraisal," *CBQ* 48 (1986) 67-80; S. Boguslawski, "Jesus' Mother and the Bestowal of the Spirit," *IBS* 14 (1992) 106-29; Brown, *Death*, 1019-26.

a child (16:21) has now arrived with the "hour" of Jesus' death, when the woman who is his mother "gives birth" to a new son, the beloved disciple.[45]

Now that the "hour" of Jesus' glorification has arrived, he invites the woman who is his mother to complete the initial family of faith she originated in anticipation of the "hour" (2:12). She must now embrace the beloved disciple as her own son, who symbolizes the significance of Jesus' death as the supreme act of love for his disciples. Full faith is only possible after the "hour" of Jesus' glorification by death. To complete the family of true believers, Jesus exhorts the beloved disciple to welcome as his own mother the woman who is the mother of Jesus, the model of unconditional faith in the word of Jesus.[46] By taking her to his own, the beloved disciple establishes the familial community of those who are nurtured to believe with the faith and commitment of the mother of Jesus, who said, "Do whatever he tells you" (2:5). This familial community thus believes in the Jesus who commands them to love one another as he loved them, the one who loved them greatly by laying down his life for them as his friends (15:11-17). By appropriating the full and authentic faith that the beloved disciple and the mother of Jesus together personify, readers can create such a familial community of mutual respect, based upon the love manifested for them in Jesus' death.

Jesus Takes Vinegar, Dies and Completes Scripture (B² 19:28-30)

28 After this, when Jesus knew that everything had already been accomplished, in order that the scripture might be completed, said, "I thirst." 29 A vessel full of vinegar was standing there. So, putting a sponge full of vinegar on a branch of hyssop, they brought it to his mouth. 30 When he then took the vinegar, Jesus said, "It is accomplished." And bowing his head, he handed over the spirit.

To complete the scripture Jesus expresses his thirst (19:28)

Creating a B-A-B intercalation with the two previous scenes, Jesus' taking of vinegar, dying and completing scripture (19:28-30) contrasts with his invita-

---

[45] Moloney, "Mary," 427-31, 439.

[46] de la Potterie, *Hour,* 117-20, interprets the beloved disciple's taking of the mother of Jesus "into his own" as his welcoming of her into the close intimacy of his life of faith. See also idem, "La parole de Jésus 'Voici ta Mère' et l'accueil du Disciple (Jn 19,27b)," *Marianum* 36 (1974) 1-39; "'Et à partir de cette heure, le Disciple l'accueillit dans son intimité' (Jn 19,27b): Réflexions méthodologiques sur l'interprétation d'un verset johannique," *Marianum* 42 (1980) 84-125.

tion for the beloved disciple to see and accept his mother (19:25-27). It also develops the Roman soldiers' taking the clothing of the crucified Jesus (19:23-24).

The Jesus who knew (εἰδὼς) everything (πάντα) that was coming upon him when he went out to meet those who arrested him (18:4) now knew (εἰδὼς) that everything (πάντα) had already been accomplished (19:28). When Jesus knew (εἰδὼς) that his hour had come to pass from this world to the Father, having loved those who were his own in the world, he loved them to the end (τέλος)—not only to the "end" of his hour but to the "perfection" or "completion" of his love (13:1).[47] The love demonstrated by the death of Jesus has been brought to its perfection or completion now that the beloved disciple, the representative recipient of that love, has accepted the mother of Jesus, the model of authentic faith, to form the community of those who love one another in faithful response to the great love Jesus has manifested for them to the "end" (19:27). Consequently, the Jesus who knew (εἰδὼς) that the Father had given everything (πάντα) into his hands (13:3) so that he could love his own to the end now knew (εἰδὼς) that everything (πάντα) had already been accomplished (τετέλεσται), that is, brought to its completion, its perfect end.[48]

Not only everything that had already been accomplished, but also Jesus' statement that "I thirst," brings the scripture to completion (19:28).[49] In the previous B scene the soldiers took the clothes of Jesus but preserved the unity of his tunic in order that the scripture might be fulfilled (πληρωθῇ) (19:24). Now, by way of development, Jesus states his thirst in order that the scripture might be perfectly completed (τελειωθῇ). The thirst of Jesus alludes to Ps 22:16, a lament uttered by the suffering just one: "My mouth is dried up like baked clay, and my tongue cleaves to my jaws; you have brought me down to the dust of death." This is from the same psalm the soldiers fulfilled by dividing and casting lots for the clothes of the dying Jesus: "They divided my clothes among themselves, and for my clothing they cast lots" (Ps 22:19). The same scripture the soldiers fulfilled and through which the dying Jesus himself

---

[47] Zerwick and Grosvenor, *Analysis,* 1.327; de la Potterie, *Hour,* 140.

[48] Brown, *John,* 908, 928-29; idem, *Death,* 1070-72; Senior, *John,* 115.

[49] de la Potterie, *Hour,* 122-23, limits the reference of the completion of the scripture to everything that had been accomplished in the previous scene and denies that the statement of Jesus' thirst is intended to complete the scripture. Brown, *John,* 908; idem, *Death,* 1072-74, however, rightly preserves the ambiguity of the final clause, "in order that the scripture might be completed," allowing it to refer both to what precedes it (everything accomplished) and to what follows it (Jesus' thirst).

acknowledged the taking of his clothes, he now begins to bring to completion by expressing his thirst.

In the previous A scene the dying Jesus drew attention to the transformed relationships that his death effects for the formation of a new community of complete and authentic faith. With his powerful and authoritative word he said (λέγει) to the mother, "Woman, behold your son!" Then he said (λέγει) to the disciple, "Behold your mother!" (19:26-27). In contrast, the dying Jesus now draws attention to himself, as he said (λέγει), "I thirst" (19:28). By expressing his "thirst," Jesus not only begins to bring to completion the scriptural plan of God the soldiers have unwittingly fulfilled (19:24), but expresses his desire, his "thirst," now to "drink" the "cup" of suffering and death that the Father has given him to drink (18:11).[50]

Jesus takes vinegar and hands over the spirit (19:29-30)

In further advancement of the preceding B scene, the scripture Jesus began to complete by expressing his thirst (Ps 22:16 in 19:28) after the soldiers took his clothes (Ps 22:19 in 19:24), the soldiers now continue to bring to its perfect completion. A vessel full of vinegar (ὄξους) was standing there. So, in response to the thirst (διψῶ) of the dying Jesus, the soldiers affix a sponge full of vinegar to a branch of hyssop and bring it to his mouth (19:29).[51] They thereby play their role in completing the scripture by adding to their fulfillment of Ps 22:19 the actualization of Ps 69(LXX 68):22, another lament uttered by the suffering just one: "They gave gall for my food, and for my thirst (δίψαν) they gave me vinegar (ὄξος) to drink."[52]

At the wedding feast in Cana Jesus wonderfully transformed the water that filled to the brim the stone water jars used for Jewish ritual washings (2:6-7) into the superior, choice wine of the messianic age (2:10). Now, as an extended irony, from a vessel full of vinegar the gentile soldiers offer Jesus only vinegar—common, sour wine—in correspondence to the bitter cup of death the Father has given him to drink (18:11).[53] As a further irony, the gentile soldiers place

[50] Brown, *John*, 930; idem, *Death*, 1073-74; Senior, *John*, 116.

[51] According to BAGD, 574, this vinegar or sour wine "relieved thirst more effectively than water and, because it was cheaper than regular wine, it was a favorite beverage of the lower ranks of society and of those in moderate circumstances, especially of soldiers." See also Brown, *John*, 909; idem, *Death*, 1063-64.

[52] Brown, *John*, 929; R. L. Brawley, "An Absent Complement and Intertextuality in John 19:28-29," *JBL* 112 (1993) 427-43.

[53] Duke, *Irony*, 113.

the sponge full of vinegar on a branch of hyssop, a gesture evocative of the Jewish Passover ritual.[54] The Israelites used hyssop to sprinkle the blood of the Passover lambs on their doorposts to save them from the destruction God was bringing upon their Egyptian oppressors. This ritual was to be commemorated in future Passover celebrations (Exod 12:21-27).[55] Now that it is the day of preparation for the Passover, when the Passover lambs are slaughtered in the temple (19:14), the gentile soldiers continue to establish Jesus as the true and universal Passover Lamb of God, who takes away the sin not only of Jews but of the whole world (1:29).[56]

In the previous B scene the soldiers took (ἔλαβον) the clothing of Jesus and thus enabled the scripture (Ps 22:19) to be fulfilled (19:23-24). In development Jesus now took (ἔλαβεν) the vinegar the soldiers offered him and enabled the scripture to be completed, declaring, "It is accomplished," as he died (19:30). Jesus thus completes the scripture not only of Ps 22:19 with Ps 22:16 but also of Ps 69:10 with Ps 69:22. His thirst in fulfillment of Ps 22:16 completes the soldiers' fulfillment of Ps 22:19 by taking his clothes. And by taking the vinegar as he dies in fulfillment of Ps 69:22, Jesus completes the scripture of Ps 69:10, "Zeal for your house will consume me" (2:17), that his disciples remembered when he drove the sacrificial commerce from the temple (2:13-16).[57] The soldiers play their part in fulfilling the scripture, but it is Jesus himself who brings the scripture to completion. Jesus is the speaker of Ps 22:19 ("*my* clothes; *my* clothing"), the one who says, "I thirst" (Ps 22:16 in 19:28), the one who predicts that zeal for God's house "will consume *me*" (Ps 69:10), the one who takes the vinegar (Ps 69:22), and the one who climactically pronounces the final accomplishment (19:30). No one takes Jesus' life from him. As the good shepherd, he lays down his life on his own in accord with the command of his Father (10:18; 18:11), as recorded in the scripture.

Now that the scripture has been completed (τελειωθῇ), Jesus authoritatively announces, "It is accomplished" (Τετέλεσται). Not only does this pow-

---

[54] On the problem and possible solutions of hoisting a sponge full of vinegar on a branch of hyssop, a rather fragile plant, see Brown, *Death*, 1075-76. His solution is "to accept the fact that John means the biblical hyssop despite the physical implausibility caused by the fragility of that plant. . . . The most famous reference to hyssop is in Exod 12:22, which specifies that hyssop should be used to sprinkle the blood of the paschal lamb on the doorposts of the Israelite homes" (p. 1076).

[55] F. G. Beetham, and P. A. Beetham, "A Note on John 19.29," *JTS* 44 (1993) 163-69.

[56] Brown, *John*, 930; idem, *Death*, 1076-78; Barrett, *John*, 553; Senior, *John*, 117-18; Schuchard, *Scripture*, 137.

[57] Schuchard, *Scripture*, 31

erful pronouncement indicate the completion of scripture, but it also climactically reinforces the narrator's report that everything the Father had given Jesus to do (13:3) has already been accomplished (τετέλεσται) (19:28).[58] Jesus has done the will of the one who sent him and completed (τελειώσω) his work (4:34). He has accomplished the works the Father gave him to complete (τελειώσω), the works that testify that the Father sent him (5:36). Having completed (τελειώσας) the work the Father gave him to do, Jesus has glorified the Father on earth (17:4). Now those who believe in him, including the audience called to believe through the word of the disciples (17:20), can be "completed" or "brought to perfection" (τετελειωμένοι) as "one" final and absolute unity, so that the world may know that the Father sent Jesus and loves them as he loved him (17:23).[59]

In the preceding A scene the beloved disciple took (ἔλαβεν) the mother of Jesus to his own at the behest of Jesus (19:27). In contrast Jesus now took (ἔλαβεν) the vinegar offered him by the Roman soldiers (19:30). Whereas the beloved disciple received Jesus' mother to form the new community of complete and authentic faith, Jesus received the vinegar so that everything, including the creation of this community, might be accomplished by his death. As Jesus pronounced, "It is accomplished," he bowed his head that had been crowned with thorns (19:2) and majestically handed over "the spirit" (19:30). He himself handed over in death his human spirit (πνεῦμα), the same spirit in which he was troubled by the death of Lazarus (11:33) and by his own handing over/betrayal to death (13:21). In taking the bitter vinegar to quench his "thirst" (19:28) for God's will, Jesus, as the good shepherd, lays down his own life in accord with the command of his Father (10:18) by "drinking" the bitter "cup" of death the Father has given him to drink (18:11).

In handing over "the spirit," Jesus handed over not only his own human spirit but the holy Spirit of God.[60] After Jesus expressed his thirst to the Samaritan woman by saying, "Give me to drink" (4:7), he disclosed his ability to give her the "living water" (4:10) that quenches one's spiritual thirst for eternal life (4:14). Jesus' giving of "living water" points to the hour of his giving of

[58] R. Bergmeier, "TETELESTAI Joh 19:30," *ZNW* 79 (1988) 282-90.

[59] We have attempted to preserve the distinction between the two closely related verbs by employing the translations "completed" (from τελειόω) and "accomplished" (from τελέω). Note the subtle progression from the work(s) (4:34; 5:36; 17:4), believers (17:23), and scripture (19:28) that are "completed" to everything that is fully and finally "accomplished" (19:28, 30).

[60] J. Swetnam, "Bestowal of the Spirit in the Fourth Gospel," *Bib* 74 (1993) 556-76.

the Spirit, so that true worshippers can worship the God who is Spirit in Spirit and truth (4:23-24). On the last and great day of the feast of Tabernacles Jesus stood up in the temple and exclaimed, "Let anyone who thirsts come to me, and let the one who believes in me drink, as the scripture said, 'Rivers of living water will flow from within him'" (7:37-38). Jesus said this about the Spirit, which believers in him were to receive; for as yet there was no Spirit, because Jesus was not yet glorified (7:39)—that is, he has not yet been lifted up or exalted in death by crucifixion.[61] As yet there was no Spirit because it can be given only when Jesus has died. But now "the hour" when Jesus was glorified by the Father through death has arrived (12:23; 13:31-32). After again expressing his thirst and tasting the bitter vinegar of death, Jesus hands over the Spirit (19:28-30), giving the "living water" for believers in him to drink and quench their thirst for eternal life.[62]

That Jesus handed over the Spirit after taking the vinegar and dying accomplishes the establishment of the familial community of true disciples, as he complements the beloved disciple's taking of the mother of Jesus to his own (19:27). Now that Jesus has handed over the Spirit by dying, he can fulfill his promise to give his disciples another Paraclete, the Spirit of truth, to be with them forever (14:16-17). This Paraclete, the holy Spirit, whom the Father will send in Jesus' name, will teach the disciples everything and remind them of all that Jesus told them (14:26). When the Spirit of truth who comes from the Father arrives, he will testify about Jesus (15:26). Whenever the Spirit of truth comes, he will guide the familial community of disciples in all truth. He will not speak on his own, but whatever he hears from Jesus and the Father he will speak, and he will declare to them the things that are to come (16:13-15).[63] Now that the dying Jesus has handed down the Spirit, his familial community of true believers, including the audience, can worship the Father, the God who is Spirit, in Spirit and truth (4:23-24) and quench their thirst for eternal life (4:14; 7:37-38).[64]

---

[61] For a discussion of the problems involved in translating and interpreting the ambiguities in 7:37-39, see G. Bienaimé, "L'annonce des fleuves d'eau vive en Jean 7,37-39," *RTL* 21 (1990) 281-310; A. T. Hanson, *The Prophetic Gospel: A Study of John and the Old Testament* (Edinburgh: Clark, 1991) 99-115.

[62] de la Potterie, *Hour,* 125-33.

[63] de la Potterie, *La vérité,* 329-466.

[64] J. Zumstein, "L'interprétation johannique de la mort du Christ," *The Four Gospels 1992: Festschrift Frans Neirynck* (BETL 100; ed. F. Van Segbroeck, et al.; 3 vols; Leuven: Leuven University, 1992) 2119-38.

Jesus' Blood and Water Invite Looking
Upon Him (A³ 19:31-37)

31 Then the Jews, since it was preparation day, in order that the bodies might not remain on the cross during the sabbath, for great was the day of that sabbath, asked Pilate that their legs be broken and they be taken away. 32 So the soldiers came and broke the legs of the first and then of the other who was crucified with him. 33 But coming to Jesus, when they saw that he was already dead, they did not break his legs. 34 Instead, one of the soldiers pricked his side with a spear, and immediately blood and water came out. 35 The one who has seen has testified, and his testimony is true, and he knows that he speaks the truth, so that you also may believe. 36 For these things happened so that the scripture might be fulfilled, "Not a bone of him will be crushed" (LXX Exod 12:10, 46; Num 9:12; Ps 34[33]:21). 37 And again another scripture says, "They will look upon the one they have pierced" (Zech 12:10).

They did not break the legs of the dead Jesus (19:31-33)

Concluding an A-B-A sandwich with the two previous scenes, the invitation to look upon the blood and water flowing from the side of the pierced Jesus (19:31-37) contrasts with Jesus' taking of vinegar, dying and completing scripture (19:28-30). It also advances Jesus' invitation for the beloved disciple to see and accept his mother (19:25-27).

As he handed over the Spirit in death and brought the scripture to completion in the preceding B scene, the Jesus who knew everything had already been accomplished solemnly announced, "It is accomplished" (19:28-30). In contrast to what Jesus has already completed and accomplished, the Jews are still preparing for what is to come. It was preparation day not only for the sabbath but for the Passover that occurred that sabbath, making that sabbath a "great day." In order that the bodies not remain on the cross to defile the great day of that particular sabbath, the Jews asked Pilate that their legs be broken and they be taken away (19:31).[65]

In the first A scene of this section it was preparation day (παρασκευὴ) for the Passover and about the sixth hour, the time the Passover lambs were being slaughtered in the temple, when Pilate presented Jesus to the Jews as their

---

[65] According to Deut 21:22-23: "When someone is convicted of a crime punishable by death and is executed, and you hang him on a tree, his corpse must not remain overnight on the tree; you shall bury him that day, for anyone hung on a tree is under God's curse. You must not defile your land that the Lord your God is giving you for possession." See also Brown, *Death*, 1174.

King, with the implication that he is also the true Passover Lamb of God (19:14). In development, the Jews, on the preparation day (παρασκευή) not only of the Passover but of the sabbath, continue to play their part in establishing Jesus as the Passover Lamb. They request that the legs of those crucified be broken to hasten their deaths and that their bodies be taken away for burial in preparation for the "great day" of that (ἐκείνου) sabbath (19:31). They thus ironically advance that (ἐκείνης) "hour" from which the beloved disciple took the mother of Jesus to his own in the previous A scene (19:27), that "hour" of Jesus' glorification by death and return to the Father (12:23, 27-28; 13:1; 17:1). In the first A scene the Jews rejected Jesus, crying out to Pilate, "Away with him (Ἆρον), away with him (ἆρον)! Crucify him!" (19:15). Now that Jesus has been crucified, they advance their rejection, requesting that his body be taken away (ἀρθῶσιν) along with those crucified with him (19:31).

In the first A scene of this section the Jews crucified Jesus, and with him two others, one on either side, with Jesus in the middle (19:18), ironically distinguishing him as a King enthroned between two attendants. But now the Jews attempt to treat Jesus, although he has already died, the same as those crucified with him. After the Jews' request to Pilate that the legs of all those crucified be broken, the soldiers came and broke the legs of the first and then of the other who was crucified with Jesus (19:31-32). But when the soldiers came to Jesus and saw that he was already dead, they did not break his legs (19:33), thus furthering the distinction of Jesus from those crucified with him.

Blood and water came out of the pierced side of Jesus (19:34)

In the preceding B scene Jesus himself, in full control of his own death and its Life-giving consequences, majestically bowed his head and handed over the Spirit as he died (19:30). In contrast, one of the soldiers, to make sure that Jesus had already died, pricked his side with a spear and immediately Life-giving blood and water came out of the dead Jesus (19:34) in ironic and symbolic correspondence to his own handing over of the Spirit.[66] In development of the previous A scene, the Life-giving blood and water flowing from the pierced

---

[66] On John 19:34, see G. Richter, "Blut und Wasser aus der durchbohrten Seite Jesu (Joh 19,34b)," *MTZ* 21 (1970) 1-21; J. Wilkinson, "The Incident of the Blood and Water in John 19,34," *SJT* 28 (1975) 149-72; E. Malatesta, "Blood and Water from the Pierced Side of Christ," *Segni e Sacramenti nel Vangelo di Giovanni* (Studia Anselmiana 66; ed. P.-R. Tragan; Rome: Anselmiana, 1977) 164-81; I. de la Potterie, "Le symbolisme du sang et de l'eau en Jn 19,34," *Didaskalia* 14 (1984) 201-30; Brown, *Death*, 1176-82.

side of the Jesus who laid down his own life as an act of greatest love for his friends (15:13) generates, nourishes, and unites the familial community of mutual love formed by the beloved disciple's acceptance of the mother of Jesus into his own (19:26-27).[67]

Water, a symbol of the Spirit, comes out of the pierced side of Jesus together with blood, a symbol of his Life-giving death. By following and flowing together with the blood, the water lends to the blood its natural cleansing and quenching qualities. That blood and water together come out of the Jesus lifted up and exalted in crucifixion brings to a climax all of the narrative's previous indications of both the salvific cleansing and quenching effects of the death of Jesus.

John came baptizing with water in order that Jesus might be manifested to Israel. John testified that he saw the Spirit descending like a dove from heaven and it remained on Jesus. The God who sent John to baptize with water told him that the one upon whom he saw the Spirit descending and remaining on him is the one who baptizes with the holy Spirit (1:31-33). But there was no giving of the Spirit before Jesus was glorified (7:39). Now that he has been glorified by death, however, Jesus "baptizes," that is, cleanses or washes, with the water that flows from his pierced side (19:34), the living water of the rivers that now flow from within him (7:38), the water that symbolically represents or contains the Spirit he handed over as he died (19:30).

The Jesus whom God revealed to John as the one who baptizes with the holy Spirit (1:33), John himself had just previously pointed out as the Lamb of God who takes away the sin of the world (1:29). That Jesus is the one who baptizes (ὁ βαπτίζων) with the holy Spirit thus parallels and complements that he is the one who takes away (ὁ αἴρων) the sin of the world. When John repeats that Jesus is "the Lamb of God" (1:36), the audience realizes that it is by baptizing or cleansing with the holy Spirit that Jesus takes or washes away the sin of the world as the Lamb of God. The cleansing water of the holy Spirit that now follows and flows together with the blood from the pierced side of the crucified Jesus empowers that blood to wash or take away the sin of the world as the sacrificial blood of the true Passover Lamb of God (see on 18:28; 19:14, 29, 31).

The blood of the slaughtered Passover lambs served a salvific purpose in Israel's liberating exodus from Egypt. The Israelites marked their doors with

---

[67] Brown, *John,* 950: "The soldier's lance thrust was meant to demonstrate that Jesus was truly dead; but this affirmation of death is paradoxically the beginning of life, for from the dead man there flows living water that will be a source of life for all who believe in him in imitation of the Beloved Disciple."

the blood of the Passover lambs to save themselves from the death God was bringing upon their Egyptian oppressors (Exod 12:7, 13, 22-23). The slaughter of the Passover lambs was considered a "sacrifice" (see θύσατε and θυσία in LXX Exod 12:21, 27 respectively).[68] And hyssop was used to apply the sacrificial blood that flowed from the slaughtered Passover lambs to their doors (Exod 12:22). But the sacrificial, salvific effects of the blood of Jesus, the new and unique Passover Lamb of God, surpass those of the Jewish Passover lambs. The soldiers used hyssop not to apply the blood of the Passover lambs but to give Jesus the vinegar that allows him to accomplish his own death (19:29-30) as the Passover Lamb. Jesus, the good shepherd-king and true high priest, lays down his own life and sacrifices himself as the Passover Lamb of God. The sacrificial blood that flows from Jesus transcends that of the exodus event. It saves not merely the Jewish people from death but takes away the sin of the whole world (1:29), saving the world from "the sin" of unbelief that brings death (8:24) in order that believers may enjoy eternal life.[69]

Nicodemus was puzzled as to how one could be born again from above by water and the Spirit in order to see and enter the kingdom of God (3:3-5, 9). The water that symbolizes the Spirit and that flows from the side of Jesus now answers his query. The blood of the pierced Lamb of God makes the water and the Spirit available for regeneration. Jesus told Nicodemus that for this rebirth it was necessary for the Son of Man to be lifted up, so that all who believe in him might have eternal life (3:14-15). Now that Jesus has been lifted up in crucifixion, his death as the Passover Lamb of God provides the Life-giving blood that takes or washes away the sin of unbelief for those reborn of the cleansing water and Spirit that follow and flow together with the blood, so that they may believe and have eternal life. By the blood and water of the Spirit flowing from his death, Jesus "baptizes" with the holy Spirit (1:33), transforming and tran-

[68] Schuchard, *Scripture*, 137-38 n. 22.

[69] de la Potterie, "Le symbolisme du sang," 208-9, denies that the blood flowing from the side of Jesus refers to the sacrificial blood of the Passover lamb. He thinks there are no ritual categories in the immediate context to indicate the expiatory value of the death of Jesus. But the hyssop (19:29) and the sixth hour on the preparation day for the Passover (19:14, 31), when the Passover lambs were slaughtered in the temple, allude to the Passover ritual. He also points out that the marking of the doors, not the flowing of the blood, was significant for the Passover. But the blood had to flow before the doors could be marked, and the flowing of blood was an important part of the sacrificial aspect of the killing of the lambs. According to Brown, *John*, 951: "One of the strict requirements of Jewish sacrificial law was that the blood of the victim should not be congealed but should flow forth at the moment of death so that it could be sprinkled." See also Carey, "Lamb of God," 97-122; B. H. Grigsby, "The Cross as an Expiatory Sacrifice in the Fourth Gospel," *JSNT* 15 (1982) 51-80.

scending John's baptism with mere water (1:31), so that believers may be baptized and reborn from above by water and the Spirit.[70] Through this baptism believers are reborn from God with power to become children of God (1:12-13) and enter the kingdom of God (3:3, 5), as well as the familial community of believers established by the beloved disciple and the mother of Jesus (19:27).[71]

During the wedding feast at Cana Jesus, prior to his "hour" (2:4) of glorification by death, transformed the water used for Jewish ritual washings (2:6) into something drinkable—choice wine (2:10). Now, during the hour of his death, the water of the Spirit transforms the cleansing blood of Jesus into something drinkable. That the water of the Spirit follows and flows together with the blood from the pierced side of Jesus answers the Jews' objection as to how Jesus can give them his flesh to eat and his blood to drink. By his death that produces blood together with the water of the Spirit, Jesus provides the true food that is his flesh and the true drink that is his blood. By eating his flesh and drinking his blood in the eucharist, those baptized and reborn of water and the Spirit have eternal life within themselves (6:51-58).[72] This sacramental food and drink resulting from the death of Jesus thus nourishes and unites the community of believers/readers with the eternal life Jesus shares with his Father (6:57).[73]

The blood of the Life-giving death of Jesus animates the water that follows and flows with it into the "living water" of the Spirit. This "living water" confirms Jesus' promise to the Samaritan woman that he can give the "living water" that definitively quenches one's deepest thirst for eternity. Indeed, the water Jesus gives will become within the person of the one who drinks it an abundant

---

[70] On sacraments in John, see F. J. Moloney, "When Is John Talking about Sacraments?" *AusBR* 30 (1982) 10-33; R. M. Ball, "S. John and the Institution of the Eucharist," *JSNT* 23 (1985) 59-68; C. H. Cosgrove, "The Place Where Jesus Is: Allusions to Baptism and the Eucharist in the Fourth Gospel," *NTS* 35 (1989) 522-39.

[71] Moloney, *Belief,* 114: "The Johannine baptismal experience of water and the Spirit introduces a believer into a community of believers: the kingdom of God."

[72] On the eucharistic allusions in 6:51-58 and 19:34, see F. J. Moloney, "John 6 and the Celebration of the Eucharist," *DRev* 93 (1975) 243-51; J. W. Voelz, "The Discourse on the Bread of Life in John 6: Is It Eucharistic?" *Concordia Journal* 15 (1989) 29-37. C. R. Koester, "John Six and the Lord's Supper," *LQ* 4 (1990) 419-37, finds a sacramental reading for 6:51-58 problematical. M. J. J. Menken, "John 6,51c-58: Eucharist or Christology?" *Bib* 74 (1993) 1-26, needlessly exaggerates the distinction between the christological and eucharistic aspects of 6:51-58. However, he rightly notes that "John puts the Eucharist in its proper place by focusing on that which gives meaning to this sacrament: Jesus' salvific death" (p. 24).

[73] Heil, *Jesus Walking on the Sea,* 161-65.

spring of water gushing up to eternal life (4:10, 13-14). The living water of the Spirit that flows with the blood of the death of Jesus enables Samaritans as well as Jews to transcend their worship on Mount Gerizim and in Jerusalem, so that they and all believers can now worship the God who is Spirit in Spirit and truth (4:21-24). The double meaning provided by grammatical ambiguity suggests that rivers of the living water of the Spirit flow not only from within the crucified Jesus but from within the believer (7:37-39).[74] This implies that believers may not only receive but also give to others the abundant living water of the Spirit (3:34) that finally quenches thirst by imparting eternal life.

Jesus laid down his clothes and washed his disciples' feet with water as a humble act of love (13:1-11) that symbolically anticipated the greater act of humble love he would demonstrate for them by laying down his life on the cross (15:13).[75] This washing was a "cleansing" (13:10-11) that gave the disciples a "share" with Jesus (13:8). He thus urged them to follow his example of love by washing one another's feet (13:14-15), thereby obeying his commandment to love one another as he has loved them—by laying down his life for them as his friends (13:34-35; 15:12-13).[76] The blood and water that flows from the death of Jesus fortifies the community of believers, by washing away their sin of unbelief in baptism and quenching their thirst for eternal life in the eucharist, to love one another as Jesus loved them.[77] From the abundant rivers of the living water of the Spirit that flows from within them (7:37-39; 3:34), believers, by loving one another as Jesus loved them, can be a source for others of the eternal life they have received and possess within themselves (4:14; 6:53-54) as a result of the loving death of Jesus.

Testimony and scripture lead readers to faith (19:35-37)

In the first A scene Pilate mockingly invited the Jews to see and accept Jesus as their king, "Behold (Ἴδε) your King!" (19:14), but they "accepted" him only for

[74] For a presentation of the various ambiguities involved in 7:37-39, see Bienaimé, "Jean 7,37-39," 281-310; Hanson, *Prophetic Gospel*, 99-115.

[75] See above on 19:23.

[76] F. J. Matera, "'On Behalf of Others,' 'Cleansing,' and 'Return.' Johannine Images for Jesus' Death," *LS* 13 (1988) 161-78; R. A. Culpepper, "The Johannine *Hypodeigma*: A Reading of John 13:1-38," *The Fourth Gospel from a Literary Perspective* (*Semeia* 53; ed. R. A. Culpepper and F. F. Segovia; Atlanta: Scholars, 1991) 133-52.

[77] On the baptismal and eucharistic connotations of the footwashing and meal in John 13 and their relation to the death of Jesus, see F. J. Moloney, "A Sacramental Reading of John 13:1-38," *CBQ* 53 (1991) 237-56. On the allusions in the footwashing to baptism and the cleansing aspect of the death of Jesus, see Thomas, *Footwashing*, 100-101.

crucifixion (19:15-16). In the second A scene the crucified Jesus invited his mother to see and accept the beloved disciple as her own son, "Woman, behold (ἴδε) your son!" (19:26). And he in turn invited the beloved disciple to see and accept his mother as his own, "Behold ("Ιδε) your mother!" (19:27). The disciple then accepted and took her to his own and thus established the familial community of authentic believers (19:27). In advancement of this theme of seeing and accepting, the one who has seen (ὁ ἑωρακὼς) the Life-giving blood and water flowing from the pierced side of the dead Jesus has testified and still testifies (μεμαρτύρηκεν, perfect tense) to the audience with true testimony. He has seen and knows that what he reports to the audience is true, "so that you also may believe" (19:35). The narrator here speaks on behalf of the beloved disciple to invite the audience to see, accept, and believe along with him, to become part of the familial community of believers (19:27), based on what he has seen and testified to be true.[78]

John the Baptist came for testimony to testify to Jesus as the Light, in order that all might believe through him (1:7-8, 15). When he saw the Spirit descending and remaining on Jesus (1:33), he reported that "I have seen" (ἑώρακα) and "I have testified" to the Jews (see 1:19) and still testify (μεμαρτύρηκα, perfect tense) to the audience that Jesus is "the chosen one of God" (1:34).[79] Although both Jesus and John have spoken and testified to the Jews, they have not accepted the testimony and believed. As Jesus solemnly informed Nicodemus, a leader of the Jews, "We speak of what we know and testify (μαρτυροῦμεν) about what we have seen (ἑωράκαμεν), but you (plural) do not accept our testimony" (3:11). The Jews have not believed (3:12; see also 3:31-36). Although the revelatory works the Father has given Jesus to complete tes-

---

[78] On the role of the narrator in 19:35, Culpepper, *Anatomy,* 44, states that "the narrator ... affirms that the Beloved Disciple's witness is true. The narrator, therefore, is not the Beloved Disciple but speaks as one who knows what is true, knows the mind of the Beloved Disciple, and knows that what the Beloved Disciple said is true." In maintaining that the beloved disciple is portrayed as the ideal author, Bauckham, "Beloved Disciple," 21-44, unnecessarily denies that he also represents the ideal disciple. Indeed, the very designation "beloved *disciple*" indicates this. See also Brown, *Death,* 1182-84.

[79] We prefer the variant, "the chosen one" (ὁ ἐκλεκτός) of God as the reading that explains the other primary variant "the Son" (ὁ υἱὸς) of God. It is difficult to explain why a scribe would introduce "the chosen one," which occurs only here in John, if "the Son" were the original reading. But if "the chosen one" is the original reading, a scribe may have introduced "the Son," which occurs quite frequently in John, to harmonize with Nathanael's confession of Jesus as the Son of God (1:49). Such harmonization, however, lessens the climactic impact of Nathanael's confession. For the manuscript evidence, see Metzger, *Textual Commentary,* 200.

tify (μαρτυρεῖ) about him, and although the Father who sent him has testified and still testifies (μεμαρτύρηκεν, perfect tense) about him, the Jews have not believed the one he sent (5:36-38; see also 8:13-19; 10:25-26). Indeed, although the scriptures in which the Jews think they have eternal life testify (μαρτυροῦ-σαι) about him, they refuse to come to Jesus with faith in order to have eternal life (5:39-40).

John has testified and still testifies (μεμαρτύρηκεν) to the truth Jesus reveals (5:33; see also 1:34; 5:31-32). Jesus was born and came into the world to testify (μαρτυρήσω) to the truth he reveals (18:37). Now the one who has seen (ὁ ἑωρακὼς) the accomplishment of Jesus' revelatory works in the death that produces the Life-giving blood and water of the Spirit (19:28-30, 34) has testified and still testifies (μεμαρτύρηκεν) with true testimony. He invites the audience to accept his true testimony and manifest the faith the Jews have refused, despite the true testimony given them, and join him in believing—that you "also" (καὶ) may believe (19.35). By testifying he anticipates and models for the audience the testifying the disciples will do, "You also will testify (μαρ-τυρεῖτε)," when the Paraclete, the Spirit of truth, comes and testifies (μαρ-τυρήσει) about Jesus (15:26-27). The audience can now believe and in turn testify to the truth, based on what the narrator, an ideal, beloved disciple, has seen and testified about the Life-giving death of Jesus.

In the first B scene the soldiers humiliated the crucified Jesus by taking his clothing so that the scripture might be fulfilled, in which Jesus is the speaker of the lament uttered by the suffering just one in Ps 22:19: "They divided my clothes among themselves, and for my clothing they cast lots" (19:24). In the second B scene Jesus declared, "I thirst," an allusion to the lament in Ps 22:16, so that the scripture might be completed (19:28). That they then gave him vine-gar to drink (19:29-30) alludes to another lament of the suffering just one in Ps 69:22: "They gave gall for my food, and for my thirst they gave me vinegar to drink." By way of contrast, "the things that happened" in this final A scene ful-fill the scripture, "Not a bone of him will be crushed (συντριβήσεται)" (19:36), that alludes not to a lament but to a thanksgiving for divine rescue of the suffering just ones in Ps 34(33):21: "The Lord watches over all their bones, not one of them will be crushed (συντριβήσεται)."[80] A hymn of praise to God

---

[80] For a discussion of the provenance and use of the scriptural quotation in 19:36, see Schuchard, *Scripture,* 133-40; M. J. J. Menken, "The Old Testament Quotation in Jn 19,36: Sources, Redaction, Background," *The Four Gospels 1992: Festschrift Frans Neirynck* (BETL 100; ed. F. Van Segbroeck, et al.; 3 vols.; Leuven: Leuven University, 1992) 2102-18; Brown, *Death,* 1184-86.

for protecting his suffering just ones now replaces the previous laments. By not breaking the bones of Jesus in distinction to those crucified with him (19:32-33), the soldiers, ironically, further fulfill the scriptural plan of God Jesus has completed. Because Jesus had already died to complete and accomplish God's scriptural plan (19:28-30), God now protects him as his specially chosen, suffering just one, not allowing a bone of him to be crushed.

That "not a bone of him will be crushed" in fulfillment of scripture also confirms Jesus as the sacrificial Passover Lamb of God who takes away the sin of world (1:29, 36). When the Israelites ate the slaughtered Passover lamb that was roasted intact (Exod 12:9), they were not to let any of it remain until morning, and "you shall not crush (συντρίψετε) a bone of it" (LXX Exod 12:10; see also Exod 12:46; Num 9:12). That God allowed not a bone of Jesus, the Passover Lamb and suffering just one, to be crushed resulted in the flowing of the Life-giving blood and water of the Spirit from the pierced side of the already dead Jesus (19:34).[81] In development of the previous A scene, then, that not a bone of Jesus was crushed enables him to provide the sacramental blood and water that generates and sustains the community of believers established by the beloved disciple and the mother of Jesus (19:27).

And again another scripture from Zech 12:10 says, "They will look upon the one they have pierced" (19:37).[82] This quote brings to a climax the theme of invitations to see and accept in the A scenes (19:14-16, 26-27), as it corresponds to the narrator's invitation to accept and believe based on what the beloved disciple has seen (19:35). That they will look (ὄψονται) upon the one they have pierced means they will see what he has seen (ἑωρακώς)—the Life-giving blood and water flowing from the pierced side of the crucified Jesus (19:34). This scripture thus invites not only the Jews who asked Pilate that the legs of those crucified be broken and they be taken away (19:31), but also the soldiers who saw (εἶδον) that Jesus was already dead so that one of them pricked his side

---

[81] Schuchard, *Scripture*, 138-39: "The stipulations in the Pentateuch concerning the sacrifice of the paschal lamb and Ps 34(33) do not share much more than their mutual references to 'bones' which will not be 'broken' and their general references to a God who delivers those who trust in him. But John's conspicuous desire to portray the Son of God as the Paschal Lamb could easily have prompted him to associate his citation of the Pentateuch with the psalm's description of God's protection of the righteous. . . . John's citation, then, suggests that Jesus is both Paschal Lamb and one of the righteous described in Ps 34(33)." See also Senior, *John*, 122; Brown, *Death*, 1186.

[82] For a discussion of the provenance and use of the scriptural quotation in 19:37, see Schuchard, *Scripture*, 141-49; M. J. J. Menken, "The Textual Form and the Meaning of the Quotation from Zechariah 12:10 in John 19:37," *CBQ* 55 (1993) 494-511; Brown, *Death*, 1186-88.

(19:33-34), to look upon the Life-giving blood and water flowing from the pierced Jesus in order to believe.[83] Readers who already believe will continuously "look upon the one they have pierced," contemplating the abundant, inexhaustible rivers of blood and water flowing from the dead Jesus, in order to sustain and renew the eternal life they enjoy by believing (4:14; 6:53; 7:37-39).

The man born blind was sent by Jesus to wash his eyes in the waters of Siloam and not only saw but believed in Jesus as the Son of Man (9:1-38). Now those who will look upon the one they have pierced will see the cleansing and quenching blood and water by which they may believe and have eternal life.[84] Now that Jesus has been "lifted up" in crucifixion as the final accomplishment and climax of his revelatory works (19:28-30) and signs (12:33; 18:32), he magnetically draws all to himself (12:32), so that all may know that he is *the* revealer of the Father (8:28; 14:7-11), and all who believe may have eternal life in him (3:14-15).

Joseph and Nicodemus Take the Body of Jesus for Jewish Burial (B³ 19:38-42)

38 After these things, Joseph of Arimathea, a disciple of Jesus, though a secret one for fear of the Jews, asked Pilate to let him take away the body of Jesus. And Pilate permitted it. So he came and took away his body. 39 Nicodemus, who had first come to him at night, also came, bringing a mixture of myrrh and aloes weighing about a hundred pounds. 40 They then took the body of Jesus and bound it in burial cloths with the spices, according to the burial custom of the Jews. 41 Now in the place where he was crucified there was a garden, and in the garden a new tomb in which no one had yet been laid. 42 There, then, because of the preparation day of the Jews, for the tomb was near, they laid Jesus.

Joseph and Nicodemus take his body for burial (19:38-40)

Concluding a B-A-B intercalation with the two preceding scenes, the taking by Joseph and Nicodemus of the body of Jesus for burial (19:38-42) contrasts with the invitation to look upon the blood and water flowing from the side of the

---

[83] I. de la Potterie, "'Volgeranno lo sguardo a colui che hanno trafitto.' Sangue di cristo e oblatività," *Civiltà Cattolica* 137 (1986) 113, excludes the Jews and the soldiers, despite their presence and responsibility for the piercing of Jesus, from those who will look upon him whom they have pierced. See also Brown, *Death*, 1187-88.

[84] B. H. Grigsby, "Washing in the Pool of Siloam—A Thematic Anticipation of the Johannine Cross," *NovT* 27 (1985) 227-35.

pierced Jesus (19:31-37). It also develops Jesus' taking of vinegar, dying and completing scripture (19:28-30).

In the previous A scene the Jews asked (ἠρώτησαν) Pilate that the legs of those crucified be broken and their bodies be taken away (19:31). Their request that the bodies be taken away (ἀρθῶσιν) continues their disowning of the Jesus they wanted Pilate to expel from their community, as they cried out, "Away with him (Ἆρον), away with him (ἆρον)! Crucify him!" (19:15). They are concerned for the preparation day not for a proper burial of Jesus, whom they treat impersonally as one of those crucified. In contrast, Joseph, a Jew of Arimathea in Judea, asked (ἠρώτησεν) Pilate to let him take away (ἄρῃ) the body of Jesus.[85] In contrast to the tacit permission he gave the Jews (19:31-32), Pilate expressly "permitted" Joseph, so that he came and personally took away (ἦρεν) Jesus' body (19:38). Like the Jews, Joseph, being from Arimathea, was a Judean Jew, not one of the belittled Galilean followers of Jesus (7:52; see also 7:41-42). But in contrast to the Jews Joseph was a disciple of Jesus, though a secret one for fear of the Jews (19:38). Despite his fear that the Jews would expel him from the synagogue (7:13; 9:22; 12:42) as they had excommunicated Jesus, he now boldly and publicly takes charge of Jesus' body, exhibiting the personal concern the Jews refuse.[86]

In further contrast to the Jews, Nicodemus, himself a Pharisee and leader of the Jews (3:1) who had first come to Jesus at night—in the darkness of unbelief, now joins Joseph (19:39).[87] When Nicodemus came to Jesus at night, Jesus invited him to see and enter the kingdom of God by being born again from above by the water and Spirit (3:2-5) now provided by the death of Jesus (19:34). Although Nicodemus did not then accept the testimony of Jesus and believe (3:11-12), he later spoke on behalf of Jesus to the Pharisees who wanted to arrest and kill Jesus, "Our law surely does not condemn a person unless it first hears from him and finds out what he does?" (7:51). But they disparaged the Galilean origin of Jesus (7:52). Nicodemus continues his favorable stance

---

[85] For possible locations, all within Judea, of Arimathea, which Luke 23:51 refers to as a "city of the Jews," see Brown, *John*, 938.

[86] Brown, *Death*, 1230-32.

[87] On the role of Nicodemus in John, see Culpepper, *Anatomy*, 134-36; O'Day, *Word Disclosed*, 16-28; Moloney, *Belief*, 106-21; J. N. Suggit, "Nicodemus—The True Jew," *Neot* 14 (1981) 90-110; J.-M. Auwers, "La nuit de Nicodème (Jean 3,2; 19,39) ou l'ombre du langage," *RB* 97 (1990) 481-503; M. Goulder, "Nicodemus," *SJT* 44 (1991) 153-68; M. M. Pazdan, "Nicodemus and the Samaritan Woman: Contrasting Models of Discipleship," *BTB* 17 (1987) 145-48; J. M. Bassler, "Mixed Signals: Nicodemus in the Fourth Gospel," *JBL* 108 (1989) 635-46; D. D. Sylva, "Nicodemus and his Spices (John 19.39)," *NTS* 34 (1988) 148-51; Brown, *Death*, 1258-68.

toward Jesus as he now comes, bringing a mixture of myrrh and aloes weighing about a hundred pounds (19:39). By bringing such a large amount of burial spices, Nicodemus, in contrast to the first A scene (19:12-22), seems to recognize the Jewish kingship of Jesus that Pilate insists upon but that the Jews reject.[88]

In the first B scene the Roman soldiers who crucified Jesus took (ἔλαβον) his clothing in fulfillment of God's plan recorded in scripture (19:23-24). In the second B scene Jesus took (ἔλαβεν) the vinegar offered him and died to complete the scripture and accomplish all the revelatory work the Father gave him (19:28-30). As the climax to this theme of "taking" to further God's plan, Joseph and Nicodemus took (ἔλαβον) the body of Jesus and bound it in accord with the Jewish burial custom (19:40). In "taking" Jesus for a proper Jewish burial, they advance God's plan in two ways: They reverse the Jews' taking (παρέλαβον) of Jesus to crucify and thus exclude him as the King of the Jews from the Jewish people (19:12-22). And they establish the definitiveness of Jesus' death as a prelude to his resurrection, an essential ingredient for the complete and authentic faith of the community formed when the beloved disciple took (ἔλαβεν) the mother of Jesus to his own (19:27). Thus, a "taking" that advances the divine plan is involved in the crucifixion (19:23-24), the death (19:28-30), and now the burial of Jesus (19:40).

That they bound (ἔδησαν) Jesus in burial cloths, as the dead man Lazarus had been bound (δεδεμένος) hand and foot with burial bands and his face bound around (περιεδέδετο) with a cloth (11:44), indicates that they did not expect the imminent resurrection of Jesus. Although Nicodemus brought a hundred pounds of myrrh and aloes for a royal burial, he did not understand that Jesus' kingship is not of this world (18:36).[89] Mary had anointed the feet of Jesus with a pound of costly perfume but wiped it off with her hair (12:3). As a result, the house was filled with the fragrance of the perfume (12:3) in contrast to the stench of Lazarus's death (11:39). She thus performed a prophetic gesture anticipating the resurrection that will follow the burial of Jesus (12:7).[90] But Joseph and Nicodemus merely bind Jesus' dead body in

[88] When King Asa was buried, they laid him on a bier filled with spices and various kinds of aromatics mixed into an ointment (2 Chr 16:14). See also Morris, *John*, 825; F. F. Bruce, *The Gospel of John* (Grand Rapids: Eerdmans, 1983) 379; Brown, *John*, 960; idem, *Death*, 1260-62; Senior, *John*, 133.

[89] Sylva, "Nicodemus," 148-51.

[90] C. H. Giblin, "Mary's Anointing for Jesus' Burial-Resurrection (John 12,1-8)," *Bib* 73 (1992) 560-64. See also N. Calduch Benages, "La fragancia del perfume en Jn 12,3," *EstBib* 48 (1990) 243 65.

burial cloths with spices without any anticipation of his approaching resurrection.[91]

They place Jesus in a new tomb in the garden (19:41-42)

Joseph and Nicodemus provided Jesus with a proper Jewish burial so that he remained a member of the Jewish community despite his ostracizing crucifixion (19:40). Similarly, by burying Jesus in a garden they preserve his relationship with his disciples despite their abandonment of him as a group (16:32). The mention of the garden (κῆπος) where Jesus was crucified and in which there was a new tomb (19:41) forms a literary inclusion with the garden (κῆπος) mentioned at the beginning of the passion narrative (18:1). As the place where Jesus habitually met with his disciples (18:2), the garden symbolizes his close relation with them—the close relation of the good shepherd-king to his sheep (10:1-5).[92] As they laid down (ἔθηκαν) the dead Jesus in the tomb in which no one had yet been laid (τεθειμένος) (19:41-42), Joseph and Nicodemus ironically contribute to the significance of Jesus' death as the good shepherd who lays down (τίθησιν) his life to win eternal life for his sheep/disciples (10:10-18, 27-28).

The contrast between the burials of Lazarus and Jesus continues. Lazarus was laid in an ordinary tomb (μνημείῳ) in a cave (11:17, 31, 38; 12:17), whereas they laid Jesus in a new tomb (μνημεῖον καινὸν) in which, with a double negative to emphasize the uniqueness, "no one had never" (οὐδέπω οὐδεὶς) been laid (19:41).[93] Lazarus was merely resuscitated from death, so that he would die again (12:10). But Jesus will be definitively raised from the dead, indicating the final triumph of life over death and providing eternal life for those who believe (11:25-26). The newness and uniqueness involved in the burial of Jesus appropriately hints at the newness and uniqueness of the one person Jesus being raised before the expected general resurrection from the dead (5:28-29; 11:23-24).

In the preceding A scene the Jews, since it was preparation day (παρα-

---

[91] Duke, *Irony,* 110: "Two men who had never dared to profess public allegiance to Jesus while he lived now seek to honor him in his death. . . The image evoked is of two remorseful half-disciples sadly piling a mountain of embalming materials onto a body they obviously think is going nowhere."

[92] Since some of the kings of Judah were buried in gardens (2 Kgs 21:18, 26), the garden of Jesus' burial may contribute to the theme of his kingship. See Brown, *John,* 960; idem, *Death,* 1268-70.

[93] Morris, *John,* 826.

σκευή), wanted the bodies of those crucified taken away, as part of their distancing of Jesus from the Jewish community (19:31). Now, by way of ironic contrast, because of the observance of that same preparation day (παρα- σκευὴν) of the Jews, Joseph and Nicodemus establish the nearness of Jesus to the Jewish people even though he has been taken away (19:38) and buried, as they laid him in the new tomb that was nearby (19:42). To the dismay of the chief priests of the Jews in the first A scene (19:21), many of the Jews read the title proclaiming the kingship of Jesus, for the place where he was crucified (ὅπου ἐσταυρώθη) was near (ὅτι ἐγγὺς ἦν) to the city of Jerusalem (19:20). In contrast, there is now no Jewish objection as Joseph and Nicodemus, themselves Jews, laid Jesus in the tomb in the garden where he was crucified (ὅπου ἐσταυρώθη), for it was near (ὅτι ἐγγὺς ἦν) (19:42).

That the tomb of Jesus was new, that no one had ever been laid in it, and that it was near (19:41-42) creates a suspenseful aura of anticipation for the resurrection of Jesus. On the deeper, ironic level the preparation day of the Jews has become the preparation day for the glorious resurrection of the King of the Jews, a resurrection that the audience expects within three days (2:19-22).

Summary

John 19:12-42 functions as yet another alternation of contrasting scenes that propel the audience through a vibrant progression of narrative intercalations. The A scenes advance the theme of invitations to see and accept that lead the audience to an authentic and profound faith in Jesus: When Pilate mockingly invites the Jews to see and accept Jesus as the Passover Lamb of God who is the King of the Jews, the Jews, instead of believing in Jesus, vehemently cry out for his removal and crucifixion (A¹ 19:12-22). After the crucified Jesus invites his mother and the beloved disciple to see and accept one another as mother and son, the beloved disciple takes the mother of Jesus to his own, establishing the familial community of complete and authentic believers (A² 19:25-27). The narrator invites the readers to join him in looking upon the pierced Jesus as the Passover Lamb of God and suffering just one, so that they may deepen their faith in the Jesus whose death produces the Life-giving blood and water of the Spirit (A³ 19:31-37).

In continuing contrast to the theme of the A scenes, the B scenes present the theme of various "takings" that advance the divine plan with regard to Jesus' death and resurrection: By taking the clothing of the crucified Jesus but not dividing his seamless tunic, the gentile soldiers fulfill God's plan as recorded in the Jewish scriptures, further illustrating the Life-giving and unifying effects of the death of Jesus as the suffering just one, the good shepherd-king, and the unique high priest (B¹ 19:23-24). Jesus himself takes the bitter vinegar of death to accomplish completely the scripture and all the revelatory work God has given him, handing down the holy Spirit as he dies (B² 19:28-30). By taking the body of Jesus for a royal Jewish burial, Joseph of Arimathea and Nicodemus advance God's plan by reversing the Jews' taking of Jesus to crucify and remove him from the Jewish people, and by establishing the definitiveness of Jesus' death as a prelude to the resurrection that will follow his unique burial in a nearby new tomb in the garden (B³ 19:38-42).

For the implied reader/audience this ongoing interchange of contrasting scenes has the following consequences:

1) The Jews' rejection of Pilate's mock invitation to see and accept Jesus in the first A scene (19:12-22) induces the reader to supply the faith both the Jews and Gentiles lack, by seeing and believing in the Jesus whose crucifixion is his royal enthronement as the good shepherd-king who lays down his own life to provide eternal life for all who believe.

2) In contrast to the Jews' taking of Jesus to crucify him as their king, the gentile soldiers' taking of the clothes and their preserving of the seamless tunic of Jesus in the first B scene (19:23-24) invites the audience to believe in the Jesus who dies as the suffering just one, the good shepherd-king, and the unique high priest to unify all who believe with the eternal life his death provides.

3) In contrast to the Roman soldiers' taking of the clothes of the crucified Jesus, the beloved disciple's seeing and taking of the mother of Jesus to form the familial community of believers in the second A scene (19:25-27) advances the theme of seeing and accepting. It challenges the reader to imitate the response of the beloved disciple to the death of Jesus as an act of the greatest love by extending to other believers the same depth and intensity of love Jesus demonstrated for the believing community by laying down his life for them (13:34-35; 15:12-17).

4) In contrast to the beloved disciple's seeing and taking of his mother, Jesus' taking of the vinegar to die and hand over the Spirit in complete accomplishment of God's plan in the second B scene (19:28-30) advances the theme of "taking" to further God's plan. It assures the audience of the divine empowerment and guidance needed to live the life of love for one another in the community of believers, who now may wor-

ship God in Spirit and truth (4:23-24) and quench their thirst for eternal life (4:14; 7:37-38).

5) In contrast to Jesus' taking of the vinegar to satisfy his thirst by dying, but advancing the theme of seeing and accepting, the piercing of the side of the dead Jesus provides the thirst-quenching and cleansing blood and water in the third A scene (19:31-37). The narrator summons the reader to an ever more profound faith by looking upon the Life-giving blood and water that flow together from the pierced side of Jesus, so that believers may be born again from above by the cleansing water of the Spirit (3:3, 5) in baptism and quench their thirst for eternal life by drinking the blood of Jesus in the eucharist (6:53-54). The blood and water flowing from the death of Jesus empowers believers to love one another as Jesus loved them, so that they can be an abundant source for others of the eternal life they have received and possess within themselves (4:14; 7:37-39) as a consequence of the loving death of Jesus.

6) In contrast to the Jews' request that the bodies of those crucified be taken away, the taking away of the body of Jesus by Joseph of Arimathea and Nicodemus for a royal Jewish burial in the third B scene (19:38-42) advances the theme of "taking" to further God's plan. It prompts the audience to complete their inadequate faith by believing in the Jesus whose unique burial not only assured his association with the Jewish people who disowned him and with his disciples who scattered, but pointed to his resurrection as the final triumph over death.

CHAPTER 5

The Disciples See and Believe in the Risen Jesus (20:1-31)

Mary Magdalene Announces That Jesus Was Taken from the Tomb (A¹ 20:1-2)

1 On the first day of the week Mary Magdalene came to the tomb early while it was still dark, and saw the stone taken away from the tomb. 2 So she ran and came to Simon Peter and to the other disciple whom Jesus loved and said to them, "They have taken the Lord from the tomb, and we do not know where they have laid him."

Mary Magdalene sees the stone taken away from the tomb (20:1)

Jesus died and was buried on the day of preparation for the "great day" of that sabbath that was also the day of Passover (19:14, 31, 42). That "great day" has passed; it is now "the first day" of a new week (20:1), a time appropriate for the resurrection of Jesus from the new tomb in which he was buried two days earlier (19:41). Jesus had promised the Jews that "within three days" of their destruction of the "temple" that is his body he would raise it up (2:19-21).

Mary Magdalene, who had stood by the cross of Jesus together with his mother, his mother's sister, and Mary the wife of Clopas (19:25), now comes to the tomb of Jesus (20:1). As a woman follower from Magdala in Galilee, her presence at the tomb contrasts yet complements that of the two Judean men who laid Jesus in the tomb—Joseph, a secret disciple from Arimathea, and Nicodemus, a Pharisee and leader of the Jews (3:1; 19:38-42). Nicodemus had first come to Jesus at night (3:2; 19:39), symbolic of the darkness of his unbelief. Mary Magdalene similarly comes "while it was still dark," but it is "early" in the dawning day that follows the "night" that characterizes the unbelief not only of Nicodemus but of the betrayer Judas and those who led Jesus to death (13:30; 18:3).[1] Darkness (σκοτία) had already arrived before Jesus came to his disciples, revealing his divine power to walk on the sea prior to their eventual confession of faith (6:17-19, 69).[2] While characterizing the unbelief of Mary, that it was still dark (σκοτίας) and early when she saw the stone taken away from the tomb anticipates the later revelation of the resurrection of Jesus, the light that overcomes the darkness of unbelief (1:5, 9; 3:19-21; 8:12; 9:5; 12:35, 46).

That the stone was taken away from the tomb continues the comparison and contrast between Jesus and Lazarus. Before he called Lazarus, who had been dead four days, back to life from his tomb in a cave, Jesus commanded, "Take away ("Αρατε) the stone" (11:39). They then took away (ἦραν) the stone (11:41). Now the stone has been taken away (ἠρμένον) from the new tomb of Jesus in the garden, although he has been dead for only three days (20:1).

Mary supposes the Lord has been taken away from the tomb (20:2)

Upon noticing the stone removed from the tomb, Mary Magdalene runs to Simon Peter and to the other disciple whom Jesus loved (20:2). Simon Peter last appeared in the narrative when he denied for the third time his discipleship and close association with Jesus (18:25-27). The disciple whom Jesus loved stood together with Mary and the other women at the cross (19:25-27), witnessing the death of Jesus (19:35).

Because the stone has been taken away, Mary concludes not that Jesus has risen from the dead but that his body has been stolen, as she announces to Peter and the beloved disciple, "They have taken the Lord from the tomb" (20:2). She evidently thinks that the Jews, who wanted the bodies of those crucified taken away (ἀρθῶσιν) (19:31), have now taken away (ἦραν) the body of Jesus from the tomb to distance him from the Jewish community. Joseph had taken away (ἦρεν) the body of Jesus (19:38), but with the help of Nicodemus gave him a royal Jewish burial in a nearby tomb in the garden where he was crucified (19:39-42).

Mary speaks not only for herself but for the group, as she continues, "And we do not know where they have laid him" (20:2). Instead of believing that

[1] See chapter 2 on 18:3.
[2] Heil, *Jesus Walking on the Sea,* 146, 168-69.

Jesus has risen from the dead, Mary thinks he is still buried, but in another place. Just as Joseph and Nicodemus laid (ἔθηκαν) Jesus in the new tomb (19:42), she surmises that those who took away Jesus have laid (ἔθηκαν) him somewhere else, but she and her group do not know where.

Peter and the Beloved Disciple Witness the Burial Cloths in the Tomb of Jesus (B¹ 20:3-10)

> 3 Then Peter and the other disciple went out and were coming to the tomb. 4 The two were running together, but the other disciple ran ahead faster than Peter and came to the tomb first. 5 And bending down he saw the burial cloths lying there, but he did not go in.
>
> 6 Then Simon Peter, following him, also came and entered into the tomb, and observed the burial cloths lying there, 7 and the cloth that had been on his head, not lying with the burial cloths but rolled up apart in one place.
>
> 8 Then the other disciple, who came first to the tomb, also went in, and he saw and believed. 9 For they did not yet understand the scripture that he must rise from the dead. 10 Then the disciples went back again to their homes.

The beloved disciple sees the burial cloths in the tomb (20:3-5)

Prompted by Mary Magdalene's announcement that Jesus has been removed from the tomb (20:2), Peter and the beloved disciple went out and were coming to the tomb (20:3). As Mary had "come to the tomb" (20:1), so now Peter and the other disciple "were coming to the tomb." But in contrast to Mary, who ran alone in haste away from the tomb, Peter and the other disciple now run together in haste back toward the tomb (20:4). The narrative focus rapidly returns to the mystery of the opened tomb of Jesus.

That the beloved disciple ran ahead faster than Peter and reached the tomb first (20:4) accords with his superiority as the ideal disciple. As the disciple who reclined in intimate association with Jesus when he predicted his betrayal by one of the disciples, he was closer to Jesus than Peter and the other disciples (13:21-25). Whereas Peter thrice denied his discipleship and association with Jesus (18:25-27), the beloved disciple stood beside the crucified Jesus and then took the mother of Jesus to his own to form the familial community of authentic and complete faith (19:26-27).

Mary merely sees (βλέπει) the stone taken away from the tomb before she quickly runs away from it, assuming the body of Jesus has been stolen (20:1-2). In contrast, the beloved disciple, after making the effort to bend down and look into the tomb, sees (βλέπει) the burial cloths (ὀθόνια) lying there—the same burial cloths (ὀθονίοις) with which Joseph of Arimathea and Nicodemus had bound Jesus when they buried him (19:40). Instead of rashly running away from the tomb like Mary, the beloved disciple remains, although he does not yet enter the tomb (20:5).

Peter enters the tomb and sees the burial cloths (20:6-7)

In contrast to Mary who ran away from the tomb without entering it (20:1-2), Simon Peter comes and enters the tomb of Jesus (20:6). When Jesus was arrested, Simon Peter and "another disciple" followed (ἠκολούθει) him (18:15). Although the other disciple, who was known to the high priest, went into the courtyard of the high priest with Jesus, Peter remained outside. After the other disciple brought him in, Peter denied his discipleship and association with Jesus (18:15-18, 25-27). Again following (ἀκολουθῶν) the lead of another disciple, Peter this time enters the tomb on his own before the other disciple to witness the evidence that can bring him to complete and authentic faith (20:6). By following the ideal, beloved disciple to the opened tomb that indicates Jesus' triumph over death, Peter is on his way to the faith that will enable him to fulfill his promise to follow (ἀκολουθείτω) Jesus as a true disciple (12:25-26) by laying down his life for him, after Jesus informed him, "Where I am going, you cannot follow (ἀκολουθῆσαι) me now, though you will follow (ἀκολουθῆσαι) me later" (13:36-37).

Inside the tomb Peter observes (θεωρεῖ) not only the burial cloths lying there (20:6), which the beloved disciple sees (βλέπει) while still outside the tomb (20:5), but also "the cloth that had been on his head, not lying with the burial cloths but rolled up apart in one place" (20:7). When Lazarus came forth from the tomb, his hands and feet were still bound with burial bands and his face was still bound around with a cloth (σουδαρίῳ), so that others had to unbind and release him (11:44). Lazarus was wondrously resuscitated from the dead but still "bound" by the power of death—he would die again (12:10). In contrast Jesus has left behind both the burial cloths in which Joseph and Nicodemus "bound" him (19:40) to the power of death and the cloth (σουδάριον) that had been on his head. Jesus has definitively triumphed over the bonds of death, never to die again.[3]

---

[3] Mahoney, *Two Disciples,* 257-58; Byrne, "The Faith of the Beloved Disciple," 83-97; J.

The elaborately detailed emphasis on the distinction and unity of the cloth that had been on the head of Jesus not only reinforces the unlikeliness that the body of Jesus has been stolen and reburied, as Mary thinks (20:2), but also symbolically concurs with the unifying function of Jesus' death. The distinction and unity of the head cloth (σουδάριον) is specifically stressed. It was lying "not with" (οὐ μετὰ) the other burial cloths (ὀθονίων) but was carefully rolled up "apart" (χωρὶς) in one place (20:7). When the soldiers crucified Jesus, they similarly kept distinct his seamless tunic that was woven from above into one whole piece of cloth. Although they divided among themselves the rest of his clothing, they preserved the unity of his seamless tunic (19:23-24), symbolically pointing to the communal unity that Jesus' death effects.[4] That the head cloth was rolled up "in one place" (εἰς ἕνα τόπον) corresponds with the purpose of Jesus' death not just to preserve the unity of the Jewish nation, but that the scattered children of God might be gathered "into one" (εἰς ἕν) (11:52), unifying all into a believing community, so that there will be one flock and one shepherd (10:15-16). Both the distinctive seamless tunic and burial head cloth, then, point to the communal unity the death and resurrection of Jesus make possible for believing readers.

The beloved disciple enters, sees, and believes (20:8-10)

Like Peter the other disciple, who came to the tomb first, enters and sees the burial cloths left behind by the risen Jesus. In accord with his superiority as the ideal, beloved disciple, reinforced by the repetition that he came to the tomb "first" (20:4, 8), the other disciple who first saw the burial cloths is the first to believe in the resurrection of Jesus, as he not only saw what Peter observed but believed (20:8). Seeing has now progressed to the insight of believing: Mary sees (βλέπει, present tense) the stone taken away from the tomb (20:1), the beloved disciple sees (βλέπει, present tense) the burial cloths from outside the tomb (20:5), Peter observes (θεωρεῖ, present tense) both the burial cloths and the head cloth inside the tomb (20:6-7), and now the beloved disciple inside the tomb not only saw (εἶδεν, aorist tense) but believed.)[5]

Winandy, "Les vestiges laissés dans le tombeau et la foi du disciple (Jn 20, 1-9)," NRT 110 (1988) 212-19; R. Robert, "Du suaire de Lazare à celui de Jésus. Jean XI,44 et XX,7," RevThom 88 (1988) 410-20; idem, "Le 'suaire' johannique: Réponse a quelques questions," RevThom 89 (1989) 599-608; L. García García, "'Lienzos', no 'vendas', en la sepultura de Jesús," Burgense 32 (1991) 557-67.

4 See chapter 4 on 19:23-24.

5 On the significance of this progression of different verb forms and tenses for the seeing that

That the beloved disciple saw and believed reinforces and advances the appeal for the audience to deepen their faith. The narrator, functioning as the beloved disciple, saw and testified to the Life-giving blood and water flowing from the pierced side of the dead Jesus, so that the readers also may believe (19:35). Now the beloved disciple inside the tomb saw the burial cloths indicating the resurrection of Jesus and believed (20:8). Through the seeing not only of the narrator, but also the progression from the seeing of Mary, Peter, and the beloved disciple, the audience may "see" and believe not only that eternal life comes from the death of Jesus but that Jesus has triumphantly risen from the dead.

Although the beloved disciple has seen and believed, Mary, Peter, and the other disciples have not yet believed. That the beloved disciple believed in the resurrection of Jesus before "they," that is, Peter, Mary, and those for whom she speaks (20:2), understood the scripture that he must rise from the dead (20:9), implies that he, as the ideal, beloved disciple, already understood the scriptural necessity for the resurrection of Jesus.[6] The way that he comes to believe assures the audience that they too can believe through the eye-witness testimony of those who have seen and believed (19:35; 20:8), along with the understanding of the scripture, without having seen the risen Lord.[7] That the disciples, Peter and the beloved disciple, who both "went out" to the tomb (20:3), "went back" again to their homes (20:10) heightens the suspense of

---

leads to belief, C. Traets, *Voir Jésus et le Père en lui selon l'évangile de saint Jean* (AnGreg 159; Rome: Gregorian University, 1967) 41-42, remarks: "Dans ces passages, nous nous trouvons donc en présence de plusieurs verbes (βλέπειν, θεωρεῖν, ὁρᾶν) qui expriment une pénétration théologique différente. La force de cette pénétration n'est pas propre à chacun des verbes comme tel, mais elle se déduit principalement du contexte. Secondairement elle est soulignée par l'aspect propre au temps verbal. Le caractère de cette pénétration provient de la spécification profane des verbes—dans notre cas: apercevoir, voir (βλέπειν, ὁρᾶν) d'une part, observer (θεωρεῖν) de l'autre. Cette pénétration se transpose au niveau théologique." See also p. 17; Mahoney, *Two Disciples*, 261-62.

[6] de la Potterie, *Hour*, 166-68, argues that the beloved disciple only began to believe here with an incipient and imperfect faith, not full Easter faith. He, along with many others, understands the indefinite subject of "they did not yet understand" (20:9) to include the beloved disciple. This is unlikely, since the beloved disciple, as the ideal, model disciple, never exhibits any deficiency in the narrative. In our interpretation the indefinite subject of "they did not yet understand" refers to those who have not yet believed—Peter, Mary Magdalene, and those for whom she speaks, when she said, "we don't know where they laid him" (20:2). The explicit mention of a definite subject, "the disciples," to refer to Peter and the beloved disciple (20:10) after the indefinite subject (20:9) that excludes the beloved disciple facilitates our interpretation.

[7] Lindars, *John*, 602.

how and whether Peter, who has seen the same burial cloths as the beloved disciple (20:5-7), will come to believe.

This first B scene (20:3-10), then, commences not only a thematic contrast but also a thematic development with the first A scene (20:1-2): That the two individuals, Peter and the beloved disciple, come and enter the tomb contrasts with the one individual, Mary Magdalene, running away from the tomb without entering it. But that both the beloved disciple and Peter observe the burial cloths inside the tomb advances Mary's seeing only the stone removed from the tomb.

Mary Magdalene Announces Her Vision of the Risen Lord (A² 20:11-18)

11 But Mary was standing before the tomb outside weeping. And as she wept, she bent down into the tomb 12 and observed two angels in white sitting there, one at the head and one at the feet, where the body of Jesus had been lying. 13 And they said to her, "Woman, why are you weeping?" She said to them, "They have taken away my Lord, and I do not know where they have laid him."

14 Having said this, she turned around and observed Jesus standing there, but she did not know that it was Jesus. 15 Jesus said to her, "Woman, why are you weeping? Whom do you seek?" Supposing that he was the gardener, she said to him, "Sir, if you have carried him away, tell me where you have laid him, and I will take him away."

16 Jesus said to her, "Mary!" Turning she said to him in Hebrew, "Rabbouni!," which means "Teacher." 17 Jesus said to her, "Do not hold on to me, for I have not yet ascended to the Father. But go to my brothers and tell them, 'I am ascending to my Father and your Father, my God and your God.'" 18 Mary Magdalene came and announced to the disciples, "I have seen the Lord!," and that he told her these things.

Mary encounters two angels at the tomb of Jesus (20:11-13)

Creating an A-B-A sandwich with the two preceding scenes, Mary Magdalene's announcement of her vision of the risen Lord (20:11-18) generates a double relationship with each of these two previous scenes: It not only contrasts with but also develops the disciples' witness of the burial cloths in the tomb of Jesus in the first B scene (20:3-10). And it not only advances but also contrasts with Mary's announcement that Jesus was taken from the tomb in the first A scene (20:1-2).

The first B scene concluded as "the disciples," Simon Peter and the beloved disciple, left the tomb in which they had witnessed the burial cloths of Jesus and went back again to their homes (πρὸς αὐτοὺς) (20:10). "But" (δὲ), in contrast, Mary was standing before the tomb (πρὸς τῷ μνημείῳ) outside weeping (20:11). In the first A scene Mary had run away from the tomb (20:2), but now, in contrast, she has returned to the tomb. And whereas Mary, the sister of Lazarus, and the Jews who had come with her were "weeping" in mourning before Jesus called the dead Lazarus from the tomb (11:33), Mary Magdalene is now "weeping" not only in mourning but in consternation outside the tomb, because it no longer contains the body of Jesus.[8]

In the first A scene Mary came to the tomb (εἰς τὸ μνημεῖον) and saw (βλέπει) the stone taken away from the tomb (20:1). In development, as she wept, she now bent down into the tomb (εἰς τὸ μνημεῖον) and observed (θεωρεῖ) two angels in white sitting there, one at the head and one at the feet, where the body of Jesus had been lying (20:11-12). Her seeing of the stone has advanced to her observing of the angels, a progression in the evidence for the resurrection of Jesus.

In the first B scene the beloved disciple, who came to the tomb (εἰς τὸ μνημεῖον) first, bent down (παρακύψας) and saw (βλέπει) the burial cloths of Jesus lying (κείμενα) in the tomb (20:4-5). Then Peter, who entered into the tomb (εἰς τὸ μνημεῖον), observed (θεωρεῖ) both the burial cloths lying (κείμενα) there and the cloth that had been on his head (κεφαλῆς), not lying (κείμενον) with the other burial cloths but in a separate place (20:6-7). In development, Mary now bent down (παρέκυψεν) into the tomb (εἰς τὸ μνημεῖον) and observed (θεωρεῖ) two angels, one at the head (κεφαλῇ) and one at the feet, where the body of Jesus had been lying (ἔκειτο) (20:11-12). The burial cloths that had enveloped both the head and the rest of the body of Jesus (19:40), but now were separated and left lying in the tomb (20:5-7), suggested Jesus' resurrection. Now the two angels, dressed in the white appropriate to their heavenly status and the realm of life rather than death, sit where the head and feet encompassing Jesus' entire body had been lying.[9] Their presence points more explicitly to Jesus' resurrection. Whereas the feet, hands, and face of Lazarus had been bound in burial cloths (11:44), indicating that his entire body was still bound to the power of death, the burial cloths and the two angels

---

[8] O'Day, *Word Disclosed,* 100-101

[9] Brown, *John,* 989: "In general, heavenly visitors are dressed in something white or bright, frequently in linen." See Ezek 9:2; Dan 10:5; 2 Macc 3:26; Matt 28:3; Mark 16:5; Luke 24:4, 23; Acts 1:10.

that now sit where the head and feet that define Jesus' entire body had been signify his complete victory over the power of death.[10]

The question the two angels ask Mary, "Woman, why are you weeping?" (20:13), implies that there is no need for Mary to weep.[11] Although their presence as heavenly visitors indicates not only that the body of Jesus has not been stolen and reburied, as Mary supposes (20:2), but that Jesus has been raised from the dead, Mary remains amazingly oblivious to the significance of the two angels clad in white. She persists in presuming that the body of Jesus has been stolen and reburied. In the first A scene she spoke for the wider group, as she reported that they have taken "the Lord" from the tomb, and "we do not know" where they have laid him (20:2). In development, she now speaks for herself and expresses her personal relationship to Jesus, as she reports that they have taken away "my Lord" and "I do not know" where they have laid him (20:13). Mary continues her agitated concern for the dead body of "her Lord," ignoring the hints of his resurrection.

Mary encounters but does not recognize Jesus (20:14-15)

Once Mary turns away, literally "backwards" (εἰς τὰ ὀπίσω), from the tomb as the realm of the dead, she observes Jesus standing there, although she does not know that it is Jesus (20:14). Her vision of the evidence of the resurrection has progressed from seeing (βλέπει) the stone removed from the tomb (20:1), to observing (θεωρεῖ) the two angels in the tomb (20:12), and now to observing (θεωρεῖ) the risen Jesus himself, in contrast to Peter in the previous B scene, who observes (θεωρεῖ) only the burial cloths and the head cloth (20:6-7). But despite her personal relation to Jesus as "my Lord" (20:13), Mary, who remains focused on the dead body of Jesus, fails to recognize the risen and living Lord.

Repeating the question of the two angels, implying that Mary need no longer weep, Jesus asks, "Woman, why are you weeping?" (20:15). But he then adds the penetrating question disclosing that he already knows why she is weeping, "Whom do you seek?" The first words Jesus spoke in the Gospel,

---

[10] P. Simenel, "Les 2 anges de Jean 20/11-12," *ETR* 67 (1992) 71-76, suggests that the two angels correspond to the cherubim positioned at the two ends of the mercy seat on the ark of the covenant (Exod 25:10, 17-22), so that the tomb that had contained Jesus' body now symbolizes the new ark of the covenant. In our opinion this is more imaginative than convincing, attributing to the tomb in itself more significance than it has in the narrative, which moves the focus away from the tomb and toward the risen Lord (20:12-14).

[11] Duke, *Irony,* 104.

"What do you seek?" (1:38), led various individuals to become his believing followers (1:38-51).[12] To those who arrested him Jesus twice asked, "Whom do you seek?," before he announced, "I am he," inviting them to believe in him as *the* divine revealer (18:4-8).[13] In now asking Mary, "Whom do you seek?," Jesus provides the question that can turn her focus from death to life and lead her to believe in him as the risen Lord.

The irony grows rich as Mary supposes that the Jesus she fails to recognize is the gardener (20:15) in the garden where Jesus had been buried (19:41). She unwittingly addresses as "Sir" (Κύριε) the Jesus she earlier referred to as "Lord" (κύριον) (20:2, 13). If the "gardener" has carried the corpse of Jesus away, and will tell her where he has laid it, Mary will personally retrieve it (20:15).[14] In declaring, "I will take him away" (ἀρῶ), Mary relates to Jesus in the same way as those whom she thinks have taken (ἦραν) the Lord from the tomb (20:2). Because she persists in "seeking" Jesus where he is not to be found—in the realm of the dead, Mary fails to recognize the Jesus who invites her to "seek" him as the risen and living Lord.[15]

Mary announces her vision of Jesus to the disciples (20:16-18)

In reply to Mary's request Jesus utters one powerful word, her name, "Mary!" (20:16). Although Mary earlier turned (ἐστράφη) away from the tomb, the realm of the dead, and observed the living Jesus, she did not recognize him (20:14). Now again turning (στραφεῖσα) upon hearing him pronounce her name, Mary recognizes Jesus, as she exclaims to him in the Hebrew/Aramaic language familiar to both of them, "Rabbouni!," which means "Teacher" (20:16). She hears the voice of Jesus, the good shepherd who has now laid down his life for his sheep, call her by name as one of the sheep whom he knows and who know him (10:3-4, 11, 14-15).[16] After Jesus asked his first followers, "What do you seek?," they addressed him as "Rabbi," which is trans-

---

[12] O'Day, *Word Disclosed*, 101

[13] See chapter 2.

[14] Duke, *Irony*, 104: "Now the irony of identity blossoms full. She weeps for a dead Jesus, and when the living Jesus stands before her asking, 'Why weep?' and inviting her to speak his name, she thinks he is the gardener. She then asks him the whereabouts of his own corpse!"

[15] O'Day, *Word Disclosed*, 101: "She is in conversation with the one whom she seeks, with the one for whom she weeps, but she does not see him. She does not see Jesus because she knows that 'they have taken him away.' She does not see Jesus because she does not really seek him. She seeks a missing corpse, not a risen Lord."

[16] Duke, *Irony*, 105; O'Day, *Word Disclosed*, 102.

lated "Teacher" (1:38), before they became his believing disciples.[17] Similarly, although Mary now recognizes Jesus, she relates to him at this point only as her Teacher. She is still on her way to full Easter faith in Jesus as the risen Lord.

The Jesus whom Mary refers to as her teacher now teaches her not to hold on to him but to allow him to complete his revelatory mission by returning to the God who sent him into the world: "Do not hold onto me, for I have not yet ascended (ἀναβέβηκα) to the Father" (20:17).[18] Jesus' ascension to the Father offers the opportunity for an authentic and perfect faith in him not just as the teacher but as the risen and ascended Lord. In his encounter with Nicodemus, who addressed Jesus as "Rabbi" and a "teacher come from God" (3:2), Jesus cryptically pointed to the ascension that would complete his "lifting up" or exaltation by crucifixion, the revelatory sign for all to believe and have eternal life in him: "No one has ascended (ἀναβέβηκεν) into heaven except the one who came down from heaven, the Son of Man. And just as Moses lifted up the serpent in the wilderness (Num 21:9), so it is necessary for the Son of Man to be lifted up, so that all who believe may have eternal life in him" (3:13-15). Corresponding to his revelation that he had come down from heaven (6:41-42), which caused the Jews and then the disciples to take offense and murmur about him (6:60-61), Jesus pointed to the opportunity they would have to believe when they see him as the Son of Man complete his revelatory mission by ascending (ἀναβαίνοντα) to where he was before (6:62), that is, going back to the Father who sent him from heaven (6:44).[19]

In the first A scene Mary ran and came to (πρὸς) Simon Peter and to (πρὸς) the other disciple whom Jesus loved and reported that the Lord had been taken from the tomb (20:2). In contrast, the risen Lord now directs Mary to go to (πρὸς) my brothers and tell them, "I am ascending to my Father and your Father, my God and your God" (20:17). And in contrast to the disciples who went back again to their homes, literally "to their own" (πρὸς αὐτούς), in the preceding B scene (20:10), Jesus is now ascending to (πρὸς) his Father who is also their Father, his God who is also their God, in order to prepare a heavenly place for them (14:2). He will come again and take them to himself (πρὸς ἐμαυτόν), so that where he is they also may be (14:3; 17:24).

[17] For additional references to Jesus as Teacher, see 3:2; 8:4; 11:28; 13:13-14.

[18] With regard to Jesus' request for Mary not to hold onto him, O'Day, *Word Disclosed*, 103, remarks: "Jesus is not rebuffing Mary with his words in verse 17, but is teaching her the first post-resurrection lesson: Jesus cannot and will not be held and controlled. Not even the 'pangs of death' can hold Jesus (cf. vs. 6-7; Acts 2:24)."

[19] Heil, *Jesus Walking on the Sea*, 166-67.

Earlier in the narrative the brothers (ἀδελφοὶ) of Jesus, although associated with his mother and his disciples (2:12), did not believe in Jesus (7:3, 5, 10). But now the term "brothers" refers to the disciples of Jesus. When the ideal, beloved disciple accepted the mother of Jesus as his own mother and took her to his own to form the familial community of believers (19:26-27), she became the mother of all disciples, who in turn became brothers and sisters with Jesus. Now Jesus and his disciples share not only the same mother but the same Father—"my Father and your Father, my God and your God" (20:17). That the disciples are now brothers of Jesus is confirmed as Mary, who was directed to tell "my brothers" (ἀδελφούς μου) of Jesus' ascension to the Father, made her announcement to "the disciples" (20:18).

Before Jesus washed his disciples' feet as a foreshadowing of his death that demonstrated his perfect love for them, he knew his hour had come to pass from this world to the Father (πρὸς τὸν πατέρα), that he had come from God and was going to God (πρὸς τὸν θεον) (13:1, 3). In his farewell discourse Jesus told his disciples that whoever believes in him will do even greater revelatory works than he does, for he goes to the Father (πρὸς τὸν πατέρα), so that whatever they ask in Jesus' name he will do, that the Father may be glorified in the Son (14:12-14). If the disciples love Jesus they will rejoice that he goes to the Father (πρὸς τὸν πατέρα), for the Father is greater than he, and his going to the Father will give them an opportunity to believe (14:28-29). It is better for the disciples that Jesus goes to the Father (πρὸς τὸν πατέρα) (16:10) who sent him (16:5; 7:33), so that Jesus with the Father can send the Paraclete, the holy Spirit, to teach them everything and remind them of everything that he told them (14:26; 16:7). That Jesus now ascends "to my Father" (πρὸς τὸν πατέρα) (20:17), then, will enable him to complete his revelatory mission of love for his disciples by returning to the Father who sent him, so that they may believe in him as the risen and ascended Lord who died for love of them. Jesus will prepare a heavenly home for the disciples, and intercede for them with divine assistance, especially by sending the holy Spirit to guide them in their revelatory mission.

The disciples, however, did not know what Jesus meant by saying that he was going to the Father (πρὸς τὸν πατέρα) (16:17). Although they have loved Jesus and have believed that he came from God (16:27, 30; 17:8, 25), their faith remains incomplete. Jesus not only came from God and entered the world, but he again leaves the world and goes to the Father (πρὸς τὸν πατέρα) (16:28). Indeed, while the disciples thought they believed, they have fulfilled Jesus' prediction that they would abandon him, each scattering to his own (16:31-32).

That is their situation now, as the disciples have gone back again to their homes (20:10). But that Jesus now sends Mary to the disciples as his brothers will enable them to complete their faith by believing not only that Jesus came from the Father, but that he, as the risen Lord, now returns, ascending "to my Father" (20:17).

In his final prayer Jesus asked the Father to protect his disciples, who are still in the world, "so that they may be one as we are one" (17:11). He prayed not only for his present disciples but for all future believers/readers, "so that all may be one, as you, Father, are in me and I in you, that they also may be one in us, so that the world may believe that you sent me. The glory that you have given me I have given to them, so that they may be one as we are one—I in them and you in me, so that they may be completed into a unity, that the world may know that you sent me and have loved them as you loved me" (17:21-23). That Jesus is now ascending to the Father and leaving the disciples in the world, but declaring that "my Father is also your Father, and my God is also your God" (20:17), enables this profound unity for which he has prayed to become a reality.

In the first A scene Mary Magdalene came (ἔρχεται) and saw the stone taken away from the tomb, and then came (ἔρχεται) to Simon Peter and the beloved disciple and told them that the Lord had been taken from the tomb and laid elsewhere (20:1-2). In contrast, Mary Magdalene now came (ἔρχεται) and announced to the disciples, "I have seen the Lord," and the things that he told her (20:18).[20] Whereas Mary had related to "the Lord" (20:2) she thought was taken from the tomb but still dead as "her Lord," whom she wanted to take away (20:13, 15), she has now seen "the Lord," the risen and living Lord who will not allow her to prevent him from ascending to the Father (20:17-18).[21]

In the first A scene Mary saw (βλέπει) the stone taken away from the tomb (20:1), the first evidence of Jesus' resurrection. Then in the first B scene the beloved disciple from outside the tomb saw (βλέπει) the burial cloths in the tomb, and Peter inside the tomb observed (θεωρεῖ) both the burial cloths and the head cloth (20:5-7), a progression in the evidence of Jesus' resurrection.

---

[20] Note that the full name, "Mary Magdalene," forms a literary inclusion, introducing (20:1) and concluding (20:18) this first A-B-A intercalation in 20:1-18.

[21] With regard to Mary's progression here, de la Potterie, *Hour,* 174, remarks: "Notice the steps she has traced. First, seeing the empty tomb, she is concerned to find *"her* Lord" (20:13); she then sees Jesus himself and takes him for the gardener (20:14-15); then she recognizes him, but only as *her* Teacher (20:16); now, after our Lord's revealing words, she finally knows that he is *the* Lord."

Then in this third A scene Mary observed (θεωρεῖ) two angels in white sitting where the body of Jesus had been in the tomb (20:12), a further progression in the evidence of Jesus' resurrection. In development, Mary now announces that she has seen (ἑώρακα) the risen Lord himself (20:18), a climactic point in the seeing of evidence for the resurrection of Jesus.[22] In the previous B scene, however, the beloved disciple saw (εἶδεν) only the burial cloths and yet this individual disciple believed (20:8). In contrast, Mary has now seen, heard, and recognized the risen Lord himself. She reports both what she has seen and what she has heard—"that he told her these things" (20:18), so that through the witness of this individual the rest of the disciples and audience may come to full and authentic faith in the risen and ascended Lord.[23]

The Disciples See the Risen Lord and Receive the Spirit (B² 20:19-23)

19 When it was evening on that first day of the week, and the doors locked where the disciples were for fear of the Jews, Jesus came and stood in their midst and said to them, "Peace be with you!" 20 And saying this, he showed his hands and side to them. Then the disciples rejoiced, seeing the Lord. 21 Then Jesus said to them again, "Peace be with you. As the Father has sent me, so I send you." 22 And saying this, he breathed on them and said to them, "Receive the holy Spirit. 23 Whose sins you forgive are forgiven them, whose sins you retain are retained."

The risen Jesus shows himself to his disciples (20:19-20)

Forming a B-A-B intercalation with the two previous scenes, the disciples' vision of the risen Lord and reception of the Spirit (20:19-23) not only contrasts with but also develops Mary Magdalene's announcement of her vision of the risen Lord in the previous A scene (20:11-18). And it not only develops but also contrasts with the disciples' witness of the burial cloths in the tomb of Jesus in the first B scene (20:3-10).

It was "early" and still dark "on the first day of the week" when Mary Magdalene came to the tomb of Jesus in the first A scene (20:1). And she again

---

[22] Note also the progression from the present tenses, "sees, observes" (βλέπει, θεωρεῖ) to the perfect tense, "has seen" (ἑώρακα) for the vision of Jesus as the risen Lord. See also Traets, *Voir*, 41-42.

[23] On the roles that both seeing and hearing play in the genesis of genuine faith within John's Gospel, see C. R. Koester, "Hearing, Seeing, and Believing in the Gospel of John," *Bib* 70 (1989) 327-48.

stood before the tomb weeping outside in the second A scene (20:11). In contrast, it is now "evening on that first day of the week" and the group of disciples is inside, behind locked doors for fear of the Jews (20:19). But that the risen Jesus now comes and stands in the midst of the disciples and announces, "Peace be with you!" (20:19), develops Mary's announcement to the disciples of what she saw and heard from the risen Lord in the second A scene (20:18).

That the group of disciples is now behind locked doors for fear of the Jews (20:19) advances the situation of the first B scene, in which the disciples, Peter and the beloved disciple, went back again to their homes after witnessing the burial cloths in the tomb (20:5-7, 10). But in contrast to the disciples, who abandoned the evidence inside the tomb for the resurrection of Jesus and went back (ἀπῆλθον) again to their homes in the first B scene (20:10), the risen Jesus himself now came (ἦλθεν) and stood in the midst of the disciples (20:19).

In contrast to Mary, who, much like Joseph of Arimathea and Nicodemus, openly and without fear of the Jews (see 19:38-39) earnestly sought to find and take charge of the dead body of Jesus in the preceding A scene (20:13, 15), the disciples are enclosed within locked doors for fear of the Jews (20:19). As Joseph of Arimathea had been a secret, private disciple of Jesus for fear of the Jews—fear that they would expel him from the synagogue (19:38; cf. 7:13; 9:22; 12:42), so fear of the Jews, who had killed and then had presumably stolen the body of Jesus (20:2), has forced the disciples into a secret and private domain, behind locked doors. But the locked doors caused by fear of the Jews cannot prevent the risen Jesus from coming and standing in the midst of the frightened disciples. His powerful pronouncement, "Peace be with you!," as he shows them his hands and side that had been crucified and pierced (19:34), transforms their fear into joy, as "the disciples rejoiced, seeing the Lord" (20:20).

In advancement of the previous A scene not only has Mary seen (ἑώρακα) the Lord (20:18), but the disciples have now likewise seen (ἰδόντες) the Lord (20:20). And in advancement of the previous B scene not only has the beloved disciple seen (εἶδεν) and believed in the resurrection of Jesus (20:8-9) after observing only the burial cloths (20:4), but now the group of disciples has rejoiced in seeing the risen Lord himself. But in contrast to the previous B scene the disciples do not yet explicitly profess their faith in the risen Lord.

In his farewell discourse Jesus promised his disciples that after he had gone to prepare a place for them in his Father's house, he would come (ἔρχομαι) again and take them to himself so that where he is they also may be (14:2-3).

He will not leave them orphans, but come (ἔρχομαι) to them. While the world will see him no longer, the disciples will see him, "for I live and you will live. On that day (ἐν ἐκείνῃ τῇ ἡμέρᾳ) you will know that I am in my Father and you in me and I in you. Whoever has my commandments and keeps them is the one who loves me. And whoever loves me will be loved by my Father, and I will love him and manifest myself to him" (14:18-21; see also 14:28). What now happens on "that day" (τῇ ἡμέρᾳ ἐκείνῃ)—the first day of the week (20:19), not only fulfills in a preliminary way for these disciples what Jesus promised, but also anticipates the future fulfillment at the final coming of Jesus for all those readers who are and who will become believers (17:20).[24] After ascending to "my Father and your Father, my God and your God" (20:17), preparing the unity among the Father, himself, and his disciples that he promised (14:20), the living Jesus now came (ἦλθεν) and stood in the midst of the disciples. He manifested himself to them, as he showed his hands and side to them. And they rejoiced upon seeing the Lord (20:19-20).[25]

When Jesus told his disciples in the farewell discourse that in a little while they would no longer see him, but that in again a little while they would see him, they did not understand what this or his going to the Father meant (16:16-19). Jesus then promised, "You will weep and mourn, but the world will rejoice (χαρήσεται); you will grieve, but your grief will become joy" (16:20). Although they now have grief, Jesus will see them again, and their hearts will rejoice (χαρήσεται), and no one will take their joy away from them. On that day (ἐν ἐκείνῃ τῇ ἡμέρᾳ) they will not question Jesus about anything (16:22-23). When they see him again, they will understand what his going to the Father means. That the disciples rejoiced (ἐχάρησαν) when they saw the risen Lord on "that first day" of the week (20:19-20) begins to fulfill this promise and anticipates its complete fulfillment for the audience when Jesus comes again for the final time. Jesus wants his own unique joy that comes from the love he demonstrated by dying to be completed in those who believe and love one another as he loved them (15:9-13; 16:24; 17:13).

That Jesus' giving of peace as he greets the disciples, "Peace be with you," alleviates their fear of the Jews and brings them joy (20:19-20) reinforces the giving of his own unique peace in his farewell discourse to them and all future believers: "Peace I leave you, my peace I give you. Not as the world gives do I give to you" (14:27). As Jesus will not manifest himself to the world (14:22), the

[24] Note also the more figurative and spiritual way that those who keep his commandments by loving one another can experience the "manifestation" of Jesus.

[25] Segovia, *Farewell,* 100 n. 75.

world cannot give the unique peace that he gives—his unity with the Father that he shares with believers: "If anyone loves me, he will keep my word, and my Father will love him, and we will come to him and make our dwelling with him" (14:23). All that Jesus has revealed to the disciples in his farewell discourse is intended to give them the peace that comes from his unity with the Father who is always with him (16:32): "I have spoken these things to you so that you may have peace in me. In the world you have suffering, but take courage, I have conquered the world!" (16:33). The peace that Jesus gives his disciples encourages them and the audience to face any suffering their living in the world, now conquered by the triumphantly risen Jesus, may bring.[26]

When Jesus drove out all those conducting business in the temple in Jerusalem (2:13-16), he admonished them, "Do not make the house (οἶκον) of my Father a house (οἶκον) of business" (2:16). His disciples later remembered that it was written, "Zeal for your house (οἶκου) will consume me" (Ps 69:10 in 2:17), a prediction not only of Jesus' being consumed by death on the cross at the hands of the Jews,[27] but also of his ascension to the heavenly "house (οἰκίᾳ) of my Father" that has many rooms to prepare a place for his disciples (14:2-3). To the Jews' request, "What sign do you show (δεικνύεις) us that you do these things" (2:18), Jesus replied by cryptically pointing to his resurrection, "Destroy this temple and in three days I will raise it" (2:19), a reference to the new temple of his risen body (2:21). Now Jesus ironically answers the request of the Jews as he showed (ἔδειξεν) his disciples not a "sign" but the very hands and side of his risen body, the new temple itself (20:20).[28]

The risen Jesus bestows the Spirit on his disciples (20:21-23)

After reinforcing his greeting and gift of peace, solemnly repeating, "Peace be with you," the risen Jesus tells his disciples, "As the Father has sent me, so I send

[26] V. Hasler, "εἰρήνη," *EDNT* 1. 396: "Behind the farewell words in John 14:27; 16:33 stands the authority of the revealer who was sent to his own chosen ones who are in the world opposed to God. He leaves to them his own supra-worldly peace, which consists in the unity of the Son with the Father. The repeated greeting of the resurrected one in John 20:19, 21, 26 indicates that the disciples remain bound together in the midst of the anxiety of the world in the indestructible security of this divine relationship."

[27] Schuchard, *Scripture*, 31-32.

[28] J. McCaffrey, *The House with Many Rooms: The Temple Theme of Jn. 14,2-3* (AnBib 114; Rome: Biblical Institute, 1988) 243: "The future 'sign' of the crucified-risen Jesus as the New Temple promised indirectly by way of response to the demand of the Jews in Jn 2,18 is now fulfilled. . . . The risen Jesus is the 'sign' of the New Temple, and is himself in his intimate union with his Father the reality signified."

you" (20:21). In development of the preceding A scene, now that Jesus has ascended to "my Father and your Father, my God and your God" (20:17), he sends his disciples to continue and extend the same revelatory mission of love on which the Father has sent him. In his farewell discourse Jesus assured his disciples that whoever believes in him will not only duplicate but surpass the revelatory works that he does, "for I go to the Father" (14:12; see also 9:4). In his final prayer Jesus already prayed for the mission he now imparts to his disciples, "As you have sent me into the world, so I have sent them into the world" (17:18; see also 4:38). The disciples will bring others to believe, so that all may be one with Jesus and the Father, and the world may believe that the Father sent Jesus and know that he has loved the disciples even as he has loved Jesus (17:20-23). Jesus demonstrated that love by laying down his life for the disciples as his friends, and gave them his commandment to love one another as he has loved them (15:12-17).

At the same time that Jesus again granted his disciples peace and sent them on their mission (20:21), he breathed on them and said to them, "Receive the holy Spirit" (20:22). When God created the first human being, he formed him out of the dust of the ground and breathed (ἐνεφύσησεν) into his face the breath of life, and the person became a living being (LXX Gen 2:7). According to the Book of Wisdom, an idolater does not recognize the Creator who formed him, inspiring him with an active soul and breathing (ἐμφυσήσαντα) into him a living spirit (πνεῦμα ζωτικόν) (Wis 15:11). When Elijah revived the dead son of the widow with whom he was staying, he breathed (ἐνεφύσησεν) on the child three times as he prayed for God to allow the child's life to come into him again (3 Kgdms 17:21).[29] God told Ezekiel to prophesy to the Spirit (πνεῦμα) to come from the four winds and breathe (ἐμφύσησον) into those slain that they may come to life. He prophesied as God commanded and the Spirit (πνεῦμα) entered into them and they came to life (LXX Ezek 37:9-10). Similarly, the risen Jesus now breathed (ἐνεφύσησεν) into his disciples the holy Spirit (πνεῦμα) that brings them to eternal life and empowers them for their mission.[30]

The disciples now receive from the risen Jesus the holy Spirit (πνεῦμα) (20:22) made available by the death of Jesus, when he bowed his head and handed over the spirit (πνεῦμα) (19:30). When Pilate handed over (παρέδωκεν) Jesus to be crucified, the Jews took or received (παρέλαβον) him

---

[29] According to the MT, Elijah "stretched himself upon the child three times" (1 Kgs 17:21) rather than breathing on him as in the LXX.

[30] Barrett, *John*, 570; Brown, *John*, 1022-23.

(19:16). In accord with that same progression from handing over to receiving, the disciples now receive (λάβετε) the Spirit Jesus handed over (παρέδωκεν) in death. That they receive the holy Spirit made available by Jesus' death proceeds from his showing them his side (πλευρὰν) (20:20)—the same pierced side (πλευρὰν) out of which flowed the blood and water (19:34), the "rivers of living water" that symbolize the Life-giving Spirit (7:38-39).[31] Now that Jesus has been glorified by his death and resurrection, there is a Spirit for the disciples and all those who believe to receive (λαμβάνειν) (7:39). The Spirit the disciples now receive from the risen Jesus, the new temple (2:19-22), makes it possible for true worshippers to worship the Father in Spirit and truth, transcending the worship on Mount Gerizim and in the temple of Jerusalem (4:20-24).

That the disciples now receive (λάβετε) the holy Spirit assures the fulfillment of Jesus' promise that the Father will give them another Paraclete to be with them forever, the Spirit of truth, that the world cannot receive (λαβεῖν) (14:16-17). The Paraclete, the Spirit of truth, that the Father will send in the name of Jesus, will equip the disciples for the revelatory mission Jesus is giving them by teaching them everything and reminding them of everything Jesus told them (14:26). When the Paraclete, the Spirit of truth, that Jesus will send from the Father, comes from the Father, he will testify to Jesus, helping the disciples to testify (15:26-27) and thus fulfill their revelatory mission. When the Spirit of truth comes, he will guide the disciples in all truth; for he will not speak on his own, but whatever he hears he will speak and he will announce to them the things that are to come (16:13), so that they can continue and extend into the future the truth Jesus has revealed.[32]

The Life-giving Spirit that the risen Jesus breathes into his disciples empowers them to bring others to eternal life by the divine forgiveness of their sins: "Whose sins you forgive are forgiven them, whose sins you retain are retained" (20:23). If the disciples forgive or "leave behind" (ἀφῆτε) someone's sins, they are forgiven or left behind (ἀφέωνται) by God (divine passive). If they retain or hold (κρατῆτε) someone's sins, they are retained or held (κεκράτηνται) by God (divine passive). Since the fundamental "sin" in John's Gospel is the failure to believe (8:24; 16:9; 19:11), the disciples' "forgiveness" of sins includes their bringing others to believe by extending the revelatory mission on which Jesus is sending them (20:21; see 1:29; 8:46; 15:22-24). Their "retaining" of sins

---

[31] See chapter 4 on 19:34.

[32] T. R. Hatina, "John 20,22 in Its Eschatological Context: Promise or Fulfillment?" *Bib* 74 (1993) 196-219.

includes the failure of others to believe despite being given the revelatory truth of Jesus by the disciples (9:39-41; 15:22-24; 16:8-9).[33] But their divine power to forgive and retain sins also extends to the faults and failures that deprive those already within the community of believers from remaining in Jesus and living eternal life.[34] Jesus had urged his disciples to remain in him by keeping his new commandment to love one another as he loved them (13:34-35; 15:1-17).

Thomas Announces His Disbelief without Seeing (A³ 20:24-25)

24 But Thomas, one of the Twelve, who was called the Twin, was not with them when Jesus came. 25 So the other disciples said to him, "We have seen the Lord!" But he said to them, "Unless I see the mark of the nails in his hands, and put my finger into the mark of the nails and put my hand into his side, I will not believe."

Thomas, the Twin, was not present when Jesus came (20:24)

Constituting an A-B-A sandwich with the two preceding scenes, Thomas's announcement of his refusal to believe without seeing the risen Jesus (20:24-25) not only contrasts with but also develops the disciples' vision of the risen Lord in the preceding B scene (20:19-23). And it not only develops but also contrasts with Mary Magdalene's announcement of her vision of the risen Lord in the preceding A scene (20:11-18).

While the risen Jesus appeared to the group of disciples in the previous B scene (20:19-23), in contrast, "but" (δὲ), Thomas, one of the twelve disciples who confessed their faith in Jesus as the holy one of God (6:69) and who were specially chosen by Jesus (6:70; 13:18), was not present with the others when Jesus came (20:24). In development of the previous A scenes (20:1-2, 11-18), which focused on the coming to Easter faith of an individual, Mary Magdalene, this third A scene likewise focuses on an individual, Thomas. But in contrast not only to Mary Magdalene, who saw the risen Lord in the preceding A scene (20:18), but also to the other disciples, who saw the risen Lord in the previous B scene (20:20), Thomas was not present and has not yet seen the risen Lord.

That Thomas is called simply "Twin" (Δίδυμος) (11:16; 20:24) subtly chal-

---

[33] See chapter 3 on 19:11.

[34] Brown, *John*, 1044; Thomas, *Footwashing*, 155.

lenges the audience.[35] On the narrative, symbolic level, with whom is Thomas to be matched as a "twin" character? There are several intriguing possibilities:

1) Is Thomas the "Twin" to Judas, the betrayer of Jesus? Only Thomas and Judas are designated "one of the Twelve" (6:71; 20:24) in John. Just as Judas left the group and was singled out as Jesus' betrayer (13:30; 18:2-5), Thomas has been absent and singled out from the rest of the group.

2) Is Thomas the "Twin" to Peter, spokesman of the Twelve (6:67-68)? Peter, who did not understand where Jesus was going and why he could not follow him, vowed to die with him by laying down his life for him, but denied Jesus three times instead (13:36-38; 18:15-18, 25-27). When Jesus wanted to go to Judea again, although the Jews were seeking to stone him to death (8:59; 10:31; 11:7-8), and Lazarus had already died (11:14), Thomas ironically misunderstood and urged his fellow disciples, "Let us also go to die with him" (11:16), thus willing to be a "twin" not only to Peter but also to both Lazarus and Jesus.[36] Like Peter, Thomas did not understand that Jesus was going to the Father via his death and resurrection (14:1-5). Although Peter observed the burial cloths in the tomb (20:6-7), he did not believe until he, along with the other disciples, saw the risen Lord (20:20). Thomas likewise will not believe until he himself sees the risen Lord (20:25).[37]

3) Is Thomas the "Twin" to Philip? After Thomas misunderstood that Jesus is "the way" to the Father, Philip misunderstood how Jesus reveals the Father, when he asked, "Lord, show us the Father, and that will be enough for us" (14:4-8).

4) Is Thomas ironically the "Twin" to the beloved disciple? The beloved disciple saw only the burial cloths in the tomb and believed (20:8). Thomas will believe only if he sees the risen Lord himself (20:25).

5) Is Thomas the "Twin" to Mary Magdalene? Mary Magdalene has an individual encounter with the risen Lord, as she personally sees and tries to hold onto him (20:17-18). Thomas likewise wants an individual

[35] H. Balz, "Δίδυμος," EDNT 1. 320: "Δίδυμος is the Greek translation of the Aramaic name and also occurs as an independent Greek name."

[36] Duke, Irony, 59: "His [Thomas's] prediction that the journey will result in death is true enough (11:53), but he is ironically wrong in presuming that the disciples will have any share in that death. Jesus will die alone (16:32), in their behalf (15:13), but not in their company."

[37] Note that Thomas called the "Twin" is mentioned immediately after Simon Peter in the list of disciples who will witness the manifestation of the risen Jesus at the Sea of Tiberias (21:2).

encounter with the risen Lord, refusing to believe unless he personally sees and touches the risen Lord who was crucified (20:25).

6) Is Thomas the "Twin" to Nathanael? Nathanael proclaimed the narrative's first climactic confession of faith in Jesus, "Rabbi, you are the Son of God, you are the King of Israel!" (1:49). Thomas will proclaim the narrative's last climactic confession of faith in Jesus, "My Lord and my God!" (20:28).[38]

In answer to these questions Thomas, on the narrative and symbolic level, is *the* "Twin" in the Gospel of John—the quintessential "twin" character to many of the other individual characters. As the "Twin" Thomas duplicates certain characteristics of the others yet exhibits his own individuality in finally coming to believe in Jesus.

Thomas will not believe unless he sees and touches Jesus (20:25)

In the previous A scene Mary Magdalene was the first individual to announce, "I have seen (ἑώρακα) the Lord!" (20:18). Although it was reported that the disciples saw (ἰδόντες) the Lord in the previous B scene (20:20), they did not yet respond to their vision. In advancement of both of these preceding scenes, the disciples now announce, "We have seen (ἑωράκαμεν) the Lord!" (20:25). Now that Mary has announced her individual experience of seeing the risen Lord to the group of disciples, they announce their group experience of seeing that same Lord to an individual disciple, Thomas.

Like Mary Magdalene who saw and held onto the risen Lord in the previous A scene (20:17-18), Thomas wants his own individual vision and encounter with the risen Lord. The disciples as a group saw (ἰδόντες) the crucified hands and side that the risen Lord showed them in the previous B scene (20:20). In an intensifying, individualizing development, Thomas wants not only to see (ἴδω) the mark of the nails in the hands of the crucified Jesus, but also personally to put his own finger into the mark of the nails and personally to put his own finger into the side (πλευρὰν) before he will believe (20:25). He will thereby personally experience and verify not only that the risen Lord is the Jesus who was crucified, but also that out of the pierced side (πλευρὰν) of the crucified but now risen Jesus flow the blood and water that provide eternal life for all who believe (19:34-35).

[38] Note that Thomas called the "Twin" is mentioned immediately before Nathanael in the list of disciples who will witness the manifestation of the risen Jesus at the Sea of Tiberias (21:2).

Individual readers can readily identify with Thomas's desire for his own personal vision and encounter with the risen Lord. Indeed Thomas can be considered the "Twin" to the individual reader, who has likewise not seen the risen Lord and must rely upon the witness of others to believe. Wishing to reinforce the witness of the group of disciples, Thomas will serve as a further, individual witness for the readers as individuals.[39] Those who have not seen can come to believe through his seeing.

The Disciples and Thomas See and Believe
in the Risen Lord (B³ 20:26-29)

26 And after eight days his disciples were again inside and Thomas was with them. Jesus came, although the doors were locked, and stood in their midst and said, "Peace be with you!" 27 Then he said to Thomas, "Bring your finger here and see my hands, and bring your hand and put it into my side, and do not become unbelieving but believing." 28 Thomas answered and said to him, "My Lord and my God!" 29 Jesus said to him, "Because you have seen me you have believed. Blessed are those who have not seen yet have believed."

The risen Jesus comes to the disciples and Thomas (20:26)

Concluding a B-A-B intercalation with the two previous scenes, Thomas's seeing and believing in the risen Lord (20:26-29) not only contrasts with but also develops Thomas's announcement of his refusal to believe without seeing the risen Jesus in the previous A scene (20:24-25). And it not only develops but also contrasts with the disciples' vision of the risen Lord in the preceding B scene (20:19-23).

It was evening on the first day of the week, and the doors were locked for fear of the Jews, when the risen Jesus came and stood in the midst of the group of disciples for the first time and said to them, "Peace be with you!," in the previous B scene (20:19). In development, it is now eight days later, the disciples are again inside the room, but now Thomas is with them. The risen Jesus again came and stood in their midst and for a third, emphatic and definitive time declared, "Peace be with you!" (20:19, 21, 26), to disciples still behind locked doors (20:26). In contrast to the preceding A scene, in which the risen Jesus was not present (20:24-25), he now came and stood in the midst of the disciples and Thomas.

---

[39] de la Potterie, *Hour*, 183-85.

Thomas sees and believes in Jesus as his Lord and God (20:27-29)

In the previous B scene the risen Jesus showed and addressed himself to the disciples as a group, empowering them for their mission in the world by bestowing on them the holy Spirit and the authority to forgive and retain sins (20:19-23). In contrast, while the group is still present, the risen Jesus now shows and addresses himself to Thomas, a still unbelieving, individual disciple within the group of implicitly believing disciples (20:27-29).

In the preceding A scene Thomas announced his refusal to believe, although the other disciples testified to him that they had seen (ἑωράκαμεν) the Lord, "Unless I see (ἴδω) the mark of the nails in his hands, and put my finger into the mark of the nails and put my hand into his side" (20:25). In advancement, Jesus now accommodates Thomas with the personal, tangible encounter he required and invites him to become a believing disciple, as he directs him, "Bring your finger here and see (ἴδε) my hands, and bring your hand and put it into my side, and do not become unbelieving but believing" (20:27).

Although the disciples saw and encountered the risen Lord in the previous B scene (20:20), they did not respond to him. In the preceding A scene they told Thomas that they had seen "the Lord" (20:25). In advancement of both of these scenes, Thomas now responds to his personal vision and encounter by exclaiming his climactic confession of faith in the risen Jesus as not only "my Lord" but also "my God" (20:28). The risen Jesus had commissioned Mary Magdalene to tell his disciples, "I am ascending to my Father and your Father, my God and your God" (20:17). Now that Jesus has ascended to the Father, Thomas's confession not only confirms but surpasses Jesus' announcement. Thomas recognizes that believers can relate not only to the Father but also to the risen and ascended Son, the revelation of the Father, as "my Lord and my God." Thomas begins to fulfill Jesus' prediction that "all may honor the Son as they honor the Father" (5:23).[40]

After John the Baptist saw the Spirit descend and remain on Jesus, he confessed, "I have seen and have testified that this is the chosen one of God!" (1:33-34). To the Jesus who already knew him, Nathanael confessed, "Rabbi, you are the Son of God, you are the King of Israel!" (1:48-49). The Samaritans confessed their faith in the Jesus who remained with them for two days, "We have heard and know that this is truly the Savior of the world!" (4:40-42). As spokesman for the Twelve, Peter confessed to Jesus, "We have believed and

---

[40] Brown, *John*, 1047.

have come to know that you are the holy one of God!" (6:69). To Jesus' question, "Do you believe in the Son of Man?," the man born blind who has now seen Jesus responded, "I believe, Lord," and worshipped him (9:35-38). To the Jesus who revealed himself as the Resurrection and the Life, Martha confessed, "Yes Lord, I have believed that you are the Christ, the Son of God, the one coming into the world" (11:25-27). To the Jesus who came into Jerusalem for the Passover, the crowds proclaimed, "Hosanna! Blessed is he who comes in the name of the Lord, the King of Israel!" (12:13). Thomas's supreme christological confession in the lordship and divinity of the risen and ascended Jesus, "My Lord and my God!" (20:28), now climactically confirms yet notably exceeds all of the narrative's previous confessions of faith in Jesus.

To the Jews who twice wanted to kill Jesus for the blasphemy of making himself equal to God (5:18; 10:33), Jesus explained rather that he is the Son of God, who is one with the Father whom he reveals; his revelatory works disclose that the Father is in him and he is in the Father (5:19-47; 10:30, 34-38). The Jews then insisted to Pilate that Jesus must die for making himself Son of God (19:7). Thomas's climactic confession confirms that Jesus has not made himself God or Son of God, but has always been the divine Word and Son of God. The audience has known from the prologue to the narrative that "in the beginning was the Word, and the Word was with God, and the Word was God" (1:1), and that the Word became human (1:14) in the person of Jesus Christ, the only Son who revealed the God whom no one has ever seen (1:18).[41] Now that the Jesus whom God the Father sent to reveal his love to the world has returned to the Father via his "lifting up" in crucifixion, resurrection, and ascension, Thomas appropriately acclaims and worships Jesus, whose risen body represents the new temple of God's presence (2:19-21), as "My Lord and my God!" (20:28).[42]

In advancement of the two preceding A scenes, now that Mary Magdalene has seen (ἑώρακα) the Lord (20:18) and the disciples have seen (ἑωράκαμεν) the Lord (20:25), Jesus acknowledges that Thomas has not only seen (ἑώρακας) him but believed (20:29).[43] In development of the first B scene, in which the beloved disciple saw (εἶδεν) only the burial cloths in the tomb and believed (20:8), Thomas, the "Twin," duplicates his seeing and believing. But in contrast to the first B scene, Thomas believes only because he sees the risen

[41] Duke, *Irony,* 77: "The reader will know that, in fact, Jesus is not a human making himself God, but God already made human." See also Brown, *John,* 1047.

[42] McCaffrey, *Temple Theme,* 243.

[43] P. J. Judge, "A Note on Jn 20,29," *The Four Gospels 1992: Festschrift Frans Neirynck* (BETL 100; ed. F. Van Segbroeck, et al.; 3 vols.; Leuven: Leuven University, 1992) 2183-92.

Lord himself. And in contrast to the second B scene, in which the disciples saw but only implicitly believed in the risen Lord (20:20), Thomas explicitly exclaims his faith that the risen Jesus is now both Lord and God (20:28).

The risen Jesus' concluding words to Thomas, "Blessed are those who have not seen yet have believed" (20:29), pertain to the audience. Even though readers have not seen the risen Lord himself like Mary, the disciples, and Thomas, nor even the burial cloths like Peter and the beloved disciple, they will still be blessed with eternal life for believing without directly seeing the risen Lord. That the beloved disciple believed (20:8) before seeing the risen Lord himself testifies to the audience that they too can believe without seeing. But readers do not have to make a totally blind leap to believe in the risen Lord. By identifying with the characters in the narrative who have seen, they may "see" through their seeing. They have the testimony of those who have seen not only the burial cloths in the empty tomb but the risen Lord himself, so that they, along with Thomas, the "Twin," can confess their faith in the risen Jesus as "my Lord and my God!" (20:28).[44]

What Has Been Written Is a Basis for the Readers' Faith (C 20:30-31)

30 Now Jesus did many other signs in the presence of his disciples, which are not written in this book. 31 But these have been written so that you may believe that Jesus is the Christ, the Son of God, and that through believing you may have life in his name.[45]

Jesus did many other signs not written in this narrative (20:30)

At this point the narrator interjects with a direct address to the audience. He informs them that there are even more revelatory signs that Jesus performed in the presence of his disciples, but he has not narrated them (20:30). Indeed, in addition to those signs specifically narrated to the readers (2:11; 4:54; 6:14; 12:18), references have been made throughout the narrative to the many other

---

[44] J. Kremer, "'Nimm deine Hand und lege sie in meine Seite!' Exegetische, hermeneutische und bibeltheologische Überlegungen zu Joh 20,24-29," *The Four Gospels 1992: Festschrift Frans Neirynck* (BETL 100; ed. F. Van Segbroeck, et al.; 3 vols.; Leuven: Leuven University, 1992) 2153-81.

[45] G. D. Fee, "On the Text and Meaning of Jn 20,30-31," *The Four Gospels 1992: Festschrift Frans Neirynck* (BETL 100; ed. F. Van Segbroeck, et al.; 3 vols.; Leuven: Leuven University, 1992) 2193-205.

signs Jesus did that attracted people to him (2:23; 3:2; 4:48; 6:2, 26; 7:31; 9:16; 11:47; 12:37). Despite the many signs Jesus demonstrated, many did not believe (12:37). Some demanded to see even more signs from him in order to believe (2:18; 4:48; 6:30). But here the narrator assures the audience that even more signs could have been narrated as a basis for their faith.

The signs that are written are for the readers' faith (20:31)

Although other revelatory signs Jesus did could be narrated, those written in this book are sufficient to generate and maintain the faith of the audience. Those signs the narrator has written are intended to bring readers to believe that Jesus is the Christ, the Son of God, so that by thus believing readers may enjoy eternal life in his name (20:31). The narrator thus reinforces the risen Jesus' appeal to the audience, "Blessed are those who have not seen yet have believed" (20:29). Although readers have not personally seen the risen Lord or the signs, they may believe by listening to the signs narrated in this book. Their faith is based on the testimony of those disciples who have seen the risen Lord and the signs.

When blood and water flowed from the pierced side of the crucified Jesus, the narrator spoke for the beloved disciple, who testified that he has personally seen this revelatory sign. And interjecting with a direct appeal to the audience, he offered his true testimony, "so that you also may believe" (19:34-35).[46] Now the narrator not only reinforces this previous appeal but advances it. All of the signs have been written "so that you may believe" (20:31). And he adds both the content, that Jesus is the Christ, the Son of God, and the consequence, eternal life, of believing. With this declaration of the purpose of the entire book the narrator climaxes all of the narrative's previous appeals for readers to believe in Jesus as the Christ (1:17, 41; 4:25-26, 29; 7:26-31, 41-42; 9:22; 10:24; 11:27), the Son of God (1:18, 49; 10:36; 11:27), in order to know and experience eternal life (3:14-18, 36; 5:24-26, 40; 6:40, 47, 53-58; 10:10, 28; 12:25, 49-50; 14:6; 17:2-3).

To Martha, the sister of Lazarus, whom he raised from the dead, Jesus proclaimed, "I am the Resurrection and the Life; whoever believes in me, even though he dies, will live, and all who live and believe in me will never die for eternity" (11:25-26). When he asked if she believed this, Martha replied, "Yes Lord, I have believed that you are the Christ, the Son of God, the one coming

---

[46] Bauckham, "Beloved Disciple," 39-41; Culpepper, *Anatomy,* 44.

into the world" (11:26-27). Now that Jesus has risen and ascended to the Father, readers may not only believe that Jesus is the Christ, the Son of God, but may actually experience and enjoy eternal life now in his name through believing (20:31), as they look forward to living eternally even after dying (11:25-26).[47] As Jesus affirmed in his final prayer to the Father who gave him, as the Son of God, authority over all people, so that he might give them eternal life: "This is eternal life, that they may know you, the only true God, and the one whom you have sent, Jesus Christ" (17:1-3).

Summary

John 20:1-31 operates as another alternation of contrasting scenes that unfold for the audience as a dynamic sequence of narrative sandwiches, but in an even richer and more complex way. The A scenes develop the theme of individuals encountering the progressive evidence that Jesus has been raised from the dead: Mary Magdalene sees the stone removed from the tomb and concludes not that Jesus has been raised but that his body has been taken away and reburied (A^1 20:1-2). But after observing two angels where the body of Jesus had been in the tomb, Mary encounters and recognizes the risen Lord himself, who sends her to the group of disciples with the message of his resurrection and ascension to their God and Father (A^2 20:11-18). Although the disciples tell him that they have seen the risen Lord, Thomas, the "Twin," refuses to believe unless he encounters and sees for himself (A^3 20:24-25).

By way of continual contrast to the A scenes, the B scenes advance the theme of the wider group of disciples encountering the progressive evidence for the resurrection of Jesus: After observing the burial cloths in the tomb, Simon Peter and the beloved disciple returned to their homes; the disciples as a group did not yet understand the scriptures that Jesus must rise from the dead (B^1 20:3-10). Then the disciples as a group see the risen Lord and receive from him the holy Spirit with the authority to forgive and retain sins for their revelatory mission in the world (B^2 20:19-23). Finally, the group of disciples along with Thomas, who had been absent, again encounter the risen Jesus, and Thomas proclaims his faith in him who had been crucified as both Lord and God (B^3 20:26-29).

But the A scenes also relate to one another in a contrasting fashion: In the first A scene Mary Magdalene runs to Peter and the beloved disciple and

---

[47] O'Day, *Word Disclosed*, 88-90.

announces that Jesus has been taken from the tomb, not realizing that he has been raised from the dead (20:1-2). In contrast, she announces to the disciples in the second A scene that she has seen the risen Lord, who is now ascending to their God and Father (20:11-18). Although Mary has announced to the disciples that she has seen the risen Lord, in contrast, the individual disciple, Thomas, announces in the third A scene that he will not believe without personally seeing and touching the Jesus who was crucified (20:24-25).

The B scenes likewise relate to one another in a contrasting manner: In the first B scene (20:3-10), although both Peter and the beloved disciple observe the burial cloths in the tomb before going away to their homes, the beloved disciple "saw and believed" (20:8). In contrast, the risen Jesus comes to the group of disciples, who see but do not yet explicitly acknowledge their faith in the risen Lord, in the second B scene (20:19-23). Although the group of disciples saw but had not yet expressed their faith in the risen Jesus, in contrast, after Thomas sees and personally encounters the risen Jesus in the third B scene (20:26-29), he exclaims his climactic confession of faith, "My Lord and my God!" (20:28).

The entire sequence of scenes in 20:1-31 presents the theme of believing based upon the progression of seeing, both by individuals and the group of disciples, the evidence for the resurrection of Jesus: In the first A scene Mary Magdalene sees the stone taken from the tomb, but thinks the dead body of Jesus has been stolen (20:1-2). In the first B scene both Peter and the beloved disciple observe the burial cloths in the tomb, but only the beloved disciple sees and believes (20:3-10). In the second A scene Mary, after observing the two angels in the tomb and then the risen Jesus whom she thinks is the gardener, finally recognizes him and announces to the disciples that she has seen the Lord (20:11-18). In the second B scene the group of disciples see the risen Lord but do not yet express their belief (20:19-23). In the third A scene, despite the disciples' announcement that they have seen the Lord, the individual disciple, Thomas, refuses to believe unless he personally sees the risen Jesus himself (20:24-25). In the third B scene Thomas sees and climactically exclaims that the crucified Jesus is now Lord and God, and the risen Lord blesses those readers who, although they have not seen, nevertheless believe (20:26-29). In the concluding C scene the narrator invites the readers, who have not seen but have the testimony of the signs seen and recorded in the narrative, to believe in Jesus as the Christ and Son of God in order to enjoy eternal life (20:30-31).

This entire progressive alternation of scenes engages the implied reader/audience as follows:

1) The audience, who knows that "within three days" of the Jews' destruction of the "temple" that is the body of Jesus he would raise it up (2:19-21), experiences the first evidence of the resurrection through the irony of Mary Magdalene. On the first day of the week, that is, within three days of the death of Jesus, she sees the stone removed from the tomb but thinks the body of Jesus has been stolen in the first A scene (20:1-2).

2) In contrast to Mary Magdalene's failure to believe despite seeing the first evidence of Jesus' resurrection, that the beloved disciple, after observing along with Peter the burial cloths in the tomb, saw and believed in the first B scene invites the reader who has not personally seen this evidence likewise to believe. This faith is based upon the beloved disciple's seeing and the scriptural necessity for Jesus to rise from the dead (20:3-10).

3) In contrast to the disciples who have left the tomb of Jesus, Mary Magdalene's observing of the two angels in the tomb and the risen Lord himself in the second A scene advances the theme of an individual seeing more evidence. It assures the audience that an individual personally saw and encountered the risen Lord who ascended to his Father, so that disciples and readers may be his brothers and sisters and relate to his Father and God as also their Father and God. In contrast to Mary's announcement that the body was stolen, but advancing the theme of coming to faith through the seeing of others, that Mary announces the resurrection and its consequences makes her a model missionary for the audience (20:11-18).

4) In contrast to Mary's remaining at the tomb for her individual experience of the risen Lord, the risen Lord's coming to the group of disciples inside locked doors for fear of the Jews and showing them that he is the crucified one in the second B scene advances the theme of the wider group seeing more evidence. It summons the audience to experience the profound peace and joy granted by the risen Jesus. In contrast to the disciples returning to their homes, but advancing the theme of bringing others to faith, Jesus commissions and empowers his disciples and thus the audience to extend his revelatory mission to the world, as he bestowed on them the holy Spirit and the authority to forgive and retain sins (20:19-23).

5) In contrast to the group of disciples seeing the risen Lord, Thomas's refusal in the third A scene to believe unless he personally sees and encounters the risen Lord as the one who had been crucified advances the theme of an individual seeing more evidence. It challenges the reader,

who has not personally seen, to believe. In contrast to Mary who saw the risen Lord, but advancing the theme of bringing others to faith, that Thomas has not yet seen and believed prompts the audience to believe by hearing the testimony of the group of disciples who have seen the risen Lord (20:24-25).

6) In contrast to Thomas's previous absence when the risen Lord first came to the disciples, that Thomas, while present to complement the whole group of disciples, sees and believes in the risen Lord in the third B scene advances the theme of the wider group seeing more evidence. It bids the audience, even though they have not personally seen like Thomas and the rest of the disciples, to believe. In contrast to the disciples' previous lack of response, but advancing the theme of bringing others to faith, Thomas's climactic confession induces the audience to heed the appeal of the risen Lord himself and likewise believe in the crucified but risen Jesus as their Lord and God (20:26-29).

7) By assuring the audience in the closing C scene that they have been given all the evidence they need in the book, the narrator's additional aside reinforces the risen Lord's appeal for the readers, who have not personally seen, to believe that Jesus is the Christ, the Son of God, in order to possess eternal life in his name (20:30-31).

CHAPTER 6

The Risen Jesus, Peter, and the Beloved Disciple
(21:1-25)

The Beloved Disciple Directs Peter to the Risen Lord Who Feeds the Disciples (A¹ 21:1-14)

1 After these things Jesus again manifested himself to the disciples at the Sea of Tiberias. And he manifested in this way. 2 Together were Simon Peter, Thomas called the Twin, Nathanael from Cana in Galilee, the sons of Zebedee, and two others of his disciples. 3 Simon Peter said to them, "I am going fishing." They said to him, "We also will come with you." They went out and got into the boat, but that night they caught nothing.

4 When it was already dawn, Jesus stood on the shore, the disciples, however, did not know that it was Jesus. 5 Jesus then said to them, "Children, you have no fish to eat, have you?" They answered him, "No." 6 He said to them, "Cast the net to the right side of the boat, and you will find some." So they cast it, and now they were not able to draw it in because of the great number of fish. 7 Then that disciple whom Jesus loved said to Peter, "It is the Lord!" When Simon Peter heard that it was the Lord, he wrapped his outer garment around him, for he was naked, and cast himself into the sea. 8 But the other disciples came in the boat, for they were not far from the land, only about a hundred yards, dragging the net of fish.

9 When they climbed out to the land, they saw a charcoal fire there with fish lying on it and bread. 10 Jesus said to them, "Bring some of the fish you have just caught." 11 So Simon Peter went aboard and drew in the net to the land, full of large fish, a hundred fifty-three of them. And though there were so many, the net was not torn. 12 Jesus said to them, "Come, have breakfast." And none of the disciples dared to ask him, "Who are you?," knowing that it was the Lord. 13 Jesus came and took the bread and gave it to them, and like-

wise the fish. 14 This was now the third time that Jesus was manifested to the disciples after being raised from the dead.

Seven disciples went fishing but caught nothing (21:1-3)

After the risen Jesus had appeared to the disciples twice—once without Thomas (20:19-23) and once to the entire group including Thomas (20:26-29)—he manifested himself again to the disciples (21:1). Previous "manifestations" of Jesus have been oriented to believing in him. The purpose of John's baptizing with water was so that Jesus might be manifested (φανερωθῇ) to Israel as the chosen one of God on whom the Spirit descended and remained (1:31-34). But many in Israel did not believe, despite the many revelatory signs Jesus performed in their presence (12:37-43). After Jesus performed his first sign by changing water into wine at Cana in Galilee and manifested (ἐφανέρωσεν) his glory, however, his disciples believed in him (2:11). Although his brothers challenged him to manifest (φανέρωσον) himself publicly to the world, they did not believe in him (7:4-5). Instead, Jesus promised to manifest (ἐμφανίσω) himself privately and interiorly to whomever keeps his commandments and not publicly to the world (14:21-22). Jesus manifested (ἐφανέρωσα) the name of God to his disciples, who believed that God sent him (17:6-8). That Jesus manifested (ἐφανέρωσεν) himself again to the disciples as the risen Lord would seem to be oriented to a further believing on their part.

Whereas the risen Jesus previously appeared to Mary Magdalene at his tomb in the garden (20:11-18) and to the disciples inside the room behind locked doors for fear of the Jews (20:19, 26), he now manifested himself to the disciples at the Sea of Tiberias (21:1). It was at the Sea of Tiberias in Galilee that Jesus miraculously fed a crowd of about five thousand with an overabundance from only five loaves and two fish (6:1-14, 23). As the narrator emphatically repeats to introduce this particular manifestation, Jesus "manifested" in the way the narrator will now recount (21:1).

At the head of the list of those disciples who were together for this particular manifestation is Simon Peter (21:2). He was last explicitly mentioned in the narrative when he and the beloved disciple observed the burial cloths in the tomb of Jesus, but he returned home without believing (20:6-7, 10).[1] He was implicitly present for the previous appearances of the risen Jesus to the group

---

[1] For the role of Simon Peter in the previous narrative, see chapter 2 on 18:10; see also 18:15-18, 25-27.

of disciples (20:19-23, 26-29). Mentioned next is Thomas, again designated the "Twin" (11:16; 20:24), who confessed Jesus as his Lord and God after seeing and tangibly verifying that the risen Lord is the crucified Jesus (20:27-28).[2] Next in the list is Nathanael from Cana in Galilee, where Jesus performed his first revelatory sign by changing water into wine (2:1-11) and a second when he saved the royal official's son from death (4:46-54). After Nathanael confessed his faith in Jesus as the Son of God and King of Israel, Jesus promised that he would see even greater things (1:49-50), and now Nathanael is present for this further manifestation of Jesus.[3] Next are the sons of Zebedee, who have not been explicitly mentioned in the previous narrative.[4] The list concludes with two other anonymous disciples to bring the total to seven, symbolically suggestive of completeness, so that this group may serve as a paradigm for the entire community of believers among the readers.[5]

Taking the lead, Simon Peter announces to the other six disciples, "I am going fishing" (21:3). They readily offer to accompany him, "We also will come with you," so that this fishing expedition becomes a group effort. In accord with the Johannine affinity for double meaning, this attempt to catch fish serves two purposes. On the one hand, it portrays the endeavor on the part of a complete, paradigmatic group of seven disciples to catch fish as food for nourishment and sustenance. On the other hand, it at the same time symbolically represents the disciples' attempt to accomplish the mission Jesus gave them to bring other people into a unity by believing in him (20:21; 17:18-21; 4:38).

In the biblical tradition the catching of fish often symbolizes the catching and gathering of people. In Jer 16:16 God proclaims that he is sending for many fishermen and "they will fish" for "them," referring to the people of Israel (Jer 16:14-15). The LXX version employs the same verb for fishing (ἁλιεύσουσιν) as Peter when he says, "I am going fishing (ἁλιεύειν)" (21:3). In Hab 1:14-15 the prophet addresses God: "You have made people like the fish of the sea, and

---

[2] For the role of Thomas in the previous narrative, see chapter 5 on 20:24-28.

[3] Brown, *John*, 1096.

[4] According to the synoptic gospels, James and John were the sons of Zebedee, fishermen who left their father in the boat at the Sea of Galilee to become "fishers of people" when Jesus called them (Matt 4:19-22; Mark 1:17-20). They were companions of Simon Peter when Jesus miraculously enabled them to catch a great number of fish in Luke 5:1-11. See also Matt 10:2; 20:20; 26:37; 27:56; Mark 3:17; 10:35.

[5] A. Pitta, "*Ichthys* ed *opsarion* in Gv 21,1-14: semplice variazione lessicale o differenza con valore simbolico?" *Bib* 71 (1990) 357-58; J. F. Drinkard, "Numbers," *HBD*, 711. Note that one of the two other anonymous disciples will prove to be the beloved disciple (21:7).

like crawling things that have no ruler. He brings them all up with his hook, he draws them in with his net, he gathers them in his seine; so he rejoices and exults." The LXX version uses the same words for fish (ἰχθύας) and drawing (εἵλκυσεν) the net in as our story (21:6, 8, 11). In the synoptic gospel tradition Jesus promised to transform the fishermen he called to be his first disciples into "fishers of people" (Matt 4:18-22; Mark 1:16-20; see also Luke 5:1-11).

The whole group of disciples went out and boarded the boat, but dramatic suspense is aroused as they failed to catch anything that night (21:3). That they could catch nothing in the darkness of that "night" accords with the Johannine symbolic contrast between the darkness of night and the light of day. In John the darkness of night can represent both lack of faith and the absence of Jesus' revelatory person and action. That Nicodemus came to Jesus at night accords with his not yet coming to believe (3:2; 19:39). Before he performed the revelatory work of healing the man born blind, Jesus told his disciples, "We must perform the works of the one who sent me while it is day, night is coming when no one can work" (9:4). Before he raised Lazarus, he told them, "If anyone walks in the night, he stumbles, for the light is not in him" (11:10). Jesus, of course, is himself the light of the world (1:4-9; 3:19-21; 8:12; 9:5; 12:35-36, 46). But when the unbelieving Judas went out to betray Jesus, it was night (13:30). That this whole group of disciples could catch nothing that "night," then, points to both their lack of faith and the absence of the revelatory action of Jesus.

Jesus enabled them to catch a large number of fish (21:4-8)

When it was already dawn, that is, the light of day was breaking, and the "night" of Jesus' absence has passed, Jesus, the "light" of the world, stood on the shore. But a further suspense is aroused, as the disciples did not know that it was Jesus (21:4). This increases the dramatic narrative conflict that begs for resolution: The disciples have caught nothing because of the absence of Jesus, but now that he is present, they have not yet recognized him.

Jesus reinforces the disciples' inability to catch anything without him, as he asks them a question worded to facilitate and force their negative response, "Children, you have no fish, have you?" And they, of course, must reply, "No" (21:5). That Jesus addresses them as "children" or more literally "little children" (παιδία) underlines their subordination and dependence upon him (see also 13:33). The word here translated as "fish to eat" more literally means "something to eat" (προσφάγιον), often used to refer to a fish relish eaten with bread.[6] It accords with that aspect of fishing as a means of procuring food, and underscores the disciples' inability without Jesus to nourish and sustain themselves for their mission.

Jesus then directs the hapless disciples to cast the net to the right side and promises that they will find some (21:6).[7] Actually he promises simply that they "will find," without any expressed object. It is naturally implied that they will find some fish. But leaving the object somewhat abruptly but tantalizingly unexpressed allows for the disciples to find more than they expected—not only a great number of fish for food but a great number of fish that represent people.

After they obeyed Jesus' instructions and cast the net to the right side, the disciples were not able to draw the net in so great was the number of fish (21:6). This resolves the story's first tension, the disciples' inability to catch anything during the night without Jesus, the "light" (21:3). Now not only do they have fish to eat (21:5), but they have caught fish symbolically representative of great numbers of people. In LXX Hab 1:14-15 the fisherman draws (εἵλκυσεν) in the people, who are like fish (ἰχθύας), with his net. But the disciples are unable to draw (ἑλκύσαι) in the net because of the great number of fish (ἰχθύων), representative of people. In LXX Ezek 47:10 it is promised that when the life-giving waters flow from the eschatological temple of Jerusalem, the fish (ἰχθύες) will be like the fish (ἰχθύες) of the Great Sea—an exceedingly great number (πλῆθος πολὺ σφόδρα). And now that the disciples have followed the direction of the risen Jesus, the new "temple" (2:19-21), they are unable to draw in the net because of the great number (πλήθους) of fish (ἰχθύων).

Then the beloved disciple resolves the story's second tension, the disciples' failure to recognize Jesus (21:4), as he exclaims to Peter, "It is the Lord!" (21:7). It was the beloved disciple who saw only the burial cloths in the tomb of Jesus and believed before Peter and the rest of the disciples, who did not yet understand the scriptural necessity for Jesus to rise from the dead (20:8-9). As the ideal disciple he now again precedes the others in recognizing the risen Lord.

Simon Peter was the disciple who impatiently and eagerly wanted to follow Jesus, to the point of laying down his life for him (13:37). He rashly cut off the right ear of the high priest's servant when Jesus was arrested (18:10). After running to the tomb of Jesus, Peter was the first to enter it, although the beloved

---

[6] *BAGD,* 719; *EDNT,* 3. 177.

[7] Although the "right side" is generally the more favorable side in the biblical tradition, as Brown, *John,* 1071, points out: "John implies a more than natural knowledge on Jesus' part and the corresponding moral duty to obey him exactly if one is his disciple."

disciple reached it before him (20:3-7). Now the impetuous Peter eagerly and hastily seeks to meet the risen Lord.[8] When the beloved disciple informed him that the one standing on the shore was the Lord, the naked Peter wrapped his outer garment around him and threw himself into the sea (21:7).[9] Peter was naked while doing the work of fishing with his companions. But now, putting on his outer garment, he ceases his work and abandons the companions who had originally offered to accompany him (21:3). Before impatiently jumping into the sea, the impulsive Peter dons proper clothing to meet the Lord.[10]

While Peter has abandoned ship and is swimming to shore by himself (21:7), the other disciples came in the boat (21:8). That they were not far from land, only about a hundred yards, underlines Peter's impatience. Dragging the net of fish, the other disciples are still struggling to bring in the great number of fish they could not draw into the boat (21:6).

Jesus fed them with bread and fish they had caught (21:9-14)

When the disciples reached the shore, "they saw a charcoal fire there with fish lying on it and bread" (21:9). It was around a charcoal fire (ἀνθρακιὰν) that Peter, after denying that he was a disciple (18:17), had warmed himself when he separated himself from Jesus and "the other disciple" and joined those who had arrested Jesus (18:18). Now, ironically, a charcoal fire (ἀνθρακιὰν) warms the meal with which the risen Jesus will nourish and reunite Peter and the disciples to himself.

Jesus is cooking a fish to be eaten with the bread (21:9) and invites the disciples to bring some of the fish he has just directed them to catch (21:10), presumably to be added to the meal he is preparing (21:5). This indicates that Jesus not only feeds the disciples himself, but also has enabled them to provide an abundant supply of food to nourish and sustain themselves for their mission

---

[8] D. H. Gee, "Why Did Peter Spring into the Sea? (John 21:7)," *JTS* 40 (1989) 481-89, rather unconvincingly, in our opinion, suggests that Peter jumped into the sea not because of joy and enthusiasm but because of fear and guilt; he sought to avoid an encounter with the Lord. This interpretation, however, does not seem to conform with the basic details and thrust of the narrative.

[9] Brown, *John,* 1072, suggests the translation that Peter "tucked in his outer garment (for he was otherwise naked)." He remarks that the verb (διεζώσατο) "can mean to put on clothes, but more properly it means to tuck them up and tie them in with a cincture so that one can have freedom of movement to do something." In John 13:4-5 the same verb is used when Jesus wraps a towel around himself before washing his disciples' feet. See also Carson, *John,* 671.

[10] Barrett, *John,* 580-81.

of catching people. The word used to refer to the fish lying on the fire as well as to the fish Jesus now bids the disciples to bring to the meal is ὀψάριον (21:9-10), in contrast to ἰχθύς, the word employed for fish when the disciples caught the great number of fish in their net (21:6, 8). In accord with the double meaning of catching fish in this story, ὀψάριον refers to fish to be eaten, whereas ἰχθύς refers to fish that represent the people the disciples are to catch and bring into the community of believers.[11]

Ever taking the lead, the eager and impulsive Simon Peter in response to Jesus' request goes aboard the boat and draws in the net to the land, "full of large fish, a hundred fifty-three of them. And though there were so many, the net was not torn" (21:11). Whereas Jesus asked the disciples to bring some of the fish (ὀψαρίων) to be eaten (21:10), Peter brings the net full of large fish (ἰχθύων) that symbolically represent the large number of people Jesus will enable the disciples to catch. The disciples were not able to draw (ἑλκύσαι) in the net because of the great number of fish/people (21:6). But now Peter, empowered by the command of the risen Lord, drew (εἵλκυσεν) in the net full of fish/people to land. This continues the unifying and universalizing purpose of the revelatory death of Jesus, who said, "When I am lifted up from the earth, I will draw (ἑλκύσω) all to myself," indicating the kind of death he would die (12:32-33). And just as the soldiers' decision not to tear (σχίσωμεν) the seamless tunic of the crucified Jesus in accord with God's scriptural plan symbolically pointed to the unity his death effects (19:24),[12] so the net was not torn (ἐσχίσθη) but kept intact by God (divine passive), unifying the great quantity of distinctly numbered—one hundred fifty-three—fish/people in it.[13]

In correspondence to the dawning day (21:4), Jesus, the "light," invites the disciples to the first meal of the day which he has provided for them, "Come, have breakfast" (21:12). This totally resolves the tension regarding the disciples' recognition of Jesus (21:4). Not only have the beloved disciple and Simon Peter recognized the Lord (21:7), but now the entire group recognizes him, as none of the disciples dared to ask who he was. Earlier at the Sea of

[11] Pitta, "*Ichthys* ed *opsarion*," 348-64.

[12] See chapter 4 on 19:24.

[13] For recent discussions of the possible symbolic significance of the one hundred fifty-three fish, see O. T. Owen, "One Hundred and Fifty Three Fishes," *ExpTim* 100 (1988) 52-54; J. M. Ross, "One Hundred and Fifty-Three Fishes," *ExpTim* 101 (1989) 375; P. Trudinger, "The 153 Fishes: A Response and a Further Suggestion," *ExpTim* 102 (1990) 11-12; K. Cardwell, "The Fish on the Fire: Jn 21:9," *ExpTim* 102 (1990) 12-14; Brodie, *John,* 586-87. Note also the caution expressed by Brown, *John,* 1074-76, with regard to the somewhat complicated symbolic interpretations that have been variously suggested.

Tiberias the disciples had gathered up the abundant leftovers after Jesus gave thanks and miraculously fed the large crowd of five thousand with only five loaves of bread and two fish (6:1-13). Then boats came from Tiberias near the place where they ate the bread, after "the Lord" gave thanks (6:23). Now the disciples know that it is "the Lord," who is similarly feeding them a meal of bread and fish (21:9, 12-13).

When Jesus fed the large crowd, he took (ἔλαβεν) the loaves of bread (ἄρτους) and gave (διέδωκεν) them to those reclining and likewise (ὁμοίως) from the fish (ὀψαρίων) as much as they wanted (6:11). Similarly, he now takes (λαμβάνει) the bread (ἄρτον) and gives (δίδωσιν) it to the disciples, and likewise (ὁμοίως) the fish (ὀψάριον) (21:13). The disciples assisted Jesus in feeding the large crowd (6:5-10) and gathered the bread that was left over into twelve baskets (6:13)—one for each of the traditional twelve tribes of the people of Israel.[14] Jesus has provided an overabundance with which the disciples may feed the people after he himself fed them. This overabundance of bread is now complemented by an overabundance of fish. Although Jesus invited the disciples to bring some of the fish (ὀψαρίων) he enabled them to catch to the meal he prepared (21:10), he fed them from the single fish (ὀψάριον) lying on the fire (21:9, 13). The disciples still have an abundance of fish to be eaten, with which they may nourish and sustain the great number of fish/people the risen Lord will enable them to draw into the community of believers (21:11).

After Jesus fed the large crowd with fish and bread (6:1-13), he eventually revealed himself as the "Bread of Life" that he gives as his flesh for the Life of the world (6:51), a reference to the eucharist (6:52-58). That Jesus again feeds the disciples with fish and bread (21:9-13) similarly suggests the eucharist. Although the Jesus who fed the crowd repeatedly disclosed that "I am" the Bread of Life that came down from heaven (6:35, 48, 51), the Jews questioned his identity as the Bread of Life (6:41-42) and his ability to give his flesh to eat (6:52) in the eucharist.[15] But none of the disciples now dares to ask Jesus, "Who are you?" They know that the one feeding them with fish and bread is the same "Lord" who fed the crowd (21:12; 6:23). That Jesus fed the crowd with fish and an overabundance of bread and the disciples with bread and an overabundance of fish points to how he overabundantly feeds believers in the eucharist with eternal life (6:54; 10:10), so that from this abundance they in

[14] Carson, *John*, 271; Bruce, *John*, 145.
[15] Heil, *Jesus Walking on the Sea*, 152-70.

turn can nourish and sustain the great number of people who will become believers.[16]

The notice that this is now the third time that Jesus was manifested (ἐφα-νερώθη) to his disciples after being raised from the dead (21:14) concludes the story. Forming a literary inclusion with the introductory notice that Jesus again manifested (ἐφανέρωσεν) himself to the disciples, the narrator has now recounted the manner in which Jesus manifested (ἐφανέρωσεν) himself (21:1). This third and therefore definitive manifestation of the risen Lord complements his first (20:19-23) and second (20:26-29) appearances to the disciples as a group, after he appeared to an individual, Mary Magdalene (20:11-18).

Jesus Commissions Peter To Feed the Sheep (B¹ 21:15-19a)

15 When they had finished breakfast, Jesus said to Simon Peter, "Simon son of John, do you love me more than these?" He said to him, "Yes, Lord, you know that I love you." He said to him, "Feed my lambs." 16 He then said to him a second time, "Simon son of John, do you love me?" He said to him, "Yes, Lord, you know that I love you." He said to him, "Shepherd my sheep." 17 He said to him the third time, "Simon son of John, do you love me?" Peter was saddened that he said to him the third time, "Do you love me?" And he said to him, "Lord, you know everything; you know that I love you." Jesus said to him, "Feed my sheep. 18 Amen, amen, I say to you, when you were younger, you used to dress yourself and go wherever you wished. But when you grow old, you will stretch out your hands, and someone else will dress you and take you where you do not wish." 19a He said this signifying by what kind of death he would glorify God.

Jesus thrice commands Peter to feed his sheep (21:15-17)

After the group of disciples had eaten the breakfast of bread and fish that Jesus cooked and fed them (21:9-13), he singles Simon Peter out from the rest and questions him: "Simon son of John, do you love me more than these?" (21:15). That he addresses him as "Simon son of John" recalls their first encounter, when Jesus distinguished him with a new name, "You are Simon the son of John, you will be called Cephas, which means Peter" (1:42). Simon Peter has

---

[16] On the eucharistic implications of 21:9-13, see Brown, *John,* 1098-1100.

just distinguished himself from the other disciples by eagerly jumping into the sea and swimming toward Jesus while the others came in the boat (21:7-8), and by again boarding the boat to draw in the net full of the great number of fish (21:11). Accordingly, Jesus inquires whether Peter will continue to distinguish himself from the others. This begins the contrast between this B scene and the preceding A scene: In contrast to the other disciples, especially the disciple whom Jesus loved (ἠγάπα) (21:7), does Peter love (ἀγαπᾷς) Jesus more than these other disciples love him?

After Peter assures Jesus of his love for him, "Yes, Lord, you know that I love you," Jesus commands him, "Feed my lambs" (21:15). The risen Jesus who fed the disciples and enabled them to catch a great number of fish for food, which Peter himself dragged to shore in the net (21:11), now commissions Peter likewise to feed "my lambs," the followers who believe and belong to Jesus, the good shepherd (10:1-18, 26-29).

A second time Jesus asks Peter, "Simon son of John, do you love me?," and Peter repeats, "Yes, Lord, you know that I love you." But this time Jesus commands him, "Shepherd my sheep" (21:16). To shepherd (ποίμαινε) my sheep, a more general and comprehensive term than the previous command to "feed" (βόσκε) my lambs (21:15), refers to caring for, protecting, guiding, leading sheep.[17] This second command of Jesus to Peter could be paraphrased, "Be a shepherd to my sheep." Jesus demonstrated what it means to shepherd his sheep, as he, the good shepherd, laid down his own life for the sheep so that they may have eternal life (10:10-11, 28). Peter wanted to lay down his life for Jesus, but denied him instead (13:37-38; 18:15-18, 25-27). Jesus first had to lay down his own life and take it up again in resurrection (10:17-18) before Peter can lay down his life. Peter had to be a sheep before he can be a shepherd. But now the risen Lord and good shepherd challenges and empowers Peter to demonstrate his love by "shepherding my sheep," laying down his life in love for them as Jesus loved them (13:34-35; 15:12-17).

An emphatic and definitive third time Jesus questions Peter, "Simon son of John, do you love me?" (21:17).[18] Peter, saddened that Jesus would thrice ques-

---

[17] Zerwick and Grosvenor, *Analysis*, 1. 347; BAGD, 683-84.

[18] This third question employs the verb φιλεῖς for "love," whereas the first two of Jesus' questions use ἀγαπᾷς (21:15, 16); Peter's response employs φιλῶ all three times (21:15, 16, 17). With respect to this variation in words for "love" the comments of W. Feneberg, "φιλέω," *EDNT* 3. 425-26, are pertinent: "Φιλέω and ἀγαπάω are synonymous in the NT. Variations in connotation or nuance by one of the two are usually taken over also by the other.... John 20:2 uses φιλέω once for the beloved disciple (otherwise 4 times ἀγαπάω); 21:15-17 uses it 5 times (4 of those

tion his love for him, climactically reinforces his affirmation of Jesus' superior knowledge. In his first two replies Peter pointed out that Jesus as Lord "knows" that Peter loves him (21:15, 16). Now an exasperated Peter asserts, "Lord, you know everything; you know that I love you." That Jesus thrice elicits from Peter an explicit acknowledgment of his love for him corresponds to Peter's three-fold denial of his discipleship, as predicted by the Jesus who knows everything (13:38; 18:15-18, 25-27).

Jesus' third command to Peter, "Feed my sheep" (21:17), serves as a climactic combination of his first two commands. Whereas Jesus first commissioned Peter to feed (βόσκε) my lambs (21:15) and then to shepherd my sheep (τὰ πρόβατά μου) (21:16), he now directs him to feed (βόσκε) my sheep (τὰ πρόβατά μου). Not only is there a progression from "my lambs" (21:15) to "my sheep" (21:16, 17) but also an alternating progression from "feeding" (21:15) to "shepherding" (21:16) to "feeding" (21:17) again. But the third command, "Feed my sheep," functions as more than a mere repetition of the first command, "Feed my lambs." It comes after the command, "Shepherd my sheep." Jesus empowers Peter now to feed his sheep not only from the overabundance of bread (6:1-13) and fish (21:9-13) that symbolically point to the overabundant, eternal life provided by the eucharist, but also to "feed," nourish, and sustain them by "shepherding" them, that is, by laying down his life for them in love.[19]

Jesus indicates that Peter's death will glorify God (21:18-19a)

The same solemn and authoritative words, "Amen, amen, I say to you," with which Jesus introduced his prediction of Peter's triple denial of him (13:38) now introduce his prediction of what will happen to Peter when he grows old (21:18). That Peter denied Jesus as predicted assures the audience that this prediction will likewise come to pass. That Peter dressed himself when he was younger and went wherever he wished was illustrated in the previous scene. Peter dressed himself when he wrapped his outer garment around himself (21:7), and went wherever he wished when he jumped into the sea (21:7) and when he again boarded the boat to draw in the net full of fish (21:11). But in

---

spoken by Peter, once in Jesus' third question to Peter as a variation of ἀγαπάω in the first two questions). Attempts to determine in these two passages distinctions that transcend mere feeling for language are not persuasive."

[19] Duke, *Irony*, 98; S. van Tilborg, *Imaginative Love in John* (Biblical Interpretation Series 2; Leiden: Brill, 1993) 154-57.

contrast to the preceding A scene, when Peter grows old, he will stretch out his hands for someone else to dress him and take him where he does not wish to go (21:18).

With an aside to the reader the narrator explains that Jesus said this to signify by what kind of death Peter would glorify God (21:19a). That Peter will be dressed and taken where he does not wish (21:18), then, refers to his eventual death. This reinforces and confirms that Jesus' commissioning of Peter to shepherd and feed the sheep (21:15-17) ultimately means his laying down his own life for them in love. Just as the death of Jesus, the good shepherd who laid down his life for the sheep, "glorified" God (12:23, 28; 13:31-32; 17:1, 4-5), so the death of Peter, who promised to lay down his life for Jesus (13:37), "will glorify" (δοξάσει) God.

In his farewell discourse Jesus told his disciples, "My Father is glorified (ἐδοξάσθη) in this, that you bear much fruit and become my disciples. As the Father loved me, so I have loved you. Remain in my love. If you keep my commandments, you will remain in my love, as I have kept the commandments of my Father and remain in his love" (15:8-10). He went on to proclaim his commandment that they love one another as he loved them, that is, to the point of dying for them. Indeed, no one exhibits a greater love than to lay down his life for his friends (15:12-13). Three times Jesus pointedly asked the Peter who thrice denied his discipleship, "Do you love me?" (21:15-17). He then challenged the Peter who affirmed his love to demonstrate that love by feeding and shepherding the sheep of Jesus, that is, by ultimately laying down his life for them in love to glorify God.[20]

Peter and the Beloved Disciple Follow the Risen Lord (A² 21:19b-23)

19b And having said this, he said to him, "Follow me." 20 Peter turned and saw the disciple whom Jesus loved following, who at the supper also leaned back upon his chest and said, "Lord, who is the one who will betray you?" 21 When Peter saw him, he said to Jesus, "Lord, what about this one?" 22 Jesus said to him, "If I want him to remain until I come, what is that to you? You follow me!" 23 So the word went out to the brothers that that disciple would

[20] For a discussion of the oral interpretation of John 21:15-19, see G. L. Bartholomew, "Feed My Lambs: John 21:15-19 as Oral Gospel," *Orality, Aurality, and Biblical Narrative* (*Semeia* 39; ed. L. Silberman; Decatur: Scholars, 1987) 69-96.

not die. But Jesus did not tell him that he would not die, rather, "If I want him to remain until I come, what is that to you?"

Jesus commands Peter to follow him (21:19b-22)

Forming an A-B-A intercalation with the two preceding scenes, Peter's and the beloved disciple's following of the risen Lord (21:19b-23) not only contrasts with but also develops Jesus' commissioning of Peter to feed the sheep in the preceding B scene (21:15-19a). It not only develops but also contrasts with the beloved disciple's directing of Peter to the risen Lord in the first A scene (21:1-14).

In the preceding B scene Jesus commanded Peter to feed and shepherd the sheep (21:15-17), and indicated that this would ultimately lead to his death that would glorify God (21:18-19a). In development, Jesus now commands Peter to "follow (ἀκολούθει) me" (21:19b), the one who has died, risen, and ascended to "my Father and your Father, my God and your God" (20:17). At the last supper Jesus told Peter that where he is going Peter could not follow (ἀκολουθῆσαι) him now, but "you will follow (ἀκολουθήσεις) later." Peter protested, "Lord, why can I not follow (ἀκολουθῆσαι) you now? I will lay down my life for you" (13:36-37). Now is the time for Peter to follow Jesus by finally laying down his life for the sheep like Jesus and following him to the Father.

In contrast to the preceding B scene, in which the beloved disciple did not participate, but in development of the first A scene, in which the beloved disciple pointed out the risen Lord to Peter (21:7), Peter turns and sees the disciple whom Jesus loved following (21:20). Peter had signalled to the beloved disciple, more intimately associated than Peter with Jesus at the last supper, to ask Jesus which one of the disciples would betray him (13:21-24). That the beloved disciple at the supper leaned back upon Jesus' chest and asked him, "Lord, who is the one who will betray you?" (21:20; 13:25) led not only to the disclosure of the betrayer (13:26-30) but also eventually to the prediction of Peter's triple denial of Jesus (13:38).

In the first A scene the beloved disciple drew Peter's attention to the risen Lord, so that Peter jumped into the sea to meet him (21:7). In contrast, Peter now sees the beloved disciple following (21:20) and draws Jesus' attention to him, as he asks, "Lord, what about this one?" (21:21). In other words, is the beloved disciple, who is "following" them, also to follow Jesus in the same way as Peter, by laying down his life for the sheep? Jesus tells Peter that it should be of no concern to him if Jesus wants the beloved disciple to remain until Jesus comes (ἔρχομαι) again (21:22). Jesus had promised the disciples that he would come (ἔρχομαι) again and take them to himself after going to the Father and preparing a place for them (14:3, 18). Bolstering his initial command (21:19b), Jesus emphatically repeats to Peter, "*You* follow me!" (21:22).

The beloved disciple will remain until Jesus comes (21:23)

The message that the beloved disciple would not die went out to the "brothers" (21:23), not only the other disciples (20:17-18) but also the believers who became "brothers" and "sisters" of the beloved disciple, when he took the mother of Jesus to his own to form the familial community of believers (19:27). But Jesus did not tell Peter that the beloved disciple would not die. Rather, as Jesus emphatically repeats, "If I want him to remain until I come, what is that to you?" (21:22, 23). Although the original beloved disciple may die before Jesus comes again, since the beloved disciple also represents the ideal and future believer (17:20), that Jesus wants the beloved disciple to remain challenges the reader to be the beloved disciple, the believer who remains until Jesus comes again.

What Has Been Written Is a True Witness for the Readers' Faith (C 21:24-25)

24 This is the disciple who testifies about these things and has written them, and we know that his testimony is true. 25 But there are also many other things that Jesus did, which, if written one by one, I do not think the world itself could contain the books that would be written.

The beloved disciple has written a true testimony (21:24)

At this point the narrator again interjects and directly addresses the audience, commenting on the entire book, much as he did in the conclusion of the previous chapter (20:30-31).[21] His affirmation that "this (οὗτός) is the disciple who testifies about these things" (21:24) functions as a further answer to Peter's previous question to Jesus about the beloved disciple following them,

---

[21] Segovia, "Final Farewell," 167-90, emphasizes the literary inclusion formed by 20:30-31 and 21:24-25.

"Lord, what about this one (οὗτος)?" (21:21).[22] The narrator now characterizes the beloved disciple as the implied and ideal author, the one who testifies about "these things," that is, the events recorded in the book, and has written them as a firm foundation for the readers to believe (21:24; cf. 20:30-31).[23] The narrator then professes in the first person plural, "we know that his testimony is true" (21:24), thus drawing in the believing community of readers. Communal confessions frame the entire narrative. The narrator similarly drew in the believing community of readers in the prologue, when he proclaimed that "the Word became flesh and made his dwelling among us, and we have seen his glory" (1:14), and "from his fullness we have all received" (1:16).[24] The narrator previously affirmed the truth of the beloved disciple's witnessing of the blood and water flowing from the pierced side of the crucified Jesus (19:34), so that the audience may believe: "The one who has seen has testified, and his testimony (μαρτυρία) is true (ἀληθινή), and he knows that he speaks the truth (ἀληθῆ), so that you also may believe" (19:35). He later asserted that the signs written in the book were written so that the readers may believe (20:30-31). As a further impetus for the audience to believe, the narrator now adds the communal confession that "we know" that the things the beloved disciple has written and testifies about in the book, "his testimony (μαρτυρία)," is true (ἀληθής).

Jesus did many other things that have not been written (21:25)

The narrator previously informed the audience that Jesus performed many other signs not written in this book, but that the ones that have been written are sufficient to provoke and strengthen their faith (20:30-31). Not only does the present book not recount all that Jesus did, but, as the narrator additionally asserts, the whole world could not contain all the books needed if all the revelatory things Jesus did were to be written down one by one (21:25). To the communal confession in the first person plural, "we know that his testimony

---

[22] Barrett, *John*, 587; Carson, *John*, 683.

[23] Culpepper, *Anatomy*, 47: "When the narrator dramatically pulls the curtain on the implied author in the closing verses of the gospel, the reader recognizes that the Beloved Disciple fits the image the gospel projects of its implied author as one who knows Jesus intimately, shares his theological perspective, and can interpret reliably, that is, 'his witness is true.' The reader is thus given yet another reason for believing the gospel: its implied author is the Beloved Disciple." See also Bauckham, "Beloved Disciple," 21-44.

[24] Culpepper, *Anatomy*, 46.

is true" (21:24), the narrator now adds his own personal conclusion in the first person singular, "I do not think the world itself could contain the books that would be written" (21:25). This rhetorical exaggeration but profound theological thought assures the readers that there exists an abundant supply of reliable testimony, even more than they have heard in this narrative, to believe that Jesus is the Christ, the Son of God, so that through believing they may have eternal life in his name (20:31).[25]

Summary

John 21:1-25 comprises a single narrative intercalation with a concluding colophon for the entire book. The two A scenes develop and contrast the different relationships of Simon Peter and the beloved disciple to the risen Lord (21:1-14, 19b-23). They frame the sole B scene, which focuses upon the risen Lord's triple commissioning for Peter alone to feed and shepherd the sheep (21:15-19a). In the conclusion (21:24-25) the narrator confirms the true testimony presented throughout the entire book so that the audience may believe.

The implied reader/audience responds to this final alternation of scenes as follows:

1) The risen Lord's feeding of the disciples with bread and fish that suggest the eucharist, after he has enabled them to catch a great number of fish to feed the diverse but unified large number of people symbolized by those same fish, empowers the audience to nourish and strengthen the future believers they will draw into the community with the same eucharistic overabundance with which they have been sustained (21:1-14).

2) In contrast to the other disciples and especially to the disciple whom Jesus loved, Peter, who thrice proclaimed his love for Jesus after thrice denying him, provides the readers with a model not only for conversion but for being empowered by the risen Lord to feed and shepherd the members of the believing community by loving them as Jesus loved them, to the point of laying down his life for his friends (21:15-19a).

[25] For similar examples of flamboyant hyperbole at the conclusion of some other ancient literary works, see Brown, *John*, 1130. And note the comment by Carson, *John*, 686, with regard to the narrator's sweeping assertion here: "The Jesus to whom he bears witness is not only the obedient Son and the risen Lord, he is the incarnate Word, the one through whom the universe was created. If all his deeds were described, the world would be a very small and inadequate library indeed."

3) In a complementary contrast to the beloved disciple, but advancing the demonstration of his love for Jesus, Peter provides the readers with a model for following Jesus by laying down their lives in love for Jesus and their fellow believers if necessary. In a complementary contrast to Peter glorifying God by laying down his life for his fellow believers, but advancing his role of drawing attention to the risen Lord, the beloved disciple provides the audience with a model for following the risen Jesus and remaining faithful witnesses, whether by dying or not, until Jesus comes again (21:19b-23).

4) In his concluding aside the narrator arouses and strengthens the continued faith of the readers by reminding them that the beloved disciple has provided in the book all the true testimony they need to believe, which is only part of the great abundance of revelatory things that Jesus did but that the whole world cannot contain (21:24-25).

CHAPTER 7

Conclusion

In chapter 1 we presented an introductory overview of the five major sections (18:1-27, 18:28-19:11, 19:12-42, 20:1-31, and 21:1-25) that comprise the narrative progression of the passion, death, and resurrection of Jesus in the Gospel of John. We provided a preliminary analysis and explanation, based upon literary criteria and details in the text itself, for the division into these particular sections and for the arrangement of the individual scenes within each section. In chapters 2-6 we in turn demonstrated how each individual section operates as an alternation of contrasting scenes that progress as a dynamic sequence of narrative "sandwiches" or intercalations, involving the implied reader/audience in an intense interplay of competing and/or complementary narrative themes. Each of these chapters concluded with a summary overview of how the audience moves through and is summoned to respond to the developing and contrasting themes of each individual section. Now, in a final summary overview, we want to put it all together and consider how the reader moves not only through each section but from section to section in the total narrative progression that concludes the Gospel of John.

The first section (18:1-27) leads the audience through the developing theme of Jesus as *the* divine revealer who challenges those who hear him to testify that he offers his own life as the good shepherd and singular "high priest" to provide eternal life for all who believe (18:1-9, 12-14, 19-24). But at the same time, in continual and progressive contrast, the reader experiences the theme of Peter's failure to understand what it means to be a disciple who follows Jesus and testifies to his divine revelation (18:10-11, 15-18, 25-27). This section warns the audience of failing like Peter and of the necessity of humbly accepting as a loved disciple/sheep the love and eternal life only Jesus provides by laying down his own life in accord with God's will. Only then can the reader like Peter become a loving disciple/shepherd, who likewise lays down his life for his fellow members in the believing community (13:34-35; 15:12-13). That Peter's triple denial fulfills Jesus' authoritative prediction encourages the audience to meet Jesus' challenge by testifying to the ultimate control and reliability of Jesus' revelatory words offering eternal life to all who believe.

Then in the second section (18:28-19:11) the audience progresses through the theme of the Roman governor, Pilate, arrogantly humiliating the Jews outside the praetorium for bringing him an innocent and apparently insignificant Jesus, whom he taunts the Jews to take back, but whom they repeatedly reject (18:28-32, 38b-40; 19:4-7). But in continual contrast the alternating scenes move the reader through the theme of Jesus revealing his transcendent identity, origin, and mission to Pilate inside the praetorium (18:33-38a; 19:1-3, 8-11). The first theme assures the audience that Jesus is laying down his own life as a "lifting up" in crucifixion that will serve as his final revelatory sign and draw all people to himself (18:28-32); it summons the reader to follow Jesus as the true king, whose kingship embraces yet transcends this world (18:38b-40); and it reveals to the reader Jesus' profound identity as the one human being, the Son of Man and the Son of God, whose crucifixion will offer eternal life to all who believe (19:4-7). The second theme challenges the audience to experience Jesus' kingship that is not of this world by hearing his voice as the shepherd/king who testifies to the truth that his death offers eternal life to all who believe (18:33-38a); in disclosing the scourged and mocked Jesus as the transcendent King whose kingship embraces both Jews and Gentiles, it provides a model for the reader who can likewise expect suffering and persecution from the world (19:1-3); and it stirs the reader to a personal decision of greater faith in the Jesus who has the authority to grant eternal life to those who become God's children by believing (19:8-11).

The third section (19:12-42) guides the reader through the theme of invitations to see and accept that provoke the reader to an authentic and profound faith in Jesus (19:12-22, 25-27, 31-37). In continual contrast the reader confronts the theme of various "takings" that advance the divine plan with regard to Jesus' death and resurrection (19:23-24, 28-30, 38-42). The first theme induces the audience to believe in the Jesus whose crucifixion is his royal enthronement as the good shepherd-king (19:12-22); it challenges the audience to imitate the response of the beloved disciple to the death of Jesus by extending to other believers the same depth and intensity of love Jesus demonstrated by laying down his life (19:25-27); and it summons the audience to an ever more profound faith by looking upon the Life-giving blood and water that flow from the pierced side of Jesus (19:31-37). The second theme invites the reader to believe in the Jesus who dies to unify all profoundly with the eternal life his death provides (19:23-24); it assures the reader of the divine empowerment and guidance needed to live the life of love for one another in the community of believers (19:28-30); and it prompts the reader to believe in the Jesus whose unique burial not only assured his association with the Jewish people and with his disciples, but pointed to his resurrection as the final triumph over death (19:38-42).

In the fourth section (20:1-31) the audience moves through the theme of individuals encountering the evidence that Jesus has been raised from the dead (20:1-2, 11-18, 24-25). In continual contrast and development, the alternating scenes lead the reader through the theme of the group of disciples encountering the evidence for the resurrection of Jesus (20:3-10, 19-23, 26-29). A concluding scene presents the audience with the purpose of the narrative (20:30-31). The first theme confronts the reader with initial evidence of the resurrection when Mary Magdalene sees the stone removed from the tomb (20:1-2); it provides the reader a missionary model in Mary, who assures the audience of being brothers and sisters with the risen Lord whose God and Father is their God and Father (20:11-18); and it challenges the reader to believe by hearing the testimony of those who have seen the risen Lord (20:24-25). The second theme invites the reader to believe in the resurrection based upon the beloved disciple's seeing and the scriptural necessity for Jesus to rise from the dead (20:3-10); it invites the reader to experience the peace and joy granted by the risen Jesus, and, empowered by the holy Spirit and the authority to forgive sins, to extend his revelation to the world (20:19-23); and through the personal seeing of Thomas it summons the audience to believe in the crucified but risen Jesus as their Lord and God (20:26-29). Based on the evidence of the entire book, the narrator appeals for the audience to believe that Jesus is the Christ, the Son of God, in order to possess eternal life in his name (20:30-31).

The fifth section (21:1-25) brings the audience through a development of the different relationships of Simon Peter and the beloved disciple to the risen Lord (21:1-14, 19b-23), in contrast to a focus upon the risen Lord's triple commissioning for Peter alone to feed and shepherd the sheep (21:15-19a). The conclusion confirms the true testimony presented throughout the entire book (21:24-25). The risen Lord's feeding of the disciples with bread and fish empowers the audience to nourish future believers with the overabundance Jesus provides in the eucharist (21:1-14). Peter's personal profession of love for Jesus provides the audience with a model for being empowered by the risen Lord to feed and shepherd the members of the believing community by loving them as Jesus loved them, to the point of laying down his life for his friends (21:15-19a). Peter and the beloved disciple provide the readers with contrasting but complementary models: Readers are called either to lay down their lives in love for Jesus and their fellow believers, if necessary, like Peter, or to follow the risen Jesus by remaining faithful witnesses like the beloved disciple, whether by dying or not, until Jesus comes again (21:19b-23). Finally, by assuring them that the beloved disciple has provided all the testimony they need in the narrative, the narrator encourages the readers to continue to believe (21:24-25).

In sum, the Johannine presentation of the passion, death, and resurrection of Jesus constitutes a highly artistic and richly complex narrative progression. It engages its implied reader/audience with a dramatic series of contrasts first between Jesus and Peter (18:1-27), then between the Jews and Pilate regarding Jesus (18:28-19:11), then between invitations for "seeing and accepting" to believe and "takings" to advance God's revelation in the dying Jesus (19:12-42), then between individuals and the group of disciples coming to believe in the risen Lord (20:1-31), and finally between Peter and the beloved disciple following the risen Lord (21:1-25). This entire dynamic sequence of contrasting and developing themes that concludes the Gospel of John involves its audience, through their encounter with the narrative progression itself, in a continual deepening and strengthening of their belief in Jesus as the Christ, the Son of God, in order to experience, ever more fully and profoundly, eternal life in his name.

Bibliography

Alter, R. *The Pleasures of Reading in an Ideological Age*. New York: Simon & Schuster, 1989.

Auwers, J.-M. "La nuit de Nicodème (Jean 3,2; 19,39) ou l'ombre du langage." *RB* 97 (1990) 481-503.

Ball, R. M. "S. John and the Institution of the Eucharist." *JSNT* 23 (1985) 59-68.

Balz, H. "χιλίαρχος." *EDNT* 3. 466-67.

——. "μαστιγόω." *EDNT* 2. 395-96.

——. "Δίδυμος." *EDNT* 1. 320.

Barrett, C. K. *The Gospel According to St. John*. 2d ed. Philadelphia: Westminster, 1978.

Bartholomew, G. L. "Feed My Lambs: John 21:15-19 as Oral Gospel." *Orality, Aurality, and Biblical Narrative. Semeia* 39. Ed. L. Silberman. Decatur: Scholars, 1987, 69-96.

Bassler, J. M. "Mixed Signals: Nicodemus in the Fourth Gospel." *JBL* 108 (1989) 635-46.

Bauckham, R. "The Beloved Disciple as Ideal Author." *JSNT* 49 (1993) 21-44.

Bauer, D. R. *The Structure of Matthew's Gospel: A Study in Literary Design*. JSNTSup 31. Sheffield: Almond, 1988.

Beck, D. R. "The Narrative Function of Anonymity in Fourth Gospel Characterization." *Characterization in Biblical Literature. Semeia* 63. Eds. E. S. Malbon and A. Berlin. Atlanta: Scholars, 1993, 143-58.

Beetham, F. G. and Beetham, P. A. "A Note on John 19:29." *JTS* 44 (1993) 163-69.

Bergmeier, R. "TETELESTAI Joh 19:30." *ZNW* 79 (1988) 282-90.

Beutler, J. "Greeks Come to See Jesus (John 12,20f)." *Bib* 71 (1990) 333-47.

——. "Two Ways of Gathering: The Plot to Kill Jesus in John 11.47-53." *NTS* 40 (1994) 399-406.

172

Bienaimé, G. "L'annonce des fleuves d'eau vive en Jean 7,37-39." *RTL* 21 (1990) 281-310, 417-54.

Böcher, O. "διάβολος." *EDNT* 1. 297-98.

Boers, H. *Neither on This Mountain Nor in Jerusalem: A Study of John 4.* SBLMS 35. Atlanta: Scholars, 1988.

Boguslawski, S. "Jesus' Mother and the Bestowal of the Spirit." *IBS* 14 (1992) 106-29.

Botha, J. E. *Jesus and the Samaritan Woman: A Speech Act Reading of John 4:1-42.* NovTSup 65. Leiden: Brill, 1991.

——. "Reader 'Entrapment' as Literary Device in John 4:1-42." *Neot* 24 (1990) 37-47.

Bottino, A. "La metafora della porta (Gv 10,7.9)." *RivB* 39 (1991) 207-15.

Brawley, R. L. "An Absent Complement and Intertextuality in John 19:28-29." *JBL* 112 (1993) 427-43.

Breck, J. "John 21: Appendix, Epilogue or Conclusion?" *St. Vladimir's Theological Quarterly* 36 (1992) 27-49.

Brodie, T. L. *The Gospel According to John: A Literary and Theological Commentary.* New York: Oxford University, 1993.

Brown, R. E. *The Gospel According to John.* AB 29-29A. Garden City: Doubleday, 1966-70.

——. "The Resurrection in John 20—A Series of Diverse Reactions." *Worship* 64 (1990) 194-206.

——. "The Resurrection in John 21—Missionary and Pastoral Directives for the Church." *Worship* 64 (1990) 433-45.

——. *The Death of the Messiah: From Gethsemane to the Grave: A Commentary on the Passion Narratives in the Four Gospels.* Anchor Bible Reference Library. 2 vols. New York: Doubleday, 1994.

Brownson, J. V. "Neutralizing the Intimate Enemy: The Portrayal of Judas in the Fourth Gospel." *SBLASP* 31 (1992) 49-60.

Bruce, F. F. *The Gospel of John.* Grand Rapids: Eerdmans, 1983.

Burkett, D. *The Son of the Man in the Gospel of John.* JSNTSup 56. Sheffield: JSOT, 1991.

Byrne, B. "The Faith of the Beloved Disciple and the Community in John 20." *JSNT* 23 (1985) 83-97.

Calduch Benages, N. "La fragancia del perfume en Jn 12,3." *EstBib* 48 (1990) 243-65.

Cardwell, K. "The Fish on the Fire: Jn 21:9." *ExpTim* 102 (1990) 12-14.

Carey, G. L. "The Lamb of God and Atonement Theories." *TynBul* 32 (1981) 97-122.

Carson, D. A. *The Gospel According to John.* Grand Rapids: Eerdmans, 1991.

Carter, W. "The Prologue and John's Gospel: Function, Symbol and the Definitive Word." *JSNT* 39 (1990) 35-58.

Cassidy, R. J. *John's Gospel in New Perspective: Christology and the Realities of Roman Power.* Maryknoll, NY: Orbis, 1992.

Charbonneau, A. "Jésus en croix (Jn 19,16b-42); Jésus élevé (3,14ss; 8,28ss; 12,31ss)." *ScEs* 45 (1993) 5-23, 161-80.

Cholin, M. "Le Prologue de l'Évangile selon Jean: Structure et formation." *ScEs* 41 (1989) 189-205, 343-62.

Cosgrove, C. H. "The Place Where Jesus Is: Allusions to Baptism and the Eucharist in the Fourth Gospel." *NTS* 35 (1989) 522-39.

Culpepper, R. A. "The Johannine *Hypodeigma*: A Reading of John 13:1-38." *The Fourth Gospel from a Literary Perspective. Semeia* 51. Ed. R. A. Culpepper and F. F. Segovia. Atlanta: Scholars, 1991, 133-52.

———. *Anatomy of the Fourth Gospel: A Study in Literary Design.* Philadelphia: Fortress, 1983.

de Boer, M. C. "Narrative Criticism, Historical Criticism, and the Gospel of John." *JSNT* 47 (1992) 35-48.

de la Potterie, I. "Le témoin qui demeure: le disciple que Jésus amait." *Bib* 67 (1986) 343-59.

———. "'Volgeranno lo sguardo a colui che hanno trafitto.' Sangue di cristo e oblatività." *Civiltà Cattolica* 137 (1986) 105-18.

———. *The Hour of Jesus: The Passion and the Resurrection of Jesus According to John.* New York: Alba House, 1989.

———. "La tunique 'non divisée' de Jésus, symbole de l'unité messianique." *The New Testament Age: Essays in Honor of Bo Reicke.* Vol. 1. Ed. W. C. Weinrich. Macon, GA: Mercer, 1984, 127-38.

———. "La tunique sans couture, symbole du Christ grand prêtre?" *Bib* 60 (1979) 255-69.

———. "La parole de Jésus 'Voici ta Mère' et l'accueil du Disciple (Jn 19,27b)." *Marianum* 36 (1974) 1-39.

———. "Jésus roi et juge d'après Jn 19,13." *Bib* 41 (1960) 217-47.

———. *La vérité dans Saint Jean.* AnBib 73-74. Rome: Biblical Institute, 1977.

———. "'Et à partir de cette heure, le Disciple l'accueillit dans son intimité' (Jn 19,27b): Réflexions méthodologiques sur l'interprétation d'un verset johannique." *Marianum* 42 (1980) 84-125.

———. "Jésus Christ, plénitude de la vérité, lumière du monde et sommet de la révélation d'après saint Jean." *Studia Missionalia* 33 (1984) 305-24.

———. "Structure du Prologue de Saint Jean." *NTS* 30 (1984) 354-81.

———. "Le symbolisme du sang et de l'eau en Jn 19,34." *Didaskalia* 14 (1984) 201-30.

Derrett, J. D. M. "Christ, King and Witness (John 18,37)." *BeO* 31 (1989) 189-98.

———. *The Victim: The Johannine Passion Narrative Reexamined.* Shipston-on-Stour, Warwickshire, England: Drinkwater, 1993.

Dewailly, L.-M. "'D'où es tu?' (Jean 19,9)." *RB* 92 (1985) 481-96.

Drinkard, J. F. "Numbers." *HBD.* 711-12.

du Rand, J. A. "Narratological Perspectives on John 13:1-38." *Hervormde Teologiese Studies* 46 (1990) 367-89.

Duke, P. D. *Irony in the Fourth Gospel*. Atlanta: John Knox, 1985.

Ehrman, B. D. "Jesus' Trial before Pilate: John 18:28-19:16." *BTB* 13 (1983) 124-31.

Ellis, P. F. "The Authenticity of John 21." *St. Vladimir's Theological Quarterly* 36 (1992) 17-25.

Eslinger, L. "The Wooing of the Woman at the Well: Jesus, the Reader and Reader-Response Criticism." *Literature & Theology* 1 (1987) 167-83.

Fee, G. D. "On the Text and Meaning of Jn 20,30-31." *The Four Gospels 1992: Festschrift Frans Neirynck*. Ed. F. Van Segbroeck, et al. BETL 100. 3 vols. Leuven: Leuven University, 1992, 2193-205.

Feneberg, W. "φιλέω." *EDNT* 3. 425-26.

Fiedler, P. "ἁμαρτία." *EDNT* 1. 65-69.

Franzmann, M. and Klinger, M. "The Call Stories of John 1 and John 21." *St. Vladimir's Theological Quarterly* 36 (1992) 7-15.

García García, L. "'Lienzos', no 'vendas', en la sepultura de Jesús." *Burgense* 32 (1991) 557-67.

Gee, D. H. "Why Did Peter Spring into the Sea? (John 21:7)." *JTS* 40 (1989) 481-89.

Genuyt, F. "La comparution de Jésus devant Pilate. Analyse sémiotique de Jean 18,28-19,16." *RSR* 73 (1985) 133-46.

Giblin, C. H. "Mary's Anointing for Jesus' Burial-Resurrection (John 12,1-8)." *Bib* 73 (1992) 560-64.

——. "Confrontations in John 18,1-27." *Bib* 65 (1984) 210-32.

——. "John's Narration of the Hearing Before Pilate (John 18,28-19,16a)." *Bib* 67 (1986) 221- 39.

Goulder, M. "Nicodemus." *SJT* 44 (1991) 153-68.

Gourgues, M. "Marie, la 'femme' et la 'mère' en Jean." *NRT* 108 (1986) 174-91.

Grassi, J. A. "The Role of Jesus' Mother in John's Gospel: A Reappraisal." *CBQ* 48 (1986) 67-80.

——. *The Secret Identity of the Beloved Disciple*. Mahwah: Paulist, 1992.

Grigsby, B. H. "The Cross as an Expiatory Sacrifice in the Fourth Gospel." *JSNT* 15 (1982) 51-80.

——. "Washing in the Pool of Siloam—A Thematic Anticipation of the Johannine Cross." *NovT* 27 (1985) 227-35.

Haenchen, E. *A Commentary on the Gospel of John*. 2 vols. Hermeneia. Philadelphia: Fortress, 1984-85.

Hanson, A. T. *The Prophetic Gospel: A Study of John and the Old Testament*. Edinburgh: Clark, 1991.

Hasler, V. "εἰρήνη." *EDNT* 1. 394-97.

Hatina, T. R. "John 20,22 in Its Eschatological Context: Promise or Fulfillment?" *Bib* 74 (1993) 196-219.

Heil, J. P. *The Death and Resurrection of Jesus: A Narrative-Critical Reading of Matthew 26-28*. Minneapolis: Fortress, 1991.

——. "The Progressive Narrative Pattern of Mark 14,53-16,8." *Bib* 73 (1992) 331-58.

——. *Jesus Walking on the Sea: Meaning and Gospel Functions of Matt 14:22-33, Mark 6:45-52 and John 6:15b-21*. AnBib 87. Rome: Biblical Institute, 1981.

——. "Mark 14,1-52: Narrative Structure and Reader-Response." *Bib* 71 (1990) 305-32.

——. "The Narrative Structure of Matthew 27:55-28:20." *JBL* 110 (1991) 419-38.

Holleran, J. W. "Seeing the Light: A Narrative Reading of John 9. I: Background and Presuppositions." *ETL* 69 (1993) 5-26.

Infante, R. "L'amico dello sposo, figura del ministero di Giovanni Battista nel quarto vangelo." *RivB* 31 (1983) 3-19.

Janssens de Varebeke, A. "La structure des scènes du récit de la passion en Joh., XVIII-XIX." *ETL* 38 (1962) 504-22.

Judge, P. J. "A Note on Jn 20,29." *The Four Gospels 1992: Festschrift Frans Neirynck*. BETL 100. Ed. F. Van Segbroeck, et al. 3 vols. Leuven: Leuven University, 1992, 2183-92.

Kelber, W. H. "The Birth of a Beginning: John 1:1-18." *How Gospels Begin. Semeia* 52. Ed. D. E. Smith. Atlanta: Scholars, 1991, 121-44.

Koester, C. R. "'The Savior of the World' (John 4:42)." *JBL* 109 (1990) 665-80.

——. "Hearing, Seeing, and Believing in the Gospel of John." *Bib* 70 (1989) 327-48.

——. "John Six and the Lord's Supper." *LQ* 4 (1990) 419-37.

Kraft, H. "στέφανος." *EDNT* 3. 273-74.

Kremer, J. "'Nimm deine Hand und lege sie in meine Seite!' Exegetische, hermeneutische und bibeltheologische Überlegungen zu Joh 20,24-29." *The Four Gospels 1992: Festschrift Frans Neirynck*. BETL 100. Ed. F. Van Segbroeck, et al. 3 vols. Leuven: Leuven University, 1992, 2153-81.

Kretzer, A. "ἀπόλλυμι." *EDNT* 1. 135-36.

Kügler, J. *Der Jünger, den Jesus liebte: Literarische,theologische und historische Untersuchungen zu einer Schlüsselgestalt johanneischer Theologie und Geschichte. Mit einem Exkurs über die Brotrede in Joh 6*. SBB 16. Stuttgart: Katholisches Bibelwerk, 1988.

Kurz, W. S. "The Beloved Disciple and Implied Readers." *BTB* 19 (1989) 100-107.

Lindars, B. *The Gospel of John*. NCB. London: Oliphants, 1972.

Mahoney, R. *Two Disciples at the Tomb: The Background and Message of John 20. 1-10*. Theologie und Wirklichkeit 6. Frankfurt/Bern: Lang, 1974.

Malatesta, E. "Blood and Water from the Pierced Side of Christ." *Segni e Sacramenti nel Vangelo di Giovanni*. Studia Anselmiana 66. Ed. P.-R. Tragan. Rome: Anselmiana, 1977, 164-81.

Manns, F. "Le symbolisme du jardin dans le récit de la passion selon St Jean." *SBFLA* 37 (1987) 53-80.

Matera, F. J. "'On Behalf of Others,' 'Cleansing,' and 'Return.' Johannine Images for Jesus' Death." *LS* 13 (1988) 161-78.

McCaffrey, J. *The House with Many Rooms: The Temple Theme of Jn. 14,2-3*. AnBib 114. Rome: Biblical Institute, 1988.

Menken, M. J. J. "John 6,51c-58: Eucharist or Christology?" *Bib* 74 (1993) 1-26.

——. "The Old Testament Quotation in Jn 19,36: Sources, Redaction, Background," *The Four Gospels 1992: Festschrift Frans Neirynck.* BETL 100. Ed. F. Van Segbroeck, et al. 3 vols. Leuven: Leuven University, 1992, 2102-18.

——. "The Textual Form and the Meaning of the Quotation from Zechariah 12:10 in John 19:37." *CBQ* 55 (1993) 494-511.

Metzger, B. M. *A Textual Commentary on the Greek New Testament.* London/New York: United Bible Societies, 1971.

Meynet, R. "Analyse rhétorique du Prologue de Jean." *RB* 96 (1989) 481-510.

Minear, P. S. "The Original Functions of John 21." *JBL* 102 (1983) 85-98.

Mlakuzhyil, G. *The Christocentric Literary Structure of the Fourth Gospel.* AnBib 117. Rome: Biblical Institute, 1987.

Moloney, F. J. *Belief in the Word: Reading John 1-4.* Minneapolis: Fortress, 1993.

——. "Mary in the Fourth Gospel: Woman and Mother." *Salesianum* 51 (1989) 421-40.

——. "John 6 and the Celebration of the Eucharist." *DRev* 93 (1975) 243-51.

——. "When Is John Talking about Sacraments?" *AusBR* 30 (1982) 10-33.

——. "The Structure and Message of John 13:1-38." *AusBR* 34 (1986) 1-16.

——. "A Sacramental Reading of John 13:1-38." *CBQ* 53 (1991) 237-56.

——. "Who is 'The Reader' in/of the Fourth Gospel?" *AusBR* 40 (1992) 20-33.

——. *The Johannine Son of Man.* 2d ed. Biblioteca di Scienze Religiose 14. Rome: Libreria Ateneo Salesiano, 1978.

Morris, L. *The Gospel According to John.* NICNT. Grand Rapids: Eerdmans, 1971.

Napole, G. M. "Pedro y el discipulo amado en Juan 21,1-25." *RevistB* 52 (1990) 153-77.

Neirynck, F. "*EIS TA IDIA:* Jn 19,27 (et 16,32)." *ETL* 55 (1979) 357-65.

——. "John 21." *NTS* 36 (1990) 321-36.

——. "La traduction d'un verset johannique: Jn 19,27b." *ETL* 57 (1981) 83-106.

O'Day, G. R. *The Word Disclosed: John's Story and Narrative Preaching.* St. Louis: CBP, 1987.

——. *Revelation in the Fourth Gospel: Narrative Mode and Theological Claim.* Philadelphia: Fortress, 1986.

Okure, T. *The Johannine Approach to Mission: A Contextual Study of John 4: 1-42.* WUNT 2/31. Tübingen: Mohr, 1988.

Owen, O. T. "One Hundred and Fifty Three Fishes." *ExpTim* 100 (1988) 52-54.

Painter, J. *The Quest for the Messiah: The History, Literature and Theology of the Johannine Community.* Edinburgh: Clark, 1991.

Panackel, C. *ΙΔΟΥ Ο ΑΝΘΡΩΠΟΣ (Jn 19, 5b): An Exegetico-Theological Study of the Text in the Light of the Use of the Term ΑΝΘΡΩΠΟΣ Designating Jesus in the Fourth Gospel.* AnGreg 251. Rome: Gregorian, 1988.

Pazdan, M. M. "Nicodemus and the Samaritan Woman: Contrasting Models of Discipleship." *BTB* 17 (1987) 145-48.

——. *The Son of Man: A Metaphor for Jesus in the Fourth Gospel.* Collegeville: Liturgical Press, 1991.

Pesch, R. "Κηφᾶς." *EDNT* 2. 292.

Pitta, A. "*Ichthys* ed *opsarion* in Gv 21,1-14: semplice variazione lessicale o differenza con valore simbolico?" *Bib* 71 (1990) 348-64.

Plank, K. A. *Paul and the Irony of Affliction.* Atlanta: Scholars, 1987.

Powell, M. A. *What Is Narrative Criticism?* Minneapolis: Fortress, 1990.

Pryor, J. W. *John: Evangelist of the Covenant People. The Narrative & Themes of the Fourth Gospel.* Downers Grove, IL: InterVarsity, 1992.

———. "The Johannine Son of Man and the Descent-Ascent Motif." *JETS* 34 (1991) 341-51.

Radl, W. "αἰτία." *EDNT* 1. 43-44.

Rebell, W. "χιτών." *EDNT* 3. 468.

Reinhartz, A. "Great Expectations: A Reader-Oriented Approach to Johannine Christology and Eschatology." *Journal of Literature and Theology* 3 (1989) 61-76.

———. *The Word in the World: The Cosmological Tale in the Fourth Gospel.* SBLMS 45. Atlanta: Scholars, 1992.

Rensberger, D. *Johannine Faith and Liberating Community.* Philadelphia: Westminster, 1988.

Rhea, R. *The Johannine Son of Man.* ATANT 76. Zürich: Theologischer Verlag, 1990.

Richter, G. "Blut und Wasser aus der durchbohrten Seite Jesu (Joh 19,34b)." *MTZ* 21 (1970) 1-21.

Robert, R. "Pilate a-t-il fait de Jésus un juge? *ekathisen epi bematos* (Jean, xix, 13)." *RevThom* 83 (1983) 275-87.

———. "Le 'suaire' johannique: Réponse a quelques questions." *RevThom* 89 (1989) 599-608.

———. "Du suaire de Lazare à celui de Jésus. Jean XI,44 et XX,7." *RevThom* 88 (1988) 410-20.

Ross, J. M. "One Hundred and Fifty-Three Fishes." *ExpTim* 101 (1989) 375.

Sabbe, M. "The Johannine Account of the Death of Jesus and Its Synoptic Parallels (Jn 19,16b-42)," *ETL* 70 (1994) 34-64.

Schaller, B. "βῆμα." *EDNT* 1. 215-16.

Schencke, H.-M. "The Function and Background of the Beloved Disciple in the Gospel of John." *Nag Hammadi, Gnosticism & Early Christianity.* Ed. C. H. Hedrick and R. Hodgson. Peabody, MA: Hendrickson, 1986, 111-25.

Schnackenburg, R. *Das Johannesevangelium: Kommentar zu Kap. 13-21.* HTKNT 4/3. Freiburg/Basel/Wien: Herder, 1976.

———. *Das Johannesevangelium: Einleitung und Kommentar zu Kap. 1-4.* HTKNT 4/1. Freiburg/Basel/Wien: Herder, 1972.

Schneider, G. "πραιτώριον." *EDNT* 3. 144-45.

Schuchard, B. G. *Scripture within Scripture: The Interrelationship of Form and Function in the Explicit Old Testament Citations in the Gospel of John.* SBLDS 133. Atlanta: Scholars, 1992.

Segalla, G. "'Il discepolo che Gesù amava' e la tradizione giovannea." *Teologia* 14 (1989) 217-44.

Segovia, F. F. "The Final Farewell of Jesus: A Reading of John 20:30-21:25." *The Fourth Gospel from a Literary Perspective. Semeia* 53. Ed. R. A. Culpepper and F. F. Segovia. Atlanta: Scholars, 1991, 167-90.

———. "John 13:1-20, The Footwashing in the Johannine Tradition." *ZNW* 73 (1982) 31-51.

———. *The Farewell of the Word: The Johannine Call to Abide.* Minneapolis: Fortress, 1991.

Senior, D. *The Passion of Jesus in the Gospel of John.* Collegeville, MN: Liturgical Press, 1991.

Simenel, P. "Les 2 anges de Jean 20/11-12." *ETR* 67 (1992) 71-76.

Smit Sibinga, J. "Towards Understanding the Composition of John 20," *The Four Gospels 1992: Festschrift Frans Neirynck.* BETL 100. Ed. F. Van Segbroeck, et al. 3 vols. Leuven: Leuven University, 1992, 2139-52.

Staley, J. L. *The Print's First Kiss: A Rhetorical Investigation of the Implied Reader in the Fourth Gospel.* SBLDS 82. Atlanta: Scholars, 1988.

———. "The Structure of John's Prologue: Its Implications for the Gospel's Narrative Structure." *CBQ* 48 (1986) 241-64.

———. "Subversive Narrative/Victimized Reader: A Reader Response Assessment of a Text-Critical Problem, John 18.12-24." *JSNT* 51 (1993) 79-98.

Stibbe, M. W. G. *John as Storyteller: Narrative Criticism and the Fourth Gospel.* SNTSMS 73. Cambridge: Cambridge University, 1992.

Suggit, J. N. "Nicodemus—The True Jew." *Neot* 14 (1981) 90-110.

Summers, R. *Behold the Lamb: An Exposition of the Theological Themes in the Gospel of John.* Nashville: Broadman, 1979.

Swetnam, J. "Bestowal of the Spirit in the Fourth Gospel." *Bib* 74 (1993) 556-76.

Sylva, D. D. "Nicodemus and his Spices (John 19.39)." *NTS* 34 (1988) 148-51.

Thomas, J. C. *Footwashing in John 13 and the Johannine Community.* JSNTSup 61. Sheffield: JSOT, 1991.

Tobin, T. H. "The Prologue of John and Hellenistic Jewish Speculation." *CBQ* 52 (1990) 252-69.

Traets, C. *Voir Jésus et le Père en lui selon l'évangile de saint Jean.* AnGreg 159. Rome: Gregorian University, 1967.

Trudinger, P. "The 153 Fishes: A Response and a Further Suggestion." *ExpTim* 102 (1990) 11-12.

van der Watt, J. G. "The Use of αἰώνιος in the Concept ζωὴ αἰώνιος in John's Gospel." *NovT* 31 (1989) 217-28.

van Tilborg, S. *Imaginative Love in John.* Biblical Interpretation Series 2. Leiden: Brill, 1993.

Viviano, B. T. "The High Priest's Servant's Ear: Mark 14:47." *RB* 96 (1989) 71-80.

Voelz, J. W. "The Discourse on the Bread of Life in John 6: Is It Eucharistic?" *Concordia Journal* 15 (1989) 29-37.

Vorster, W. S. "The Reader in the Text: Narrative Material." *Reader Perspectives on the New Testament.* Ed. E. V. McKnight. *Semeia* 48. Atlanta: Scholars, 1989, 21-39.

——. "The Growth and Making of John 21." *The Four Gospels 1992: Festschrift Frans Neirynck.* BETL 100. Ed. F. Van Segbroeck, et al. 3 vols. Leuven: Leuven University, 1992, 2207-21.

Wanke, J. "Ἕλλην." *EDNT* 1. 435-36.

Wiarda, T. "John 21.1-23: Narrative Unity and Its Implications." *JSNT* 46 (1992) 53-71.

Wilkinson, J. "The Incident of the Blood and Water in John 19,34." *SJT* 28 (1975) 149-72.

Winandy, J. "Les vestiges laissés dans le tombeau et la foi du disciple (Jn 20, 1-9)." *NRT* 110 (1988) 212-19.

Wyatt, N. "'Supposing Him to Be the Gardener' (John 20,15): A Study of the Paradise Motif in John." *ZNW* 81 (1990) 21-38.

Zeller, D. "Jesus und die Philosophen vor dem Richter (zu Joh 19,8-11)." *BZ* 37 (1993) 88-92.

Zerwick, M. and Grosvenor, M. *A Grammatical Analysis of the Greek New Testament.* 2 vols. Rome: Biblical Institute, 1974, 1979.

Zumstein, J. "L'interprétation johannique de la mort du Christ," *The Four Gospels 1992: Festschrift Frans Neirynck.* BETL 100. Ed. F. Van Segbroeck, et al. 3 vols. Leuven: Leuven University, 1992, 2119-38.

Author Index

Scripture Index